Studies in Empowerment: Steps Toward Understanding and Action

The *Prevention in Human Services* series:

- *Evaluation & Prevention in Human Services*, edited by Jared Hermalin and Jonathan A. Morell

- *Helping People to Help Themselves: Self-Help and Prevention*, edited by Leonard D. Borman, Leslie Borck, Robert Hess, and Frank L. Pasquale

- *Early Intervention Programs for Infants*, edited by Howard A. Moss, Robert Hess, and Carolyn Swift

- *R_x Television: Enhancing the Preventive Impact of TV*, edited by Joyce Sprafkin, Carolyn Swift, and Robert Hess

- *Innovations in Prevention*, edited by Robert Hess and Jared Hermalin

- *Strategies for Needs Assessment in Prevention*, edited by Alex Zautra, Kenneth Bachrach, and Robert Hess

- *Aging and Prevention: New Approaches for Preventing Health and Mental Health Problems in Older Adults*, edited by Sharon Simson, Laura B. Wilson, Jared Hermalin, and Robert Hess

- *Studies in Empowerment: Steps Toward Understanding and Action*, edited by Julian Rappaport, Carolyn Swift, and Robert Hess

Studies in Empowerment: Steps Toward Understanding and Action

Edited by
Julian Rappaport, Carolyn Swift, and Robert Hess

The Haworth Press
New York

Studies in Empowerment: Steps Toward Understanding and Action has also been published as *Prevention in Human Services*, Volume 3, Numbers 2/3, Winter 1983/Spring 1984.

The Haworth Press, Inc., 28 East 22 Street, New York, NY 10010

Library of Congress Cataloging in Publication Data
Main entry under title:

Studies in empowerment.

Published also as Prevention in human services, v. 3, no. 2/3, winter 1983/spring 1984.
Includes bibliographies.
1. Power (Social sciences)—Addresses, essays, lectures. 2. Community psychology—Addresses, essays, lectures. 3. Community power—Addresses, essays, lectures. 4. Helping behavior—Addresses, essays, lectures. 5. Community development—Addresses, essays, lectures. I. Rappaport, Julian. II. Swift, Carolyn F. III. Hess, Robert, 1948- .
HM271.S878   1984   303.3   84-4461
ISBN 0-86656-283-4

Studies in Empowerment: Steps Toward Understanding and Action

Prevention in Human Services
Volume 3, Numbers 2/3

CONTENTS

Foreword
Empowerment:
An Antidote for Folly

Carolyn Swift

This volume raises two major issues for prevention practitioners. First, it introduces an empowerment model of human services as a substitute for the paternalistic model that has dominated human service delivery during this century. A second, more subtle issue has to do with the relationship between empowerment and prevention. The positive, proactive imagery of empowerment and its explicit repudiation of paternalism make it an attractive model for theorists and practitioners committed to social system change. Whether empowerment represents an extension and refinement of prevention theory, or an alternative (Rappaport, 1981) is not explicitly addressed in these contributions. The question invites the discussion and debate of the field.

Human service professionals have long been divided in choosing between helping individuals in need and changing the conditions that distribute needs unequally within a population. The economic contingencies of the health and mental health industries maintain an army of human service providers contributing to the solution of individuals' problems. Tackling the redistribution of resources is significantly more difficult. The principal model for doing this is our culture is paternalistic. Paternalism has shaped both our government's attempts to provide assistance to other countries and our efforts to help those in need within our own borders. The process has been to seek "expert" opinion about the needs of target populations, to back this expert opinion with an infusion of funds administered by a bureaucracy of experts, and to wonder at the resistance of indigenous populations to our efforts to improve their lives.

The result has sometimes been beneficial. Too often it has been folly. Historian Barbara Tuchman's (1984) brilliant analysis of folly in government is instructive. In her recent book she focuses on the follies of governments in dealing with each other. But the concept is too rich and the parallels too great to restrict her analysis of state folly to matters of international relations. The syndrome she outlines also provides insights into the flawed human service policies of the public sector. Tuchman identifies the mark of folly in government as the pursuit of policies contrary to its own interests. She offers three criteria for state ''wooden-headedness'': the policy must have been perceived as counterproductive within its own lifetime; a feasible alternative must have been available; the policy must have had the support of a group, not just a single leader, and it must have spanned more than one political lifetime. Paternalism as a philosophy for the distribution of human service resources fits the three criteria for folly.

First, paternalism has been perceived as counterproductive by an articulate series of spokespersons (Albee, 1959; Iscoe, 1974; Rappaport, 1981; Ryan, 1971).

> The mainstream reform position in the United States between 1900 and 1965 was largely an attempt to translate the biological model of the caring parent into a program for social action. The prime moving rationale was belief in the state as parent, not simply as metaphor but literally. This belief informed both the questions and the answers. For the first two-thirds of this century the legislative, governmental, and administrative social policy makers built an apparatus to provide services to the needy with little concern about the possibility of abuse and loss of rights. In this scheme of things the helping professions were the frontline soldiers in an army that would benevolently care for the poor, the retarded, the mentally ill, and the downtrodden. Those in need were more or less like children, to be helped, told what to do, and kept off the streets . . . The thrust of community mental health came as a last-ditch effort to parent the entire society by means of the noble ambition of extending the reach of services via catchment areas to the heretofore unreached. (Rappaport, 1981, 10-11)

The President's Commission on Mental Health was informed by an array of task panel reports. These reports confirm the omission of large geographic and demographic segments of the public from access to mental health resources (see especially the Reports of the

Task Panel on Prevention, and the Task Panel on Community Support Systems). Paternalism as a model for human service delivery has been extensively documented to be insensitive to a variety of citizens' needs.

Second, a feasible alternative to paternalism is available. The roots of the ideology of empowerment go deep into the political and philosophical foundations of this country. The concept of democracy and its embodiment in our political institutions are based on the principle of empowering citizens to participate in decisions affecting their welfare. The political ideology of empowerment has been eloquently translated to the mental health arena by Rappaport (1981). He outlines two requirements of an empowerment ideology.

> On the one hand it demands that we look to many diverse local settings where people are already handling their own problems in living, in order to learn more about how they do it . . . On the other hand, it demands that we find ways to take what we learn from these diverse settings and solutions and make it more public, so as to help foster social policies and programs and make it more rather than less likely that others not now handling their own problems in living or shut out from current solutions, gain control over their lives. (p. 15)

The contributions in this volume provide diverse applications of the empowerment model to the promotion of mental health and the prevention of mental illness.

Third, the dominence of paternalism in social policy spans multiple political lifetimes. The most visible federal assumption of the parental role in human service delivery has occurred over the last quarter-century in the administrations of Kennedy ("The New Frontier"), Johnson ("The Great Society"), Carter, Nixon and Reagan. The generosity of the first three administrations cited is in contrast with the impecuniosity of the last two. The difference is between more and less generous parental authorities. The constant throughout is the state's arrogation of power to determine who will share in the benefits of state resources and what form these resources will take.

Within the paternalistic structure of human service delivery, prevention has emerged as an increasingly strong competitor for resources that have traditionally been allocated to treatment programs. The ideology of primary prevention has attracted advocates across the spectrum of human services. A body of literature, professional organizations, college level curricula, and administrative offices at the federal and state levels have given prevention the status of a discipline. Not surprisingly, the paternalism modeled by local and federal governments is reflected in the attitudes and intervention strategies of many prevention professionals in both the public and private sectors.

Another troublesome concomitant of prevention ideology—in addition to the paternalistic structure within which it has been developed—is the negative semantic baggage it carries. To prevent something is to stop it from happening. It is a reaction in advance of an expected event—the termination of a sequence of events already in motion. Prevention calls up images of blocking, impeding, obstructing, retarding. The often tedious disputes about classification of preventive interventions as primary or secondary are rooted in this reactionary posture of prevention ideology to a stream of ongoing events.

The concept of empowerment as developed by Rappaport (1981) avoids these shortcomings. He provides empowerment with a positive formulation and an alternative set of symbols. The connotations and denotations of prevention and empowerment are overlapping but clearly distinct. Prevention is primarily concerned with the goal, empowerment with the process. Empowerment insists on the primacy of the target population's participation in any intervention affecting its welfare. It is the antithesis of paternalism.

While many prevention practitioners subscribe to an empowerment philosophy and practice, they are not required to do so by ideology. Prevention addresses health and mental health goals. The processes may be left to expediency or the resources of the intervener: legislation (e.g., mandating the use of seatbelts), regulation (e.g., prescribing safety procedures in industry), or mediation (e.g., facilitating and enforcing of agreements reached by opposing factions) may be used singly or in combination in pursuit of the elimination of negative health or mental health outcomes. Empowerment requires the acquiescence and participation of those affected by the intervention; the assumption here is that interventions that do not subscribe to this process will fail—seatbelts will not be worn, safety procedures will not be followed and agreements will not be honored.

This compilation of applications of empowerment invites debate—on the continued pursuit of the folly of paternalism, and on the relationship between prevention and empowerment. One of Rappaport's (1981) major contributions to this debate is his argument for the necessity of paradoxical approaches to the resolution of social problems. In the selection of writings that appear in this volume he has leveraged this argument to advance the field.

REFERENCES

Albee, G. *Mental health manpower trends.* New York: Basic Books, 1959.

Iscoe, I. Community psychology and the competent community. *American Psychologist,* 1974, *29,* 607-613.

Rappaport, J. In praise of paradox: A social policy of empowerment over prevention. *American Journal of Community Psychology,* 1981, *9,* 1-25.

Ryan, W. *Blaming the victim.* New York: Random House, 1971.

Tuchman, B. *The march of folly.* Knopf, 1984.

Studies in Empowerment: Steps Toward Understanding and Action

Studies in Empowerment:
Introduction to the Issue

Julian Rappaport

Half a dozen years ago, after completing a textbook on community psychology I wrote:

> In the future (we) will need to study, experience, and understand. . . the communities and naturally occurring helping systems that evolve in families, neighborhoods, and social networks in which people find meaning in life and a psychological sense of community. By understanding these systems we may be able to do more to provide alternatives for those who do not 'fit in' than by trying to force such people into the existing limited options developed under professional control. (Rappaport, 1977, p. viii)

As it turns out, my sense of this need seems to have been felt by others as well. Recent papers by Chavis, Stucky, and Wandersman (1983), Gottlieb (1983) and by Tyler, Pargament, and Gatz (1983) have addressed similar themes.

Four years after the textbook was published, on the occasion of my presidential address to the Division of Community Psychology of the American Psychological Association, I was given a second opportunity to reflect on the ''state of the art.'' At that time I introduced the concept of ''empowerment'' as one which, combined with the study of naturally occurring helping systems, might energize and guide mental health social policies. Following publication of that address (Rappaport, 1981), I have been fortunate to have heard a wide variety of commentary, both positive and negative, about my assessment. This issue of *Prevention in Human Services* was stimulated by that reaction and it is therefore useful to present here the essence of my viewpoint as well as the crux of the reactions to it. This will set the stage for what follows. Of course, I cannot here provide the detailed philosophical underpinnings or reasoning which led to my conclusions; for that I must ask the reader to pursue the earlier (1981) paper.

My thesis is that the *idea*[1] of "empowerment" is uniquely powerful as a model for policy in the field of social and community intervention. The reason for postulating the power of this idea is directly derived from a philosophy of social problems which makes several assumptions. Key among these assumptions is the belief that the most important and interesting aspects of community life are by their very nature paradoxical in that there is always more than one solution to whatever problem is presented.

Among the many possible solutions to community problems some will be contradictory to others. Phrased otherwise, potential solutions to social problems may be found among equally compelling opposites. One will not necessarily lead to the other; one may hinder the other. The example of freedom and equality is well known. Both are positively valued in our society, yet one actually hinders the other. Limits on freedom to do as one pleases are often required in order to achieve steps toward equality for others. Similarly, rights and needs are often pitted against one another in human service programs. Providing for the perceived needs of people may sometimes infringe on their rights, and assuring rights does not necessarily satisfy needs. In short, most social problems are more complex and involve interrelationships among opposites in such a fashion that there is no single solution which "solves" the problem. Consequently, the method of investigation required, because of the very nature of social problems, is a dialetical one, governed by divergent, rather than convergent reasoning.

Divergent reasoning is more appropriate than convergent reasoning when there are a variety of solutions possible. For social problems the pursuit of many different solutions is appropriate. That is, the nature of the phenomena are such that diversity of approaches is a true reflection of the things studied, which may be best understood in more than one way. In the domain of prevention in human services, in order to avoid being what I have called "one-sided," it is useful to be very attentive to both the ideas and solutions developed by professionals and those developed by successful people living out

---

[1]The *idea* is more important than the thing itself. We do not know what empowerment is, but like obscenity, we know it when we see it. The idea stimulates attempts to create the thing itself. Those are imperfect but useful representations of it, like the papers in this issue.

their own lives. It is this latter set of ideas and solutions which mental health professionals too often ignore.

As one looks to various (very different from each other) people solving problems (in various, very different from each other) settings and adds this data to professionally developed solutions, we may be expected to develop a more complete understanding of the possibilities for solutions to problems in living. As we turn to such study we should expect to find many different, even contradictory, solutions, depending on time, place, and context.

What has all of this to do with empowerment? Empowerment is viewed as a process: the mechanism by which people, organizations, and communities gain mastery over their lives. However, the content of the process is of infinite variety and as the process plays itself out among different people and settings the end products will be variable and even inconsistent with one another. The inconsistency is in the ends rather than in the process; yet the form of the process will also vary.

The recognition that a drug without a brand name may have exactly the same ingredients as a brand name drug can save us a great deal of money. The understanding that empowerment can be the active ingredient in a wide variety of human interactions, and that the end result can take on a variety of forms, is similar. For some people the mechanism of empowerment may lead to a *sense* of control; for others it may lead to actual control, the practical *power* to effect their own lives. Empowerment can be either understood as an internationalized attitude, or as an observable behavior.

Empowerment is easy to define in its absence: powerlessness, real or imagined; learned helplessness; alienation; loss of a sense of control over one's own life. It is more difficult to define positively only because it takes on a different form in different people and contexts.

Understanding that H_2O can be in liquid, gas, or solid form and still be H_2O is like the realization that empowerment for a poor, uneducated black woman can look very different than for a middle class college student or a thirty-nine year old businessman, a white urban housewife or a single elderly person resisting placement in a nursing home.

The only way to "see" empowerment as an end product or to concretize it as a process is to "triangulate" with varying measures as in converging operations (Garner, Hake, & Eriksen, 1956). Like perception, which is not an entity and therefore impossible to "see" apart from cognition, empowerment is a process knowable only in the form it takes. However, we must not reify empowerment in the measurement of the end product, or the process, or in the particular intervention or means by which it comes about. The way it is measured is not the thing in itself. Nevertheless, each measurement, intervention, and description in a particular context adds to our understanding of the construct.

The idea of empowerment does suggest certain parameters within which we might look for understanding. Under what conditions do we find people reporting a sense of control over their own lives? We need not limit our questions to particular contents of control. It may include political, economic, interpersonal, psychological, or spiritual control. Empowerment may be the result of programs designed by professionals, but more likely will be found in those circumstances where there is either true collaboration among professionals and the supposed beneficiaries, or in settings and under conditions where professionals are not the key actors. For understanding of this process we must look to diverse settings, people, strategies, and tactics because the thing itself is diverse. We must look to many different local settings where people are already handling their own problems in living. If we are to inform a social policy of empowerment and to develop interventions useful for those who are not now empowered we need to find ways to intervene in a form and with a style that is consistent with the idea of empowerment rather than the idea of controlling others.

Empowerment implies that many competencies are already present or possible, given niches and opportunities. It implies that new competencies are learned in a context of living life, rather than being told what to do by experts. It means realizing that the forms, the strategies, and the contents achieved will be quite variable from setting to setting. It means diversity of form. It means fostering local solutions by a policy which strengthens rather than weakens the mediating structures between individuals and the larger society: neighborhoods, families, churches, clubs, and voluntary associations. We need to learn from those ''natural'' support systems which are successful and to transmit what we learn to those which are less successful. ''Success'' cannot be defined in a single way. It needs to be self-defined by the people of concern, otherwise we undercut by our metacommunications the very essence of empowerment.

Given this view of empowerment, the most frequent critical response to my thesis has been: "Fine, I understand and agree with this idea, but tell me what to do about it; how does all this translate into research and action?"

A good deal of what I have previously written in order to concretize the idea of empowerment was based on a reinterpretation of the work of others, after they had published it. In developing this issue I was presented by the editors with an opportunity to invite those who I know to be thinking about empowerment to present their own work in an empowerment context. This issue then is a partial answer to the question of research and action. It is not the case, of course, that these are the only answers, or even the best. The papers are merely illustrative of self-conscious attempts by these authors to relate their own endeavors to the idea of empowerment.

In this issue the reader will find various definitions of empowerment. Its meaning is concretized in the context of individual, organizational, and community development. Participation of people in their own empowerment is a key theme which runs through these papers. As a corollary, the role of the professional as observer, researcher, and intervener is frequently discussed. The issue purposely presents a variety of populations and settings including women's groups and feminist organizations, native American residents of a reservation, the Puerto Rican poor, members of white ethnic neighborhoods, non-Western tribes people, political activists, members of a nondenominational religious community, and a variety of other specific citizen groups with goal oriented aims.

Topics presented here span the developmental trends of empowerment as an individual achievement, as a community experience, and as a professional aim orienting social intervention strategies and tactics. Research strategies include the methodologies of anthropological, behavioral, and community organization research. Data presented range from the purely descriptive through the application of complex, multivariate data analytic procedures. Each paper fleshes out the meaning of empowerment in general as well as its specific contextual meaning. Taken as a whole the issue provides a link between an intuitively appealing theoretical construct and its operationalization in research aimed at the development of a public policy of empowerment. It is food for thought more like appetizers rather than the full course meal. It is hoped that the readers' appetites will be stimulated and that they will look for recipes of their own.

The papers in this issue begin with Charles Kieffer's study of the process of empowerment as it transforms the individual lives of political activists, followed by Maton and Rappaport's study of individual differences among members of a religious community. Despite dissimilarity in the end product of the process, i.e., the experience of political efficacy as opposed to a spiritual-interpersonal change, and in the methodology—Kieffer uses multiple intensive interviews with a small number of people while Maton and Rappaport use a relatively large number of people, measurement development and multivariate quantitative assessment methodologies—both studies stress an understanding of the individual experience of empowerment.

Michael O'Sullivan, Natalie Waugh, and Wendy Espeland describe how a Native American tribe living on a reservation learned, as a community, to deal with government pressure to relocate. They describe their own research and collaboration with the tribe. Again, empowerment is seen as a transformation from an initial sense of powerlessness, this time for an entire community. Stephanie Riger's description of feminist organizations, using the language of the sociology of social movements presents questions of empowerment at the organizational level of analysis.

The papers by David Biegel, Steven Fawcett and his colleagues, and Irma Serrano-García, each address the role of the interventionist as collaborator with local communities. Each present their own suggestions for strategies and tactics as well as the special concerns of work with the particular population. Biegel's paper discusses research using the strengths of local neighborhoods to reduce obstacles to seeking help among white ethnic groups. Fawcett et al. emphasize the use of behavioral technologies to enhance the aims of local citizen groups, while Serrano-García presents us with the reality of the difference between psychological and political change in her efforts to empower the residents of a poor rural community.

The final paper, by Richard Katz, extends the theme of professional and community collaboration in the task of empowerment by drawing on the implications of his research among the people in Botswana and Fiji. His premise, that the resources created by human activity, including helping and healing are intrinsically renewable and expanding, rather than scarce, has tremendous implications for a psychology of empowerment and for the transformation of relationships between the would be healer and the community.

Taken together, this issue is a step toward understanding the mechanism of empowerment, hypothesized as the key to a genuine psychology of prevention in human services.

REFERENCES

Gottlieb, B. H. Social support as a focus for integrative research in psychology. *American Psychologist*, 1983, *38*, 278-287.

Rappaport, J. *Community psychology: Values, research and action.* New York: Holt, Rinehart, & Winston, 1977.

Rappaport, J. In praise of paradox: A social policy of empowerment over prevention. *American Journal of Community Psychology*, 1981, *9*, 1-25.

Tyler, F. B., Pargament, K. I., & Gatz, M. The resource collaborator role: A model for interactions involving psychologists. *American Psychologist*, 1983, *38*, 388-398.

Garner, W. R., Hake, H. W., & Eriksen, C. W. Operationism and the concept of perception. *Psychological Review*, 1956, *63*, 149-159.

Chavis, D. M., Stucky, P. E., & Wandersman, A. Returning basic research to the community: A relationship between scientist and citizen. *American Psychologist*, 1983, *38*, 424-434.

Citizen Empowerment:
A Developmental Perspective

Charles H. Kieffer

ABSTRACT. Since the late 1970s, the notion of empowerment has appeared with increasing frequency in discussion of preventive social and community intervention. While the *idea* of empowerment is intuitively appealing both for theory and practice, its applicability has been limited by continuing conceptual ambiguity. Based on a small *N* study of emerging citizen leaders in grassroots organizations, this article proposes a view of empowerment as a necessarily long-term process of adult learning and development. In this framework, empowerment is further described as the continuing construction of a multi-dimensional participatory competence. This conception encompasses both cognitive and behavioral change. Implications for practice are also addressed.

"The more you get involved in making power, the more your understanding of power changes. . ."—Felipe, Migrant Laborer

"Developing a sense of powerfulness is really a question of developing new perspective. . ."—Ellen, Working-Class Accountant

"A man doesn't know his rights, ain't got no rights. . ."—Jim, Appalachian Storekeeper

"I'm not radicalized. . . I'm more humanized. . ."—Emily, Public Health Nurse

Charles H. Kieffer is Executive Director of the SOS Community Crisis Center in Ypsilanti, Michigan and Lecturer in the Department of Psychology at The University of Michigan. The dissertation research on which this article is based received the first Dissertation Award of the Community Psychology (Division 27) Division of APA in August 1982. All correspondence should be addressed to Charles H. Kieffer, 263 Crest, Ann Arbor, MI 48103.

9

"Empowerment" is coming of age in the 1980s. An idea rooted in the "social action" ideology of the 1960s, and the "self-help" perspectives of the 1970s, empowerment appears with increasing frequency in discussions of strategies for prevention and community intervention (Berger & Neuhaus, 1977; Engelberg, 1981; Rappaport, 1981). There is an enticing promise in this orientation; we seem to resonate intuitively to its psychosocial, political, and ethical connotations. But we have yet to define this term with sufficient clarity to establish its utility either for theory or practice. It is often used as though it were synonymous with concepts as varied as "coping skills," "mutual support," "natural support systems," "community organization," "neighborhood participation," "personal efficacy," "competence," "self-sufficiency," and "self-esteem." Indeed, all of these notions may be related to the idea of empowerment.[1] There is need, though, for much greater precision in establishing a more functional definition of this term.

Rappaport's (1981) exploration of the ideology of emphasis on rights and abilities rather than deficits and needs is a crucial opening of dialogue in this direction. His discussion is especially important because it incorporates an unabashedly political conception of human being—addressing the person as "citizen" embedded in a political as well as social environment. Accepting this perspective as fundamental, this paper adapts the findings of a recent study of grassroots activists (Kieffer, 1981) in extending the dialogue on empowerment. It will emphasize, in particular, a view of empowerment as a long-term process of adult learning and development.

BACKGROUND

Social research seems obsessively preoccupied with why people *don't* do the things we think they "should," or why they do do the things we think they "shouldn't." Over the past several decades, for example, social scientists have produced a preponderance of studies regarding the experience of helplessness and alienation (Finifter, 1972; Gaventa, 1980; Rubin, 1976; Seeman, 1959; Sennett & Cobb, 1973; Seifer, 1976). Numerous publications from the "War on Poverty" era focused on explaining the "failure" of "de-

---

[1] The research on which this paper is based suggests that the most meaningful definition of empowerment encompasses the area in which all these ideas intersect.

prived" cultures, the "pathology" of the "underprivileged," and "obstructions" to the empowerment of the "culturally disadvantaged" (see Clark, 1974; Ganon, 1963; Freire, 1970; Moynihan, 1970; Piven & Cloward, 1977; Ryan, 1971; Sexton, 1965). Complementary research has documented a decline in feelings of internal control (Rotter, 1971), a loss of meaning and satisfaction (Ransford, 1968; Seeman, 1972), and a generally increasing sense of detachment and surrender (Coleman, 1974). Many studies illuminate, in particular, the processes through which the sense of powerlessness is constructed and internalized (Fromm, 1961; Henry, 1967; Lerner, 1979; Lewis, 1961; Liebow, 1967; May, 1972; Whyte, 1943). Other efforts further explicate the self-perpetuating or cyclical generation of social impotence, through concepts such as locus of control (Abramowitz, 1974; Phares, 1973; Rotter, 1966), learned helplessness (Maier & Seligman, 1976), and expectancy of success (Gurin & Gurin, 1970). Furthermore, acceptance of this sense of powerlessness is assumed to be manifest in consistent trends of declining voter participation, particularly among lower-income and economically displaced populations (Fahrquhar & Dawson, 1979; Harris, 1976; Schlozman & Verba, 1979; Verba & Nie, 1972). It is also seen as evidenced in the decline of society's "mediating structures" (Berger & Neuhaus, 1977) and the pervasive "erosion of social competence" (Lasch, 1979).

At the same time, however, the number and influence of community organizations—which have as their implicit function the counteracting of impotence and disenfranchisement—has blossomed and continues to grow (Boyte, 1980; Perlman, 1976). There has been a dramatic increase in activity, for example, among mass-based multi-issue grassroots groups (e.g., ACORN, Fair Share) and the community-based citizen organizations (Boyte, 1980; Fahrquhar & Dawson, 1979; Green, 1978; Langton, 1978; Perlman, 1976).

From my own direct experience in community settings it was also evident that many individuals who are living in the most oppressive social and economic conditions evolve as active and effective citizen-leaders nonetheless. This seeming "paradox" of emergence of citizen activism in the midst of more general apathy and hopelessness helped provoke this investigation of citizen empowerment. Rather than continue to focus on conditions of powerlessness, I was eager to illuminate the phenomenon of emergence from its midst. I believed that there was much to be learned from examining the manner in which formerly politically ineffectual individuals reconstruct their personal and social realities to become assertive and committed grassroots activists.

Throughout the broad literatures of citizen participation and community organization, there is a striking absence of attention to issues of individual empowerment. In several comprehensive reviews of the citizen participation literature (Cook, 1979; Davies & Zerchykov, 1978; Gittell, Hoffacker, Rollins, & Foster, 1979; Kelly, Snowden, & Muñoz, 1977; Spivak, 1973; Yin, Lucas, Szanton, & Spindler, 1973), for example, there is virtually no reference to the relationship between citizen involvement and the development of individual participatory competence. Both the extensive conceptual literature on community organization (see Alinsky, 1969; Boyte, 1980; Kahn, 1971; Spiegel, 1968), and a growing body of research on the structure and process of grassroots organizations (Andersen, Spiegel, Suess, & Woods, 1979; Gittell et al., 1979; Green, 1978; Perlman, 1976) suffer this same insufficiency. Neither the individual nor his/her process of development are seriously considered. Scouring these literatures, I found not a single study of citizen empowerment as an issue of adult learning and development. Through my experience as a clinician, an educator, and an organizer, I had the sense that this perspective could be fruitful. In this conviction, and amidst the scarcity of prior related findings, I framed an exploratory study of the emergence of individual activists in citizen organizations who had succeeded in increasing their real and self-perceived sense of participatory competence. Explicitly from the perspective of individual development, this research sought to illuminate the patterns and processes of transition from powerlessness to socio-political empowerment.

METHOD

Approaches to Investigation

The nature of the problem posed, the researcher's commitments and assumptions, and the concomitant logistical complexities underlay the use of innovation in qualitative/ethnographic methodology. Because "empowerment" was conceptualized as an interactive and highly subjective relationship of individuals and their environments, this inquiry required a special strategy to capture the intense experience of human struggle and transformation it explored. This was further complicated by my interest in constructing a generic descriptor of experience in widely varied community organizations. Invested both in depth of meaning and in breadth of applicability, I relied upon the traditions of small *N* research, purposive sampling, and phenomenological investigation for guiding principles.

At the same time, I was committed to a study which would not reify or further propagate the relations of powerlessness it was exploring. It was essential, then, that the design build on active collaboration and the promotion of participants' self-interests. My experience in community practice reinforced the importance of adopting this approach in every facet of the study, from problem definition and research design to analysis and interpretation of the data.

The solution to these challenges lay in combining elements of established practices of naturalistic, phenomenological, and depth-interview methodologies. The central facet of this strategy was an approach I have labeled "dialogic retrospection" (see description below).

Population

Fifteen individuals were included in the study. All participants had emerged through activity in "grassroots organizations" (Perlman, 1976) which were citizen-initiated, pragmatically oriented, and community-based (see Gittell et al., 1979). Selection was limited to those who had become active in the latter 1970s. Each was characterized by (1) self-acknowledgement of personal transformation, (2) recognizable transition into proactive and multi-issue engagement, and (3) evidence of continuing commitment to involvement in local political processes or grassroots leadership roles. They were all identified through networking with formal leaders in regional advocacy and training organizations.

Of this sample, five were male and ten were female—a fairly typical proportion of gender distribution in community organizations. Ages ranged from thirty to sixty-five. While most had not moved beyond a high school diploma, two had recently completed Bachelor's degrees, and one had attained a Master's degree in nursing. One was a migrant laborer, two came from Spanish Harlem, four were residents of ethnic, working-class neighborhoods in the Northeast and Midwest, four were from communities in the Central Appalachians, and four were from Southern agrarian and industrial areas. Typical of the individuals involved were a working-class mother who had become the prime force in constructing a community health clinic, a migrant laborer who had become an organizer and boycott coordinator, a former junkie and gang leader who had become a leader in an urban homesteading program, and a retired laborer leading efforts against brown lung disease.

Collection and Analysis of Data

All interviews were conducted in the subjects' natural settings. Individuals were prompted to articulate as fully as possible—in their own most meaningful terms—a description of their personal transition. These dialogues were open-ended, reflective, and critical, and were patterned after Levinson's (1978) "biographical interview" and Sardello's (1971) "reciprocal exchange." Verbatim transcripts sent to each individual provided opportunity for more intensive and critical self-reflection and followup. These were also the basis for continuing participant "ownership," or collaboration, in the generation, refinement, and analysis of data.

Followup interviews were conducted several months later with ten of the fifteen participants. (Financial and logistical complications precluded inclusion of the others.) Based on the researcher's preliminary analysis and the subjects' opportunity for self-critical reflection, these dialogues encouraged participants to extend, to correct, and to clarify their earlier conversations, and to validate and refine emergent interpretations. Again, verbatim transcripts of these interviews were shared with each of the participants for further and final clarification.

Tentative interpretations constructed throughout the research process were consistently referred back to the participants for response and refinement. This "elaboration of meaning through joint inquiry" (Von Eckartsberg, 1971) is consistent with the general tenets of phenomenological tradition (Colaizzi, 1978; Giorgi, 1975; Stevick, 1971). It is, in fact, this strategy which insures rigor, reliability, and intersubjective "objectivity" in phenomenological terms (Becker, 1978; Colaizzi, 1978; Giorgi, 1975; Natanson, 1978; Von Eckartsberg, 1971).

Aggregate analysis was grounded in these individual collaborations and followed parallel procedures of construction and refinement. Following conclusion of all interviews, all transcripts were reviewed to generate a comprehensive and exhaustive thematic portrait of each individual. These were then compared to reduce all identified themes to those essential, verifiable, and nonredundant categories of description applicable to *all* of the participants.

Analysis, itself, proceeded in a dialogic fashion. The data suggested categories for interpretation, which were then checked back against the interview material. Discrepancies or anomalies provoked "re-vision" of the emerging structure and patterns of analysis. "Pre-dominance," "intensity," and "verifiability" served as guiding principles in this process. A much more complete description of this procedure is available elsewhere (see Kieffer, 1981).

ON POWERLESSNESS

Understanding empowerment demands that we first clarify a conception of the condition from which it evolves. In this study that counterpoint is referred to as the "sense of powerlessness." Seeman's (1959) view of "powerlessness" as the "expectancy. . . held by the individual that his own behavior cannot determine the occurrence of the outcomes. . . he seeks" (p. 784) is most useful in framing our discussion. More specifically, the sense of powerlessness is approached as an attitude of being which incorporates past experience, ongoing behavior, and continuing cognition. Stokols' (1975) construction of a "psychological conception of alienation" further amplifies this perspective. While not seen as unilaterally imposed on the individual by his/her environment, powerlessness is viewed as an experience embedded in and reinforced by the fabric of social institutions. Cloward and Ohlin's (1960) "opportunity theory," Fanon's (1963) "colonial model," and Lewis' (1961) notion of the "culture of poverty" are reflective of this perspective. A well-established consequence of such conditions is entrapment in a cycle of victimization and self-blame (Ryan, 1971).

Freire's (1970, 1973) conceptions are also instructive. In his view, the individual becomes powerless in assuming the role of "object" acted upon by the environment, rather than "subject" acting in and on the world. As such, the individual alienates him/herself from participation in the construction of social reality. Powerlessness, for Freire, results from passive acceptance of oppressive cultural "givens," or surrender to a "culture of silence." Another way of understanding this is as submersion in a system of social relations to such an extent that the individual loses the sense of control over those relations. In a similar vein, Gaventa (1980) refers to this phenomenon as one of "acquiescence."

In sum, the sense of powerlessness is viewed as a construction of continuous interaction between the person and his/her environment. It combines an attitude of self-blame, a sense of generalized distrust, a feeling of alienation from resources for social influence, an experience of disenfranchisement and economic vulnerability, and a sense of hopelessness in socio-political struggle.

This perspective is more effectively portrayed through self-descriptions of the daily experience of powerlessness from which the study's participants emerged. Sharon, for example, a Native American now living in Harlem, recalls that in her growing up:

> It would never have occurred to me to have expressed an opinion on anything. . . It was *inconceivable* that my opinion had any value. . . that's lower than powerlessness. . . You don't even know the word "power" exists. It applies to *them*. . . I didn't question that that's the way the world was. . . It was *their* world. . . And I was an intruder, you know?

Such feelings of isolation and impotence were echoed by all the participants. Felipe, a migrant laborer, remembers:

> When you're in the "stream," you feel powerless, you feel helpless. You just feel like you're in there and you can't get out. And if you get out of the "stream," like a fish getting out of the water, you'll just die. . . I always felt like I was trapped.

The flow of day-to-day social relations reinforces the expectations of inability to impact on one's own life-world. The politics of silence is so deeply embedded that abdication to ineffectuality perpetuates itself. As Faith, from a small town in Central Appalachia, sums up:

> The people around here. . . don't believe that things *can* change. . . . You go in a community and break people's spirit, they can't hardly overcome it.

Major public institutions—i.e., schools, church, the press, and local government—function as partners in the suppression of individual initiative. Their intimidation is especially intense in relation to the experience of economic insecurity. Indebtedness and financial dependency are *concrete* realities in lower-income life-worlds; they are not merely emotional constructs. Lower-income citizens are thus understandably reticent to jeopardize whatever small economic ground they may have gained through overt challenge of established interests. Because networks of political and economic resources are so extensively intertwined, vulnerability to economic loss, for all these individuals, is quite real.

Moreover, survival is, in itself, a full-time occupation. As such, engagement in citizen action is inescapably an additional burden— particularly for those whose incomes are already so very low. As Felipe, the migrant laborer, underscores:

> People don't have time. . . they're tired, they work too late. . . you don't have a chance to stop and think. All you're worried about. . . is making sure you earn enough to feed your stomach and feed your children.

This feeling is echoed by Emily, a public health nurse:

> People like us. . . have a hard enough time copin' with every-day livin'. When you have to work every day for your basic food, shelter, clothes, and safety, you're not very much apt to have a lot of energy left to go to meetin's. . . . People. . . are so busy earnin' a livin' they don't really stop and think about. . . what real impact they may have as a citizen.

As a consequence of these issues, as Emily reiterates:

> You feel like you just *can't* do things. You're reluctant to stand up and voice your point of view. You'd rather give up than get involved.

In view of these experiences, the central question posed by this study is all the more dramatic. How *do* individuals manage to move beyond these situations of powerlessness and oppression? In what ways do the shared experiences of a scattered group of individuals illuminate the elusive idea of empowerment? What emerges from their lengthy and detailed retrospections is a common and consistent conception of empowerment as a process of becoming, as an ordered and progressive development of participatory skills and political understandings. Empowerment then assumes a dual mean-ing. It refers both to a longitudinal dynamic of development and to attainment of a set of insights and abilities best characterized as "participatory competence." Discussion here will focus primarily on the notion of empowerment as a developmental process.

EMPOWERMENT AS A DEVELOPMENTAL PROCESS

As portrayed by all participants in this study, the transition from powerlessness to participatory competence can best be characterized as a dynamic of long-term development from socio-political illiteracy or "infancy" to socio-political "adulthood." The primary themes revealed in participants' interviews cluster in sequential patterns which comprise a life span analogy in their emergence. There appear to be four distinct and progressive phases of involvement as these individuals construct the skills and the insights which constitute a fully matured attainment of participatory competence.

The "Era of Entry"

Despite the sense of powerlessness which characterized the prior life-worlds of all participants, these individuals also shared a common sense of "integrity" in their sensed self-identity and daily lives. Aspects of this underlying attitude include a strong sense of pride and determination, a deeply felt rootedness in community, a commitment to self-reliance, and feelings of attachment and support within a caring community of peers. It is only as this sense of integrity is directly violated or attacked that these individuals respond. The common or daily experience of injustice and exploitation is insufficient in its provocation. For all of the study's participants, only tangible and direct threats to individual or familial self-interests provoke the initiation of what ultimately evolves as an empowering response.

Emily, for example, speaks of her concern regarding the proposed construction of an electric power facility which would flood and destroy her native valley:

> My heart and soul, my way of life, everything is here. . . That valley is *me*. It's a part of us. . . . Now are they just goin' to come in here and destroy all this? No! And I'm goin' to stay in here and fight until somebody shoots me down one way or another.

It is important to note that these initial reactions are never fostered by "consciousness-raising," intellectual analysis, or other merely educative intervention. Only the immediate and physical violation of the sense of integrity described has sufficient force to mobilize initial participation. In one case, for example, a woman is assaulted in her own yard, and only then becomes active in a burgeoning community organization. In another, the betrayal of years-long trust in a relationship with a farmer incites a migrant laborer finally to respond. In each case, the mobilizing episode has some particular symbolic or emotional significance for the person involved. The incident or episode, of itself, is never of such objective force or magnitude that it would predictably energize others. The provocation of empowerment, it must then be understood, is necessarily a consequence of a personally experienced sense of outrage or confrontation.

The mobilizing episode is analogous to the "birth" of emergency of participatory competence. It initiates a period of a year or more of reactive engagement which we may refer to as the "era of entry." During this period, participation is exploratory, unknowing, and unsure. Individuals are first discovering their political muscles and potential for external impact. In Ellen's words, "In the beginning, emotionally. . . you think nobody could possibly be as nervous as I am, or as ill equipped. . ." Through awkward initial—often trial-and-error—efforts, they begin to develop their first sense of themselves as active political beings. As Martha attests:

> The longer you're involved, the more you begin to realize—I *can* say. I have the *right* to say everything! I am a taxpayer, I am a citizen. . . . If I feel that somebody is doing me wrong, I'm gonna speak out.

Moving through this initial phase demands especially that each individual alter his/her sense of relation to long established symbols and systems of authority. The symbolic "power" of authority in its various manifestations is confronted and demystified through the dynamics of conflict and engagement. Lucinda, for example, who initially experienced herself as "scared to death" of city officials, comes to appreciate, through years of effort in the community, that "titles. . . do not make you any different," that officials "do not have all the answers," and ultimately that "people *can* change things!" The de-mythification of power and reorienting of self in relation to authority is the central developmental demand of this initial post-mobilization phase.

The "Era of Advancement"

With relative success in the developmental tasks of the era of entry, individuals progress into an "era of advancement," which parallels the development of later childhood. The three major aspects of empowering evolution in this phase are the centrality of a mentoring relationship, the enabling impact of supportive peer relationships within a collective organizational structure, and the cultivation of a more critical understanding of social and political relations. Much like the initial period of reaction, this phase also encompasses at least a year of intensive engagement and reflection.

All participants rely extensively on the assistance of an external enabler, or an outside community organizer. This is particularly true in the first years of community involvement, and in the tasks of demystification of political process and negotiation of new authority relations. Often described much like a benevolent parent, the enabler helps evoke latent strengths, nurtures independent action, and supports autonomous experimentation in unpracticed political skills. In Lucinda's words, again:

> When I first got involved. . . the (local organizers) all saw beyond me. . . they just didn't see me. They saw what I was *capable* of, what I *could* be. . . . It was so important that somebody cared enough to be there encouraging me, pushing me. . .coming back after me. . . no matter how afraid I was.

To these ends, the "organizer" acts as a role model, mentor, ally, instructor, and friend. While providing concrete aid in helping define appropriate actions, he/she also provides emotional support in the maintenance of effort amidst daily frustration and conflict.

Continuing engagement in citizen action, in and of itself, tends to subvert cycles of helplessness and oppression. But this is only true in the context of reflective and focused participation. Over time, through ongoing efforts, individuals construct more viable strategies for political action, more effective mechanisms for collective expression and support, and more sophisticated capacities for social analysis and resource development. Action informs understanding to the extent that individuals accept responsibility for their choices and engage in self-critical reflection on their efforts. As Ellen describes:

> My confidence grows from doing and failing and saying to myself, "Try again!" I try always to learn from mistakes that I've made.

Or, in Barbara's words:

> It all didn't happen easy. We often made mistakes. . . but I think that's the *best* way to do it. . . . It was a very long process of learning. But slowly we built it up.

Involvement in an organization of peers appears to be the essential ingredient in cultivation of rudimentary political skills. In the short term, the grassroots organization generates a sense of strength in numbers and provides an arena in which equally unknowing companions can collaborate in mutually supportive problem solving. Over the long haul, it nurtures the maturation of incipient skills by providing an environment in which risks can be taken, frustrations can be shared, fears can be allayed, and support can be reinforced. In this fashion, it functions much as a traditional self-help group. It differs, however, in its emphasis on external causation and political dynamics. Rather than serving mainly to increase emotional support, it strives to articulate the embeddedness of individual conflicts in a more explicitly political frame of reference. As such, engagement in an organization helps to recast both consciousness and capacity in social and political, rather than simply personal and emotional terms. Together, participants in the organization learn and create the strategies, resources, and basic grammar of elementary political literacy.

As engagement in political activity continues, participants increase both the breadth and the depth of their involvements. Gradually, they become aware of the interconnections of social, political, and economic relations. Cultivation of more critical analysis, in turn, provokes continuing political action. The unfolding illumination of political process and deepening clarification of the relations through which exploitation and alienation are maintained lead eventually to a maturation of empowerment. This phenomenon is aptly illustrated in Felipe's poignant remarks:

I was thirty-five years old and never knew that I had rights to certain laws. . . It's hard for people to see what's really goin' on. You spend half your life helping to keep yourself down. . . The more that you get involved in making power, the more your understanding of power changes. The more I'm out there in the struggle, the more I'm realizing. The more I'm involved, the more I'm learning.

The longer participants extend their involvement, the more they come to understand. The more they understand, the more motivated they are to continue to act. The more they continue to act, the more proactive they are able to be. The more proactive they are able to be, the more they further their skill and effect. The more they sense their skill and effect, the more likely they are to continue. The cultivation of rudimentary strategic capacities and construction of more critical political awareness constitute this period's essential developmental tasks.

The "Era of Incorporation"

Having sustained participation through these first two eras of mobilization, these individuals advance into a subsequent "era of incorporation." In this period, self-concept, strategic ability, and critical comprehension substantially mature. Through continuing struggle, participants confront and learn to contend with the permanence and painfulness of structural or institutional barriers to self-determination. Emily refers to this ongoing frustration:

These corporations have the resources to do whatever the hell they please to support their position. But we're just a bunch of old tobacco farmers and workers who've got little more than our investment in a piece of land and a piece of history and a prayer to battle back with. . . . And you don't get any help. You don't get any help from government. You don't get any help from private corporations. You don't get any help from the media. But then we start to learn to apply ourselves to the corporate and societal issues in this thing. We have to "grow."

Organizing skills are sharpened, leadership skills are honed, and survival skills, of necessity, are constructed. Participants also are required to resolve the multiple role-conflicts and social strains generated by enduring community involvement. This task is particularly straining for women. Martha's feelings are particularly illustrative of this point:

> You get to the point when you're so involved with an organization that you can't help but feel that you're ignoring your family. . . I think [all women] feel the same way. They have that gnawing question hanging over their heads all the time— "How am I going to do all these things? How can I be a wife and mother and an organizer and a leader and be able to do them all well?"

Overcoming these obstacles helps to strengthen skill and resolve. And as these participatory capacities continue to evolve, the sense of mastery and competence are gradually incorporated in the individuals' sense of being in the world.

Incorporating self-acceptance of new levels of political competence and alteration of one's fundamental sense of relation to the socio-political world are this period's focal developmental concerns. Once again, this third phase seems to demand at least another full year's involvement. The elaboration of technical skill, the awakening of more abstract capacities, the increasingly self-conscious awareness of self as a visible and effective actor in the community, and continuous reflection on one's role and identity which characterize this phase of involvement directly parallel the central concerns of adolescence. It is intriguing that many participants refer to this transition themselves through the metaphor of "growing up." Most describe its conflicts in terms remarkably similar to those of adolescent "identity crisis." In Emily's words:

> I've changed. . . I think I'm understanding more of the structure of our society, and understanding more of how people operate within our society. But I've still not gotten it straight in my mind where is my little niche. Or do I have one? And what can I really do? One thing's for sure, I won't ever be the same self as I was when this thing first started.

Or, as Martha describes:

> All of a sudden, I "grew up". . . You grow up awfully fast.

You know, your mind, your values, and everything really change.

Not only must they resolve ongoing personal conflicts regarding their sense of self-competence and self-esteem, they must also reconstruct their sense of themselves as authors of—as well as actors in—the socio-political environment. Barbara summarizes this emergence:

> I'm a firm believer that anything in this life that affects you, you have control over. . . I think my skills have gotten sharper, and I think my conception in my own head has gotten clearer. . . I'm not in there just knocking around, doing this and hoping that reaction happens. . . I can go in now and deal with an issue and have in my head a very clear-cut process that you go through. . . I know it.

Just as the resolution of the "identity crisis" ushers individuals from adolescence into adulthood, so the resolution of this crisis of transformation ushers participants into a more mature state of empowerment.

The "Era of Commitment"

Those who develop a fully realized participatory competence are those who succeed in reconstructing their sense of mastery and awareness of self in relation to the political world. In the final "era of commitment," participants continue to struggle with integrating new personal knowledge and skill into the reality and structure of their everyday life-worlds. As Lucinda reveals:

> What I've learned in the past four years, I'm applying to *all* my life. It's changed my whole life—personal, professional, everything. My values have changed. My priorities have changed. Everything has changed.

Much like in young adulthood, they search for viable and personally meaningful ways of applying their new abilities and insights. Many transpose their capacities into new careers helping others. Some commit themselves to more traditional political roles. All have committed themselves to adapting their recent empowerment to continuing proactive community mobilization and leadership. Martha describes her involvement this way:

> I've learned enough where I think I can make some type of impact on people. . . . to make them aware of their neighborhood, or how it works. . . just as a resident of the neighborhood. You have experience. . . you have knowledge. . . . It's up to you to help those new leaders.

In this period, then, participatory competence attains its "adulthood." While this investigation did not examine the experience of post-transition survival, it is clear that the struggle of personal evolution continues. This continuity, too, is consistent with what we know of the continuity of life span development.

Underlying Developmental Themes

By way of summation, we can identify at least two pervasive themes which underlie movement through all phases of the developmental process portrayed. First is the function of a continuing internal "constructive dialogue," or the maintenance of the creative force of internal contradiction. From the very initiation of empowering mobilization, the internal perception of dissonance is fundamental—i.e., people must *feel* the confrontation to respond. This is the essence of what organizers have always referred to as finding "gut issues." In one participant's words:

> You can't empower people unless you can get them involved. And to get them involved, you've got to have an issue that smacks people somewhere inside that something is wrong. . . . It's got to be an issue that touches them in the gut.

In the struggle towards empowerment, conflict and growth are inextricably intertwined. It is essential that individuals continue to experience conflict to sustain their emergence. As the woman above continues: "If you don't have conflict. . . you're dead. . . . The moment at which you try to stop conflict is the moment at which you stop growing." It is also essential that there be constructive channels and supportive resources for resolution of these continuing internal confrontations. The maintenance of this internally creative tension, however, is the force which propels the developmental process.

In addition to this function of constructive conflict is the essential contribution of the dynamic of "praxis." Praxis, here, refers to the circular relationship of experience and reflection through which actions evoke new understandings, which then provoke new and more effective actions. As one participant remarks, "It's like the more I see, the more I want to stay in it. . . The more I learn, the more I want to struggle. . . All these little things just keep pushing you into more." Involvement generates insight, which, in turn, promotes more knowing participation.

Experience, then, is at the core of empowering learning. The "building up" of skills progresses only through repetition of cycles of action and reflection. In another participant's words:

> You've got to live it. You've got to *do* it. It's like, you can take an instruction course on how to do sex best, but if you don't go do sex, if you don't go and try it, then all you know is the hypothesis. . . It's the same way with going through experience with community organizing. You go through these steps of developing your anger. . . . You're getting angrier each time you take the next step. . . . You have to *build* it up.

While this research sought to illuminate empowering transitions as processes of development, I had never anticipated the consistency and clarity of the developmental model which ultimately emerged. The preceding paragraphs merely sketch the outlines of a much more fully developed and complicated descriptor of empowering transformation (see Kieffer, 1981). What this outline lacks, in particular, is the vitality and forcefulness of the words of the participants themselves. I find again and again that I am frustrated terribly by an inability to reduce their elaborate and dramatic personal retrospections into an appropriately respectful theoretical summary. That is, at least partially, because those persons clearly hold little respect for the abstraction of theory. It is not that they act without thought—much to the contrary. It is simply that they see thought's fundamental function as informing action. They are little concerned with conceptual description of their acts, except to the extent that it may render their future acts—or those of their peers—more effective. It is this critical idea which most appropriately leads us into discussion of the policy and practice implications of this developmental model of citizen empowerment.

IMPLICATIONS FOR PRACTICE

Generally this developmental perspective establishes the specific importance of *time* and of *practice* in the evolution of participatory skills. Empowerment is inescapably labor-intensive. For all of these participants, at least four years of intensive experience underlies attainment of enduring commitment. While individuals may expand their political fluency or grow in their sense of self-competence in more limited time frames, only those who evolve through all identified eras of involvement establish a fully mature participatory competence. The significantly transformative transitions portrayed can grow only from long-term engagement. In becoming empowered, individuals are not merely acquiring new practical skills; they are reconstructing and reorienting deeply engrained personal systems of social relations. Moreover, they confront these tasks in an environment which historically has enforced their political repression, and which continues its active and implicit attempts at subversion of constructive change. It is completely unrealistic to presume that the cumulative effects of domination can be reversed in any other than a long-term frame of reference. As such, it would be frivolous to pretend that there can ever be developed a ''short course'' in individual empowerment.

It is not simply the issue of ''time'' that is so crucial, but more importantly the question of practice. Empowerment is not a commodity to be acquired, but a transforming process constructed through action. Throughout the proposed developmental model, reflective experience is the irreducible source of growth. Individuals must learn to overcome internalized expectations of helplessness, conflicts inherent in maintaining collective support, the strains of familial disruption, the frustrations of inequities in tactical resources, and the endurance of political intimidation. These capacities evolve only through practice. In one participant's recollection, struggling through such conflicts is the most critical process in learning:

> It's important for people to go through the process and to see what you have to do in order to get something done in the system. It's important for them to have to feel all the agony, and all of that. . . . Growing is an awful painful process.

As she emphasizes, the knowledge, skills, and commitments of participatory competence are constructed primarily through actions in, and on, the environment. There is no substitute for learning through experience. More passive forms of training and instruction may be useful in instances where specific information is required; but the didactic approach apparently has little relevance in promoting the most critical elements of empowerment. As another participant remarks:

> People can't really learn the things that I've learned through workshops or through classes or courses. . . You have to experience it yourself to really know.

While we cannot simulate or cognitively duplicate the fundamental dynamic of empowering learning, we can actively facilitate individuals, or citizen organizations, in their own critical and constructive examination of their efforts toward changing social and political situations.

In most of these tasks, the grassroots organization can best serve as the locus of learning and support. While empowerment is, at root, an individual demand, it is nurtured by the effects of collective effort. Because the citizen organization is the arena in which sociopolitical literacy is most naturally and effectively nourished, practitioners can utilize or adapt the broad existing knowledge of organizational development and group process to assist in building grassroots organizations that can thrive. Much of what we know of leadership development, group problem solving, peer support, and motivation can easily be applied. But the keyword throughout is "collaboration."

Among the central lessons of this study is the conclusion that we should not seek to do for others what they must do for themselves. We should not focus so much on designing programs "on behalf of" others; rather, we must strive to collaborate *with* others in developing the emotional and practical resources they require. The participants refer with great emotional intensity to the importance of the role of an external enabler, or mentor, as they struggle through their empowering growth. This role is a useful model to build on as we consider how best to work with persons or programs in fostering empowering or participatory skills. In such facilitating relationships, we can function more effectively in addressing the many conflicts each individual confronts in evolving toward participatory competence. Some personal issues relate to the demands of developing and maintaining effective political and organizational problem-solving skills. Others relate to the personal stress and strain which result from the inherent role demands of citizen leadership and changing social roles which are consequent to empowerment. Facilitation oriented to such needs will help evoke and maintain involvement while reducing the risks of "burnout" and frustration. The mentoring role is most promising in this task.

Another manner in which we can utilize traditional skills in a nontraditional fashion (with distinctly empowering effect) is in assisting with the development of action-research capabilities. The more accurately and extensively individuals are able to perceive and describe their environments, the more effective they become in their political action. To the extent that knowledge of one's setting helps to deal with one's setting more effectively (Engleberg, 1981), generation of knowledge is empowering. As one participant asserts:

> The only way you can change a system is by knowing what the system is about. . . . The more you know, the more you can handle. . . knowing is power.

The construction of critical awareness is an essential component in developing the capability to competently challenge established systems or political interests. This was manifest in this study in areas as diverse as exploring investment policies of financial institutions and their relation to neighborhood development, assessing community needs for low-cost health care, and examining the impact of industrial poisons on workers and community residents. The generation of such data can be useful both in provocation of mobilization and in application as a political tool. Aiding in the development of related research skills has a significant empowering potential.

The articulation of a progression of developmental stages—as portrayed—also suggests the need to orient facilitation to the particular conflicts confronting individuals at varying points in the developmental continuum. The life span analogy suggests the importance of designing facilitation to be responsive to changing capabilities in changing phases of personal evolution. For example, the initial phases of involvement are often most concerned with the individuals' perceptions of self in relation to authority. Training, support, or aid in this period might then focus best on helping individuals in working through these conflicts. In the following period, individual concerns revolve around developing practical organizing strategies and skills. This could then be seen as the most appropriate emphasis

of assistance in this time. Effective intervention towards empowerment respects the assumption of a graduated cultivation of participatory skills. And, in every case, we must build on assumptions of
citizens' strengths and capabilities, not needs and inabilities. While
we cannot substantially alleviate the most pervasive and painful of
social inequities, we can work to help others develop the capacities
and resources which will enable them to act more efficaciously on
their own.

Traditionally, we limit our thinking regarding preventive interventions to the promotion of psychological health or the reduction of
emotional disorder. More recently we have added emphasis in the
areas of engendering proactive social and cognitive capabilities and
strengthening social support. In most instances we have contained
our discussion within the boundaries of social well-being or personal
mental health. To this end, we teach "problem-solving skills" and
"assertiveness training." We offer instruction in "stress reduction
techniques" and create programs which foster "coping skills."
While these programs and the skills they engender may well have
some degree of empowering consequence, they fall well short of the
concept of empowerment portrayed by the participants in this research. This study illuminates a view of empowerment as an extensively political—as well as psychosocial—conception. What
could be more fundamentally preventive—or political—than individuals' capabilities for conscious and effective involvement in mold-
ing the myriad systems and dynamics which define their daily lives?
Should we not then consider efficacious citizenship as a critical
preventive outcome variable? Ira Iscoe (1974) said almost a decade
ago:

> If the poor were articulate, knew their way around the system,
> and had time to spend building up their resources, then they
> most likely would not be poor and lacking in power. (p. 612)

The wisdom of this perspective—and the loss entailed in our continuous evasion of it—ought to be painfully self-evident by now.

REFLECTIONS ON THE MEANING OF EMPOWERMENT

In closing, we return to the question of the meaning of "empowerment." This study suggests that we articulate a distinction between empowerment as a development of empowering skills and

empowerment as attainment of participatory competence. The thrust of this article has been to illuminate the idea of empowerment as a long-term and continuing *process* of adult development.

At the same time, however, empowerment can be viewed as attainment of an abiding set of commitments and capabilities which can be referred to as "participatory competence." This state of being and ability incorporates three major intersecting aspects or dimensions: (a) development of more positive self-concept, or sense of self-competence, (b) construction of more critical or analytical understanding of the surrounding social and political environment, and (c) cultivation of individual and collective resources for social and political action. It is important to emphasize that these are interconnected elements of a unitary notion of socio-political competence.

Interventions or self-initiated efforts which promote development of any of these competencies can be seen as "empowering," at least in a limited way. To the extent that efforts promote development in *all three* dimensions simultaneously, they have greater empowering capability. A fully established attainment of empowerment, however, implies attainment of extensive and abiding competence in each of these areas—all of which are essential participatory skills. Participatory competence thus refers to the combination of attitudes, understandings, and abilities required to play a conscious and assertive role in the ongoing social construction of one's political environment. It is essentially an enabling evolution which implies the establishment of self as subject, or author, of one's own history (Freire, 1970; Sartre, 1963).

While this view of participatory competence emerges directly from the data of this study, it is consistent with several prior related conceptions. It can be seen as parallel, for example, with Hunter and Harman's (1979) notion of "functional literacy" as attainment of skills for self-determination. It similarly encompasses Kozol's (1980) description of "functional literacy" as the ability to question the legitimacy of social institutions and to participate in their transformation. This approach is also clearly linked to conceptions of "competence" familiar in the psychological literature (Albee, 1980; Bond & Rosen, 1980; Inkeles, 1966; Smith, 1968; White, 1959). These refer variably to elements of self-esteem, sense of causal importance, efficacy in new or traditional social roles, effective management of stressful events, and capacity for resource mobilization. The essential difference in the definition proposed here from those referred to above is twofold: (a) it places the notion of competence and coping within an explicitly political context, and (b) it suggests that participatory competence be conceptualized explicitly as the intersection of *all* of the above aspects of competence.

This conception of empowerment also departs from the more traditional notions of political power—which is usually described as "possession" of sufficient influence or authority to produce or to force change (Wrong, 1979). The participants in this study did not view themselves as *"having* more power," but rather as *"feeling* more powerful."* They had not necessarily gained significant social influence or political control, but they did see themselves becoming more efficacious participants in the political process and local decision making. While they did not assess themselves as having acquired any more absolute power to dictate the shape of their environments, they did believe they were growing better able to engage effectively in the dynamics of social and political exchange.

The fundamental empowering transformation, then, is in the transition from sense of self as helpless victim to acceptance of self as assertive and efficacious citizen. Achieving empowerment also implies developing the skills and resources needed to confront the root sources which create and perpetuate victimization. The "preventive" impact of this model resides in the development of competencies required to counteract the dehumanizing and destructive social forces which underlie most human stress and dysfunction. In developing political literacy, or attaining the participatory competence of political "adulthood," individuals create the most promising preventive capacities conceivable.

REFERENCES

Abramowitz, S. I. Research on internal-external control, locus of control and social political activism. *Psychological Reports*, 1974, *34*, 619-621.

Abramson, L. Y., Seligman, M. E. P., & Teasdale, J. D. Learned helplessness in humans: Critique and reformation. *Journal of Abnormal Psychology*, 1978, *87*, 49-74.

Adams, F. *Unearthing seeds of fire: The idea of highlander.* Winston-Salem, N.C.: John F. Blair, 1975.

Albee, G. W. A competency model must replace the defect model. In L. A. Bond & J. C. Rosen (Eds.), *Competence and coping during adulthood.* Hanover, N.H.: University Press of New England, 1980.

Alinsky, S. D. *Reveille for radicals.* New York: Vintage Books, 1969.

Allport, G. The psychology of participation. *Psychological Review*, May 1945, pp. 117-132.

Andersen, W. G., Spiegel, H., Suess, T. A., & Woods, W. K. *Profiles of participation.* New York: National Municipal League, 1979.

Becker, C. S. *Phenomenology: An overview of theoretical and methodological issues.* Paper presented at the meeting of the American Psychological Association, 1978.

Becker, H. S. Interviewing medical students. *American Journal of Sociology,* 1956, *62,* 199-20.

Berger, P. L., & Luckmann, T. *The social construction of reality.* New York: Anchor Books, 1967.

Berger, P. L., & Neuhaus, R. J. *To empower people: The role of mediating structures in public policy.* Washington, D.C.: American Enterprise Institute, 1977.

Bond, L. A., & Rosen, J. C. (Eds.). *Competence and coping during adulthood.* Hanover, N.H.: University Press of New England, 1980.

Boyte, H. *The backyard revolution.* Philadelphia: Temple University Press, 1980.

Clark, K. *Pathos of power.* New York: Harper & Row, 1974.

Cloward, R. A., & Ohlin, L. E. *Delinquency and opportunity.* New York: The Free Press, 1960.

Colaizzi, P. F. Psychological research as the phenomenologist views it. In R. S. Valle & M. King (Eds.), *Existential-phenomenological alternatives in psychology.* New York: Oxford University Press, 1978.

Coleman, J. S. *Power and the structure of society.* New York: W. W. Norton & Company, 1974.

Cook, N. C. *Citizen participation issues.* Charlottesville, VA: Mid-Atlantic Consortium for Community Education—University of Virginia, 1979.

Cottrell, L. S. The competent community. In R. L. Warren (Ed.), *New perspectives on the American community* (3rd ed.). Chicago: Rand-McNally, 1977.

Cowen, E. Social and community interventions. *Annual Review of Psychology,* 1973, *24,* 423-472.

Cowen, E. The wooing of primary prevention. *American Journal of Community Psychology,* 1980, *8*(3), 258-284.

Danish, S. J., & D'Augelli, A. R. Promoting competence and enhancing development through life development intervention. In L. A. Bond & J. C. Rosen (Eds.), *Competence and coping during adulthood.* Hanover, N.H.: University Press of New England, 1980.

Davies, D., & Zerchykov, R. *Citizen participation in education.* Boston: Institute for Responsive Education, 1978.

Engleberg, S. Toward explicit value standards in community psychology. *American Journal of Community Psychology,* 1981, *9*(4), 425-434.

Erikson, E. H. *Identity and the life cycle* (Reissue). New York: W. W. Norton & Company, 1980.

Fahrquhar, E., & Dawson, K. S. *Citizen education today: Developing civic competencies* (Office of Education Publication No. 79-07007). Washington, D.C.: U.S. Government Printing Office, 1979.

Fanon, F. *The wretched of the earth.* New York: Grove Press, 1963.

Finifter, A. W. Dimensions of political alienation. *American Political Science Review,* 1970, *64*(2), 389-410.

Freire, P. *Pedagogy of the oppressed.* New York: Seabury Press, 1970.

Freire, P. *Education for critical consciousness.* New York: Seabury Press, 1973.

Fromm, E. *Marx's concept of man.* New York: Ungar, 1961.

Gaventa, J. *Power and powerlessness.* Urbana: University of Illinois Press, 1980.

Giorgi, A. *Psychology as a human science.* New York: Harper & Row, 1970. (a)

Giorgi, A. Toward phenomenologically based research in psychology. *Journal of Phenomenological Psychology,* 1970, *1*(1), 75-98. (b)

Giorgi, A. Phenomenology and the foundations of psychology. In W. J. Arnold (Ed.), *Nebraska symposium on motivation, 1975.* Lincoln: University of Nebraska Press, 1976.

Gittell, M., Hoffacker, B., Rollins, E., & Foster, S. *Citizen organizations: Citizen participation in educational decisionmaking.* Boston: Institute for Responsive Education, 1979.

Green, G. *Who's organizing the neighborhood?* Washington, D.C.: U.S. Government Printing Office, 1979.

Gurin, G., & Gurin, P. Expectancy theory in the study of poverty. *Journal of Social Issues*, 1970, *26*, 83-104.

Harris, L. *Confidence and concern: Citizens view American government.* Washington, D.C.: U.S. Government Printing Office, 1973.

Henry, J. *Culture against man.* New York: Random House, 1963.

Hunter, C. S. J., & Harmon, D. *Adult illiteracy in the United States.* New York: McGraw-Hill, 1979.

Inkeles, A. Social structure and the socialization of competence. *Harvard Educational Review*, 1966, *36*(3), 255-283.

Iscoe, I. Community psychology and the competent community. *American Psychologist*, 1974, *29*, 607-613.

Jennings, K., & Niemi, R. J. Patterns of political learning. *Harvard Educational Review*, 1968, *38*(3).

Joffe, J. M., & Albee, G. W. (Eds.). *Prevention through political action and social change.* Hanover, N.H.: University Press of New England, 1981. (a)

Joffe, J. M., & Albee, G. W. Powerlessness and psychopathology. In J. M. Joffee & G. W. Albee (Eds.), *Prevention through political action and social change.* Hanover, N.H.: University Press of New England, 1981. (b)

Kahn, S. *How people get power.* New York: McGraw-Hill, 1971.

Kelly, J. G. Antidotes for arrogance: Training for a community psychology. *American Psychologist*, 1970, *25*, 524-531.

Kelly, J. G., Snowden, L. R., & Munoz, R. F. Social and community interventions. *Annual Review of Psychology*, 1977, *28*, 323-361.

Kessler, M., & Albee, G. W. Primary prevention. *Annual Review of Psychology*, 1975, *26*, 557-591.

Kieffer, C. H. *The emergence of empowerment: The development of participatory competence among individuals in citizen organizations.* Unpublished Doctoral Dissertation. Ann Arbor: University of Michigan, 1981.

Klein, D. C., & Goldston, S. E. (Eds.). *Primary prevention: An idea whose time has come* (DHEW Publication No. ADM 77-447). Washington, D.C.: U.S. Government Printing Office, 1977.

Konopka, G. Social change, social action as prevention: The role of the professional. In J. M. Joffee & G. W. Albee (Eds.), *Prevention through political action and social change.* Hanover, N.H.: University Press of New England, 1981.

Kozol, J. *Prisoners of silence.* New York: Continuum, 1980.

Langton, S. *Citizen participation in America.* Lexington, Mass: Lexington Books, 1978.

Lasch, C. *The culture of narcissism.* New York: Warner Books, 1979.

Lerner, M. P. Surplus powerlessness. *Social Policy*, 1979, *2*(4), 18-27.

Levinson, D. J. *The seasons of a man's life.* New York: Ballantine Books, 1978.

Lewis, O. *The children of Sanchez.* New York: Random House, 1961.

Liebow, E. *Tally's corner.* Boston: Little, Brown & Company, 1967.

Maier, S. F., & Seligman, M. E. Learned helplessness: Theory and evidence. *Journal of Experimental Psychology*, 1976, *105*, 3-46.

May, R. *Power and innocence.* New York: Delta, 1972.

Mead, G. H. *Mind, self and society.* Chicago: University of Chicago Press, 1934.

Moynihan, D. *Maximum feasible misunderstanding.* New York: The Free Press, 1970.

Natanson, M. Phenomenology as a rigorous science. In T. Luckmann (Ed.), *Phenomenology and sociology.* New York: Penguin Books, 1978.

Pateman, C. *Participation and democratic theory.* Cambridge: University Press, 1970.

Perlman, J. E. Grassrooting the system. *Social Policy*, 1976, *7*(2), 4-20.

Phares, E. J. *Locus of control: A personality determinant of behavior.* Morristown, N.J.: General Learning Press, 1973.

Piaget, J. *The development of thought: Equilibrium of cognitive structures.* New York: Viking Press, 1977.

Piven, F. F., & Cloward, R. A. *Poor people's movements.* New York: Vintage Books, 1977.

Ransford, H. E. Isolation, powerlessness, and violence: A study of attitudes and participation in the Watts riot. *American Journal of Sociology,* 1968, *73,* 581-591.

Rappaport, J. *Community psychology: Values, research and action.* New York: Holt, Rinehart and Winston, 1977.

Rappaport, J. In praise of paradox: A social policy of empowerment over prevention. *American Journal of Community Psychology,* 1981, *9*(1), 1-25.

Rappaport, J., Davidson, W. S., Wilson, M. N., & Mitchell, A. Alternatives to blaming the victim or the environment: Our places to stand have not moved the earth. *American Psychologist,* 1975, *30,* 525-528.

Rotter, J. B. Generalized expectancies for internal versus external control of reinforcement. *Psychological Monographs,* 1966, *80*(1), (Whole No. 609).

Rotter, J. B. External control and internal control. *Psychology Today,* June 1971.

Rubin, L. B. *Worlds of pain.* New York: Basic Books, 1976.

Ryan, W. *Blaming the victim.* New York: Vintage Books, 1971.

Sardello, R. J. A reciprocal participation model of experimentation. In A. Giorgi, W. F. Fischer, & R. Von Eckartsberg (Eds.), *Duquesne studies in phenomenological psychology* (Vol. 1). Pittsburgh: Duquesne University Press, 1971.

Sartre, J. P. *Search for a method.* New York: Vintage Books, 1963.

Schlozman, K. L., & Verba, S. *Injury to insult.* Cambridge: Harvard University Press, 1979.

Seeman, M. On the meaning of alienation. *American Sociological Review,* 1959, *24,* 783-791.

Seeman, M. Alienation and engagement. In A. Campbell & P. Converse (Eds.), *The human meaning of social change.* New York: Russell Sage, 1972.

Seifer, N. *Nobody speaks for me!* New York: Simon & Schuster, 1976.

Sennett, R., & Cobb, J. *The hidden injuries of class.* New York: Vintage Books, 1973.

Sexton, P. C. *Spanish Harlem: Anatomy of poverty.* New York: Harper Colophon, 1965.

Sidel, V. W., & Sidel, R. Beyond coping. *Social Policy,* 1976, *7*(2), 67-69.

Sigel, R. Assumptions about the learning of political values. In E. S. Greenberg (Ed.), *Political socialization.* New York: Atherton Press, 1970.

Smith, M. B. Competence and socialization. In J. A. Clausen (Ed.), *Socialization and society.* Boston: Little, Brown, & Company, 1968.

Spiegel, H. B. C. (Ed.). *Citizen participation in urban development* (Vol. 1-3). Washington, D.C.: NTL Institute for Applied Behavioral Science, 1968-1974.

Spivak, H. *School decentralization and community control.* New York: Center for Urban Education, 1973.

Steinberg, L. S. *Social science theory and research on participation and voluntary associations.* Boston: Institute for Responsive Education, 1977.

Stevick, E. L. An empirical investigation of the experience of anger. In A. Giorgi, W. F. Fischer, & R. Von Eckartsberg (Eds.), *Duquesne studies in phenomenological psychology* (Vol. 1). Pittsburgh: Duquesne University Press, 1971.

Stokols, D. Toward a psychological theory of alienation. *Psychological Review,* 1975, *82*(1), 26-44.

Unger, D. G., & Wandersman, A. Neighboring in an urban environment. *American Journal of Community Psychology,* 1982, *10*(5), 493-509.

Verba, S., & Nie, N. *Participation in America: Political democracy and social equality.* New York: Harper & Row, 1972.

Von Eckartsberg, R. On experiential methodology. In A. Giorgi, W. F. Fischer, & R. Von Eckartsberg (Eds.), *Duquesne studies in phenomenological psychology* (Vol. 1). Pittsburgh: Duquesne University Press, 1971.

Wandersman, A., Jakubs, J. F., & Giamartino, G. A. Participation in block organizations. *Journal of Community Action,* 1981, *1*(1), 40-47.

White, R. W. Motivation reconsidered: The concept of competence. *Psychological Review*, 1959, *66*, 297-333.

Whyte, W. F. *Street corner society*. Chicago: University of Chicago Press, 1943.

Withern, A. Helping ourselves: The limits and potential of self-help. *Social Policy*, 1980, *11*(3), 20-28.

Wrong, D. H. *Power: Its forms, bases, and uses*. New York: Harper Colophon, 1979.

Yin, R. K., Lucas, W. A., Szanton, P. L., & Spindler, J. A. *Citizen organizations*. Santa Monica, CA: RAND, 1973.

Empowerment in a Religious Setting: A Multivariate Investigation

Kenneth I. Maton
Julian Rappaport

ABSTRACT. This study examines the correlates and contexts of empowerment among members of a Christian, nondenominational religious setting. The research approach combines participant-observation and measurement development methodology to capture the empowering aspects of religious experience in a form which lends itself to quantitative analysis, without excessive loss of the phenomenological meaning of that experience. The criterion of empowerment is progress toward a salient goal of members—interpersonal behavior change in the direction of group ideals (i.e., in the direction of becoming more like Jesus). Present and retrospective past measurement of perceived interpersonal behavior yielded eight predictor variables from member peer, self-report, and interviewer sources. These variables include religious orientation, locus of control, spiritual experience, group involvement, and religious history. The relationship of the predictors to interpersonal behavior change was assessed in canonical correlation analyses. Results from multiple data sources find that those seen by themselves and by others as empowered are committed to a relationship with God and with others in the setting. They may be described, in part, as experiencing

---

This paper is based on the first author's masters thesis, under the direction of the second author. A more detailed version of the study, including complete descriptions of all measurement devices and item pools which could not be included due to space limits, is available on request. Requests for reprints should be sent to the authors at the Department of Psychology, University of Illinois, 603 E. Daniel Street, Champaign, IL 61820.

The authors wish to express their gratitude to the Elders and members of New Covenant Fellowship, Urbana-Champaign, for their willingness to openly share so much of their intimate experiences. The fellowship Elders were particularly helpful in assisting us in the conduct of the study in such a way as to maximize cooperation and veridical reports by the members. We are also grateful to Thom Moore of the University of Illinois for his insightful collaboration during much of the study and to several reviewers whose candid critiques of methodology and data analysis helped us to improve our handling of the difficult problems encountered in such a project. We are particularly grateful for the constructive critique of an earlier version of this manuscript offered by Carolyn Swift who, as Associate Editor of this journal, provided many helpful suggestions for revision.

a "psychological sense of community." In addition, they report a
life crisis prior to joining the setting and a sense that God is in control of the events of their life. Follow-up data, three years later, finds
a relationship between commitment and life satisfaction. Two years
of participant-observation provide hypotheses, consistent with
several psychological theories, for suggesting salient setting
variables which provide a context for understanding the results.

RESEARCH STRATEGY

The relationship between religion and psychological well-being
has been of interest to researchers for several decades (Argyle,
1959; Dittes, 1971; Donaldson, 1976; Sanua, 1969; Stark, 1971). A
renewed interest has emerged among those who emphasize the importance of natural support systems for social policies and programs
(e.g., President's Commission on Mental Health, 1978). Natural
support systems are those relationships (e.g., family, friend, neigh-
bor) and settings (e.g., voluntary and religious associations) which
constitute the enduring social fabric of individual lives. In American
life religious groups represent one of the most prevalent of such
natural settings (Jacquet, 1972). They constitute a potential resource
for those who believe that the efficacy and reach of traditional mental health services as sources of empowerment are limited. However, at present little is known about the processes and impacts of
most natural support systems, including religious settings. The research reported here is aimed at contributing to the understanding of
the processes by which members of a particular religious setting
come to experience empowerment.

Since much of religious experience is subjective, it has not readily
lent itself to analysis by conventional scientific approaches. Nevertheless, a great deal of our psychological understanding of human
beings is grounded in attempts to objectify phenomenology. In principle, religious experience may be describable by using many of the
familiar methods of personality assessment and multivariate data
analysis which can be applied to understand other complex internal
processes. This paper is, in part, an attempt to capture the empowering aspects of religious experience in a form which lends itself to
quantitative analysis, without excessive loss of the phenomenological meaning of that experience.

In order to lend validity to our understanding of the quantitative
measures, we have selected a strategy for research which relies on

participant-observation as a means to allow us to interpret the more objective data collected. The selection of that strategy necessarily meant that we had the advantage of knowing a great deal about almost every individual who completed our measures, as well as about the internal organizational processes of the setting. Presumably, we could interpret the responses to our questionnaires in light of that knowledge. Similarly, we were able to construct measures based on our knowledge of the setting as well as our knowledge of measurement development technology. This approach has the disadvantage, given the time investment, of limiting our work to one setting and of leaving us open to charges of "bias" in our interpretation of data. That charge may be partly overcome by our use of multiple sources of data—self-report, reports of peers who are a part of the setting and those who are outside the setting, and by use of several independent interviewers who were not participant-observers. We do our best to describe our methodology such that the readers may draw their own conclusions as to the wisdom of our research strategy.

It is useful to note at the outset several additional limitations of such a study, as well as some of the advantages. We attempt to use what we have learned from our data to understand those who are "empowered" in a particular religious community. As such, this data is viewed as a case study of a particular setting which generates hypotheses about other similar settings. When we first approached this setting as observers we expected to find it to be one wherein a significant portion of the members would express the belief that their experience is empowering. The members of the setting were only later asked to participate in systematic individual analysis when, following a year of participant-observation, we became convinced that the setting was successful in facilitating empowerment among many of its members.

Our year long observation of setting participants and of certain leadership qualities and structural arrangements (some of which are described later in this paper) led us to the decision that our initial belief that we would find a reasonable number of people who would experience a sense of empowerment was correct. Given the likelihood of finding enough people who would experience a sense of empowerment, we only then decided that it would be profitable to look at individual differences among those who did and did not experience such a change, and to continue a second year of participant-observation. Thus, within our case study we were able to conduct a comparative study of individual differences. However, this study does not attempt to verify the assessment of the setting *per se* as "empowering" by comparing it to other settings—rather, it should be understood as a case study of people in a particular organization. We make no claim as to the relative impact of the setting as a vehicle for empowerment. Quantitative assessment is limited to within-setting analysis of individual differences on certain criterion behaviors which have been selected as an index of empowerment.

The thrust of this research is to look for multivariate relationships among a set of individual predictors and a set of criterion variables so as to describe the perceived experiences of those who score relatively highest on the criterion measures of empowerment. In simple terms we ask: Within this religious setting how can we describe those who are seen by themselves and by others as empowered?

The multiplicity of perspectives from which the empowerment construct can be viewed and the diversity of goals and contexts of natural settings place special demands on research in the area. For instance, a natural setting can be said to empower individuals to the extent it helps members to: (1) develop a personal sense of being able to effect important life aims and/or (2) acquire psychological or material resources necessary for the accomplishment of life aims and/or (3) actually achieve (or make progress towards achieving) personal aims. The meaning of personal control and the nature of the resources and goals defined as important varies from setting to setting and individual to individual. Researchers must be careful to be sensitive to the nature of each setting to determine the meaning of the empowerment construct. For example, in religious settings a sense of too much personal control, to the exclusion of the sense of God's control, is often viewed by members as a negative, rather than a positive attribute.

The criterion of empowerment employed here is *perceived interpersonal behavior change in the direction of group ideals* (described in detail in the measures section). Perceived interpersonal behavior change was chosen as the criterion of empowerment because it represents a salient goal of group members. In the members' view, as measured by their ratings of ideal behavior, empowerment is best indexed by a sense of closeness with a loving God who actively transforms (i.e., empowers) members' lives in the direction of becoming more like Jesus (i.e., increased compassion and humility and a desire to serve and help others). This way of selecting the criterion measure is an attempt to meet the demand that the variables studied are central to the phenomenology of the people under study. In this setting empowerment is understood by the members to enable them to behave in particular interpersonally appropriate ways.

In addition to self-reports, the research design employed member and nonmember peer ratings of members' interpersonal behavior. Measures were taken retrospectively for the time period prior to joining the group and again with reference to the present. The anchor point for the criterion scales is the mean of members' ideal ratings for each dimension of interpersonal behavior, again an attempt to be consistent with the phenomenology of the group. The specific dimensions selected emerged from principal components analysis of members' ratings.

The predictor (individual differences) variables studied emerge from a combination of observation, theoretical considerations, and empirical analyses. Participant-observation revealed two especially salient dimensions of individual difference. One is the extent of love, forgiveness, and expectation for positive outcomes experienced in a personal relationship with God and Jesus. This dimension contains elements which diverse psychological theorists such as Sullivan, Rotter, and Rogers indicate as important conditions for behavior change and development. Individuals also differ in their involvement in the setting, an important dimension since extent of involvement should influence the impact of the setting on the person.

Since these two dimensions are salient both to the population under study and mainstream psychological theories, a set of summary items assessing them was designed for interviewer and member peer ratings. In addition, self-report "intrinsic religion" and locus of control items were included since one or both variables have been found to be correlated with psychological criteria in studies of other populations (Entner, 1977; Kahoe, 1974; McClain, 1978; Pargament, Tyler, & Steele, 1979). In keeping with a multidimensional perspective, and consistent with our belief that multivariate data analytic procedures are an appropriate tool for understanding individual differences, first order components analysis for each source and set of items separately, and second order components analysis across first order scales were used so that the final set of predictor scales would be based on empirical characteristics of the population under study. It was expected that the emerging (individual difference predictor) dimensions would be positively related to perceived interpersonal change (the criterion) measures generated from self, member, and nonmember peers.

METHOD: PARTICIPANT OBSERVATION,
PEER AND SELF-REPORT

Research Setting

This research is part of a larger, continuing study of a non-denominational Christian fellowship in a medium sized midwestern city. The fellowship evolved from a small Bible study group in the early 1970s into a congregation of 150-200 members at the time of this research. The diversity of backgrounds of those who constitute the formal and informal leadership of the group is distinctive: some came to the fellowship from social or student activist backgrounds; others from intensive involvement in local "street" or "drug" cultures; some were Christians just beginning to seek a relationship with a personal God; others already claimed a strong, personal relationship with Jesus; many had been strongly disillusioned with what they saw as rigidity or a lack of spirituality in mainline denominations. Of the 150-200 members who attend Sunday services, approximately 75-125 are also involved in one of the four "house churches" which meet one evening per week. The congregation is led by three "lay ministers," one of whom was financially supported by the congregation at the time of this research.

Although there is some variation among individuals, most fellowship members believe in a God who has been active throughout history and who continues to be active in everyday life in the present. Central to their faith is that Jesus is the Son of God who died to liberate mankind and who rose from the dead. Most members experience a personal relationship with God or Jesus in which they communicate through prayer. God or Jesus is seen as personally guiding their lives and growth. The Bible is seen as the revelation to man of God's word.

Many members verbalize: a desire for increased closeness with God and for God to meet personal needs together with a desire to become more compassionate and self-sacrificing as people; the goal of developing deep trust and childlike dependence on God together with the need to retain intellectual honesty in dealing with doubts and personal responsibility for one's decisions; and a desire for the fellowship to be a "family" which provides both interpersonal and material support for members together with a desire to involve everyone in decision making and to be able to change structures and traditions whenever they begin to rigidify and interfere with members' spiritual and personal growth.

Sample

Eighty-six of the 125 individuals listed on the then most current fellowship telephone-address listing at the time of the formal onset of data collection constitute the primary sample in the study. Thirty-eight are male and forty-eight female. The ages range from 19 to 54 with a mean of 29. Forty-four are married; all but one are white. Fifty-nine reside with one or more other fellowship members. Of these 59 members, 28 live with nuclear family members only, 18 reside in one of three communal fellowship households, and 13 have one or two fellowship roommates. The number of years of education completed ranges from 9 to 20, with a mean of 15 (three years of college). Twenty-three work in human services capacities in educational, social service, religious, or medical settings; seven are skilled tradesmen or hold positions of responsibility in business or technical settings; thirteen are graduate students; thirteen are undergraduates; eleven are homemakers; sixteen work at unskilled or semiskilled office or technical jobs and three are unemployed. Membership at the time of data collection ranged from four months to six years (when the congregation began), with a mean membership of 2.9 years.

Research Role

The investigators' role in the setting is that of participant-observers. In September, 1977 the membership was asked, and agreed, to participate in ongoing research about the setting. Shortly thereafter regular participation in Sunday morning worship, one of the weekday evening house church groups, and a diversity of social, recreational, and social action activities began. This involvement averaged about five to seven hours per week. It continued for two years. After the first year individual assessment devices were developed and administered. When asked, the investigators informed members that they were involved in research about the fellowship and interested in exploring personal spiritual questions.

Procedure

After one year in a participant-observation role, an extensive semistructured interview instrument was constructed as part of a larger study of this setting. Although details of that interview are not analyzed in the present study, specific interviewer ratings (described below) are. The interview includes sections on religious history, present religious beliefs and relationship with God or Jesus, fellowship involvement, past and present psychological, interpersonal, and social network characteristics, life crises, and social action orientation and activities. Seven graduate students (including the first author) and one graduate student's husband had five weeks of training before interviews commenced.[1] There were four male and four female interviewers, ranging in age from 22 to 35 and encompassing a wide diversity of religious backgrounds.

Stratified, random procedures were used to select potential interviewees from the fellowship address list and to assign interviewees to interviewers. Stratification was based on age, sex, and number of years of involvement in the fellowship (Table 1). Table 1 reveals that a relatively representative sample of the fellowship population was obtained.

Each interviewee was initially contacted by an investigator, who invited participation in a study that would describe various aspects of the fellowship and of members' group involvement, spirutual involvement, and personal lives. They were informed that interviewers were from a diversity of religious backgrounds, and asked if they were willing to be interviewed by whomever was free to do the next interview. They were informed that all interviews would be tape-recorded, and assured of the confidentiality of all information.

Random assignment of interviewees to interviewers was not fully possible. Six individuals requested to be interviewed by one of the investigators. One of the interviewers was able to do interviews on-campus during daylight hours only. Of the other interviewers, only two could do "full time" interviewing—these two were assigned the majority of interviewees that the investigator (due to "requested" interviews) and the other full time interviewer (due to scheduling/transportation limitations) could not do.

Over a seven month period, 86 interviews were completed. The interviews ranged from two and a half to ten hours, encompassing from two to five separate interview sessions per person. At the end of each one-and-one-half to two-and-one-half hour session, the interviewer completed relevant items from the interviewer rating measure.

---

[1]Interviewers were selected by asking for volunteers among graduate students in the Personality & Social Ecology and the Clinical Psychology programs at the University of Illinois, Urbana-Champaign.

TABLE 1

Stratification of Fellowship Members by Age and Time in Group

Age	Months in Fellowship	0-6	7-12	13-24	25-48	49+	Totals
				Male			
15-21		-	2 (2)	5 (3)	2 (2)	-	9 (7)
22-25		1 (1)	2 (1)	3 (2)	5 (3)	2 (2)	13 (9)
26-29		1 (0)	1 (1)	2 (0)	3 (2)	4 (2)	11 (5)
30-34		1 (0)	-	3 (2)	6 (5)	2 (2)	12 (9)
35+		-	-	2 (2)	3 (3)	3 (3)	8 (8)
Totals		3 (1)	5 (4)	15 (9)	19 (15)	11 (9)	53 (38)
				Female			
15-21		4 (4)	3 (2)	5 (3)	2 (1)	1 (1)	15 (11)
22-25		2 (1)	2 (0)	4 (2)	7 (6)	2 (1)	17 (10)
26-29		1 (1)	3 (3)	3 (3)	5 (3)	4 (2)	16 (12)
30-34		2 (2)	1 (1)	2 (2)	4 (3)	2 (1)	11 (9)
35+		-	-	4 (2)	5 (2)	4 (2)	13 (6)
Totals		9 (8)	9 (6)	18 (12)	23 (15)	13 (7)	72 (48)
						Grand Totals	125 (86)

Notes: Numbers in parentheses indicate the number from that cell who completed
the interview. All told, 100 of 125 fellowship members were contacted
for interviews; 88 agreed to be interviewed, and 86 completed the
interview.

At the conclusion of the interview, the interviewee was given a
self-report questionnaire to be completed during the next several
weeks and returned in a pre-addressed, pre-stamped envelope. Interviewees were also asked to provide the names of two or more fellowship and two or more non-fellowship peers who knew them well
and who they thought might be willing to fill out questionnaire
items.

Since some of the member peers were also interviewees, if they
were named as a peer they were contacted only after they had completed their own interviews and returned their own self-report
forms. When contacted, both member and nonmember peers were
told that as part of a study of the fellowship the person who had
given their name had already taken part in an extensive interview
and filled out a lengthy self-report form. They were assured that the
project was a study of the fellowship in general and not of individ-

uals, and that confidentiality of information and anonymity of individuals was guaranteed. If they agreed to take part, they were mailed peer rating forms (described below) and asked to return them within several weeks in the pre-stamped envelope provided.

Initial Item Pool: Predictor Variables

Adequate measures of personal belief and involvement developed for or validated on populations comparable to this fellowship do not exist. For the self-report source, this required beginning with measures developed on quite different populations and empirically generating new scales from the items. It was expected that the new scales emerging from the empirical analysis would differ from the initial ones. For member peer and interviewer sources a new set of items was designed as a basis for the empirical generation of rating scales. The initial pools of items on which measurement generation was based is described below. The first order and final set of measures which emerged from empirical analyses of all groups of items are presented in the Preliminary Analyses section.

Religious orientation and motivation item pool (self-report). A number of different conceptual and empirically-based formulations have been proposed to assess general categories of religious orientation and motivation (e.g., Allport & Ross, 1967; Glock & Stark, 1965; King, 1967). Unfortunately, none have demonstrated consistent reliability, validity, and utility across diverse samples nor have any been used with a sample as homogeneous and committed in religious orientation as are the members of this fellowship. Nonetheless, Batson's (1976) work was chosen for use in this study with the hope that at least some of the items would cluster together to form meaningful scales.

Batson (1976) used factor analytic techniques to analyze his own Internal, External, Interactional, and Doctrinal Orthodoxy scales and the Allport and Ross (1967) intrinsic and extrinsic religious orientation scales.[2] He found three basic categories of religious orientation: "Religion as End," "Religion as Means," and "Religion as Quest." The items from all but the Doctrinal scale were used in the present study. Each item was rated on a seven-point scale ranging from "strongly disagree" to "strongly agree."

---

[2]Intrinsic religion refers to Allport's (Allport & Ross, 1967) use of the term which assesses the desire for religious experience for its own sake, rather than as a means to some other ends, such as social life or conformity to one's community.

Locus of control item pool (self-report). The locus of control items of Levenson (1973) and Kopplin (1976) were used to assess attributions the individual makes regarding the factors that influence events in his or her life. Levenson's scales assess the individual's perceptions of internal control over his or her life (Personal Control), control by powerful others (Powerful Others), and control by chance (Chance Control). Kopplin added a fourth scale which assesses the perception of control over one's life events by God (God Control). Each item was rated on a seven-point scale ranging from ''strongly disagree'' to ''strongly agree.''

Social desirability; Demographic information (self-report). Respondents completed Marlow-Crowne's Social Desirability Scale (Crowne & Marlow, 1964). They also supplied information about their age, sex, marital status, educational status, current living situation, and current work situation.

Spiritual life and group involvement item pool (rated by member peers and interviewers). Fellowship member peers and interviewers received a rating measure of items designed to assess dimensions of present spiritual life and group involvement. These items were constructed by the investigators following the first year of participant-observation. They indicate dimensions of the lives of fellowship members which were hypothesized to have a potential connection with social and psychological processes related to interpersonal development. One item for each of thirteen dimensions was included (Maton, Note 1). Each item was rated on a five-point scale.

Religious history item pool (rated by interviewers). Four items were constructed to assess the process leading the fellowship member to become a Christian (Maton, Note 1). These items assess the influence of childhood religion, life crises, spiritual experiences, and cognitive choice. Each item was rated on a five-point scale ranging from ''to a small extent or not at all'' to ''to a large extent.''

Criteria Variables

Interpersonal behavior (self-report and rated by member and nonmember peers). Perceived pre-joining-the-fellowship, present, and ideal interpersonal qualities were assessed with Leary's (1957) Interpersonal Checklist. The measure contains 128 adjectives, composing 16 scales of eight items each. The scales are constructed to conform to a circumplex ordering. Although Leary suggests two underlying dimensions of the scale, dominance-submission and hostility-love, factor analytic solutions yield from two to four dimensions (Briar & Bieri, 1963; Golding & Knudson, 1975; Wiggins, 1973). LaForge (1977) reports reliability, validity, and utility results establishing the instrument's reasonably sound psychometric properties.

For the self-report, retrospective account the individual was asked to think about a specific period of time before involvement in the fellowship became important, and to indicate the month and year of the beginning and end of the time period on which they are reflecting.[3] Then, the respondent was asked to mark "true" for each adjective that generally described themselves, then, and "false" for those that did not. After completing the retrospective account, the individuals completed the same sets of adjectives to describe themselves in the present, and then a third set to describe their ideal self.

For member and non-member peers the retrospective past directions read, "Now we'd like you to reflect back to *John* in the period *he or she named, e.g., June, 1975* to *June, 1976.* Remembering him/her then. . ." The dates were filled in prior to sending the form to the peers and were the same ones given by the member on his/her self-report form if the rater knew him/her during the pre-fellowship period. Otherwise, for member peers the dates filled in were those corresponding to when the member peer informed the investigator (when first contacted about the study) he/she first knew the individual well. For nonmember peers, if they did not know the person during the pre-fellowship period, nor during the same time period after fellowship involvement during which member peers first knew the person, then the time period during which the nonmember peer first knew the individual well was used. After completing the retrospective past ratings, the peers completed ratings of their perception of the member in the present. Member and nonmember peers did not receive an ideal interpersonal form as part of the rating measure; member peers did, however, complete the ideal interpersonal checklist as part of their own self-report form.

Self-esteem (rated by member and nonmember peers). A one-time rating of perceived past and present self-esteem was completed for

---

[3]The exact time on which the interviewee is reflecting was not standardized since we sought a time frame relevant to each individual. While this method obviously pulls for the person to select a previous period of time when they were not meeting their own criterion of satisfactory interpersonal behavior, it should be recalled that this is not a study of the relative effectiveness of the fellowship setting *per se.* Rather, the aim is to look for individual differences in the extent of perceived change among the membership and their nominated peers.

each member by member and nonmember peers. The past rating is based on the same time period as the interpersonal behavior ratings. The rater is asked to assess the member's "feelings about himself/herself" for the past, and then in the present, on a five-point scale ranging from "very negative" to "very positive."

A summary of the different item pools completed by the different sources is provided in Table 2.

Setting Level Variables

The qualitative assessment of setting variables is based on observations obtained during two years of participant-observation. The major modalities for obtaining evidence include observation, listening, formal interviews, informal probing, self-analysis of experience, and written documents. The major situations observed include Sunday worship, weeknight house-church, informal social contact, recreational activities, and special decision-making or discussion meetings. Over the two year period, systematic sampling of formal group situations was observed, but the sample of informal contacts and contexts is less systematic due to particular friendships and acquaintances developed.

One group of setting variables includes private, small group and large group prayer, worship and Bible study, distribution of role responsibilities in the setting, explicit and implicit group expectations, emotional and material support offered during times of stress and

TABLE 2

Item Pools by Source of Data

Item Pools	Source of Data:	Self-Report	Member Peer	Nonmember Peer	Interviewer
Predictors					
Religious Orientation and Motivation		XXX			
Locus of Control		XXX			
Spiritual Life and Group Involvement			XXX		XXX
Religious History					XXX
Criteria					
Interpersonal Checklist		XXX	XXX	XXX	
Self-Esteem			XXX	XXX	

exposure to models of appropriate interpersonal behavior and opportunities for self-disclosure, guidance and emotional insight about personal problems.

A second group of setting variables are those which provide the context for the development and maintenance of these specific activities and associated experiences. Those noted include organizational goals, qualities of leaders, authority structure, setting climate, balance between community and freedom, and individual and setting history.

Setting variables are not operationalized into quantitative items and scales. Since the primary use of the information is to provide a context for understanding individual level findings, qualitative description of these variables is not presented in the Results section, but reserved for presentation in the Discussion as a means to inform our interpretation of the data.

RESULTS: COMMITMENT, CRISES AND COMMUNITY

Preliminary Analyses

Since extensive preliminary analyses for the purpose of measurement development are performed in this study, only an overview of these results is presented, with most of the tables and details of analyses reported in Maton (Note 1). First, participation and completion rates are reported. Next, the results of empirical analyses to generate a first order set of predictor scales are presented. Evidence relating to the reliability and validity of these scales is then reported. The results of a second order principal components analysis to generate the final set of predictor scales are next described. Then, the results of analyses used to generate the interpersonal criteria scales are presented. Finally, evidence relating to the reliability and validity of the criteria measures is reported.

Participation and completion rates. Table 3 presents the completion rates for each of the measures obtained for study participants. As may be seen from the table, completion rates ranged from 49% to 83% of the total number of people contacted.

Generation of first order predictor scales. The self-report religious orientation and locus of control items have most often been used for samples from populations more heterogeneous in religious orientation than the population of fellowship members. The peer and interviewer rated spiritual life and group involvement items,

TABLE 3

Data Completion Rates for Study Participants

Data Source	Number for Whom Data are Available
Interviewees Contacted	100
Consented to be Interviewed	88
Completed Interview	86
Interview Ratings Available	83 (94%)[1]
Completed and Usable Self Report Forms	71 (81%)[1]
Interviewees with Member Peer Forms completed and usable	78[2] (89%)[1]
Interviewees with Nonmember Peer Forms completed and usable	49[3] (56%)[1]

[1]Percentage of those who consented to take part in the study for whom completed and usable measures were available.

[2]Ratings of interviewees were obtained from two different member peers for 46 interviewees and from one member peer for 32 interviewees.

[3]Ratings of interviewees were obtained from two different nonmember peers for 26 interviewees and from one nonmember peer for 23 interviewees.

and the interviewer rated religious history items, were generated specifically for this study. Consequently, empirical analysis was necessary in order to generate scales with adequate measurement properties for this sample. The general procedure followed for each set of items (see Maton, Note 1, for details and for variation across sets) was: (1) elimination of items with low endorsement frequencies, (2) principal components analysis (for the religious orientation items a rational scale generation phase was necessary as well), (3) item-scale analyses to test the components solution, and (4) unitary weighting of items to form first order scale scores.

Five scales emerged from the initial set of religious orientation self-report items. *Intrinsic-committed* refers to a religious orientation in which religious belief and religious experience are of primary importance to the individual. *Models* reflects the influence of key religious individuals in a member's religious beliefs in life situations. *Quest for meaning* refers to the importance of religion for an individual's search for identity. *Instrumental* reflects an orientation in which religion is primarily a means to achieve personal goals.

Three scales emerged from the set of locus of control self-report items. *God in Control* assesses the perception that the outcome of events in one's life is the result of God's activity. *Personal Control* reflects the perception that the outcome of events is under one's direction. *Powerful Others Control* measures the perception that people in positions of power influence the outcome of one's life events.

The peer rating items of spiritual life and group involvement formed two scales. *Social and spiritual* assesses the perceived level of integration into congregational life and values, and a closeness of relationship with God attributed by peers to the member. *Private spiritual* taps the intimacy of a personal relationship with God which is attributed to the member by his or her peers.

Two scales also emerged from the interviewer rating items of spiritual life and group involvement. *Social, private, and spiritual* encompasses the two peer rating dimensions of integration into the congregation and intimacy of a personal relationship with God. *Cognitive orientation* reflects a primarily intellectual basis to one's religious experience.

The interviewer rating items of religious history also formed two scales. *Life crisis* assesses the importance of painful life experiences rather than childhood religion in leading the person to a personal relationship with God and Jesus as an adult. *Encounter* reflects the importance of spiritual experience rather than cognitive considerations as the basis of conversion.

Reliability and validity of first order scales. Of the eight self-report scales, only Models is significantly (albeit a small correlation) associated with social desirability ($r = -.20$, $p < .05$), and this is an opposite direction than might be expected if the Models scale reflected social desirability. That is, the higher the reported influence of key religious leaders the lower the social desirability score. Given the lack of a systematic relationship to social desirability, all self-report scales were retained for second order analysis.

Intraclass reliability coefficients on the peer member rating scales of Social and spiritual and Private spiritual are .72 and .58 respectively. The lower reliability on the Private spiritual scale is probably explained by the fewer number of items and the more inferential nature of the qualities rated in comparison to the Social and spiritual scale. The correlations of raters' scores on the social desirability measure and their individual ratings of members on the two spiritual scales are .10 and .05 respectively. The levels of interrater reliability and lack of relationship with social desirability indicate the scales' acceptable psychometric qualities. Peer ratings were averaged to obtain members' scores on each dimension.

Analysis of variance of the ratings of the interviewers reveals significant differences on two of four scales. Additional analyses, however, lead to the interpretation that these differences represent the result of limitations in the random assignment process and are reflective of true member differences rather than interviewer effects. The findings on interviewer differences are such that when they do occur, they are in correspondence with differences found on independent measures of similar dimensions as rated by peers (Maton, Note 1). Intercorrelations among predictors are reported in Maton (Note 1). They demonstrate overall convergent and discriminant validity among self-report, member peer, and interviewer first order scales.

Second order components analysis. Second order components analysis is a measurement development technique based on the convergence of evidence across differing measurement modalities and the minimization of method variance inherent in any given modality (Golding & Seidman, 1974). In this study it is used to generate a final set of predictor scales based on the convergence of first order self-report, peer rating, and interviewer rating measures. Only the two religious history scales and the living situation measure were not included in this analysis since they are not intended to assess underlying, present psychological and spiritual dimensions.

The five self-report religious orientation scales, three self-report locus of control measures, two peer rating spirituality scales, and two interviewer rating spirituality scales were subjected to a principal components analysis with varimax rotation. Based on a criterion of eigenvalues greater than one, a five component solution emerged (Table 4). Component one has high loadings for the peer rating scales of Social and spiritual and Private spiritual, the interviewer rating measure of Social, private and spiritual, and the self-report measure of Intrinsic-committed religion. Since these scales reflect high levels of commitment to a relationship with God and the congregation, this component is named *Commitment*.

The second component has a positive loading for the self-report scale God in control, and high negative loadings for the interviewer scale Cognitive orientation and the self-report scales of Personal and Powerful others control. It is named *God not man* since it reflects a perception of God as influencing the outcome of events in one's life,

TABLE 4

Second Order Components Analysis of Predictor Scales
(Principal Components; Varimax Rotation)

Scale	Commit-ment	God not man[1]	Consis-tency	Guid-ance	Instru-mental	Commu-nalities
Self-Report: Religious Orientation						
Intrinsic-committed	.50				(.42)	.58
Models				.61		.64
Instrumental					.83	.71
Consistency			.83			.72
Quest for meaning				.86		.80
Self-Report: Locus of Control						
God		.44	(-.48)			.64
Personal		-.76				.67
Powerful others		-.64			(.45)	.75
Member Peer Ratings						
Social and spiritual	.88					.79
Private spiritual	.71					.57
Interviewer Ratings						
Social, private and spiritual	.67					.60
Cognitive orientation		-.74				.65

Notes: Loadings less than $|.4|$ are not shown. Solution accounts for 67.6% of the total variance.
Parentheses indicate that scale is loaded on another component.

[1]The direction of the loadings of the four scales which compose this factor have been reversed to facilitate naming the factor and ease of discussion.

rather than complex perceptions of human (i.e., self, others) in control.

Component three has a high single loading for self-reported *Consistency* in attempting to apply religious beliefs to life situations. The fourth component has high loadings for the self-report scales of Quest for meaning and Models influence on religious development. This component is named *Guidance* as it reflects the influence of models in a guiding capacity. *Instrumental* religious orientation has a high single loading on the fifth factor.

Unitary weighting of scales with high loadings yields five second order measures, which together with the Life crisis, Encounter, and

Living situation measures results in a final set of eight predictor scales.

Generation of interpersonal behavior criteria—peers. Four separate principal components analyses with varimax rotations were performed on the sixteen Leary scale scores (eight items per scale) for retrospective past and present member peer, and retrospective past and present non-member peer ratings. Based on an eigenvalue criterion of one, a three components solution emerged in all four cases. The component congruence scores (Harman, 1967) were .97, .94, and .93 for the past and present member peer solutions and .99, .99, and .97 for the past and present non-member peer solutions. The past and present scales for member, and nonmember, peers were then analyzed together, again with principal components analysis with orthogonal rotation. The three components solution, which emerged across both sources, had factor congruence scores of .96, .94, and .95. Finally, principal components analysis of past and present nonmember peer scale scores combined together were performed. A three components solution again emerged (Table 5).

The three components conform closely to those obtained in previous analyses of the Leary circle (Briar & Bieri, 1963; Golding & Knudson, 1975; LaForge, 1977; Wiggins, 1973). Two of the dimensions, *Dominance-submission* and *Hostility-caring*, are bipolar in nature. They represent the basic dimensions of the interpersonal behavior measure originally theorized by Leary. The third is unipolar and includes loadings from both the caring and submission quadrants of the circle. Since the Leary summary measure of the total number of items checked also loads high on this component, LaForge (1977) suggests that it is best viewed as a measure of acquiescence/social desirability. Others, however, have viewed it as a substantive dimension and named it friendly-submissiveness (Golding & Knudson, 1975) or love with conformity overtones (Briar & Bieri, 1963). Since in the present study no relationship was found between Marlowe-Crowne's measure of social desirability and scores given by peer raters on this dimension (r = .05), and especially since a combination of attributes from these two quadrants represents a dimension of behavior often discussed as an ideal in this population, it is retained as a substantive factor and named *Giving-and-open*. Unitary weighting was applied to those scales with the highest loading on each of the three components.

The Leary measure is constructed so that extreme high or low scores represent maladaptive interpersonal qualities. However, na-

TABLE 5

Factor Structure of Leary's Interpersonal Check List (16 Scales)
Member and Nonmember Peer Ratings from Past and Present
Time Periods – Collapsed

(Principal Components; Varimax)

Scale	I	II	III	Communalities
A Managerial	.84			.73
B Narcissistic	.80			.69
C Competitive	(.40)		.53	.45
D Sadistic	.62			.56
E Aggressive	(.43)		.71	.71
F Rebellious			.83	.71
G Distrustful			.83	.71
H Self-Effacing	-.72			.66
I Masochistic	-.66	(.52)		.71
J Docile		.66		.55
K Dependent		.78		.68
L Cooperative		.79		.67
M Over-Conventional		(.55)	-.61	.70
N Hypernormal		.63	(-.54)	.69
O Responsible		.64	(-.40)	.58
P Autocratic	.65			.49

Notes: Loadings less than $|.4|$ are not shown.
Solution accounts for 64.4% of the total variance.
Parentheses indicate that item loads higher and is therefore scored on another component.

tional norms indicating adaptive anchor points and intervals do not exist. In keeping with the phenomenological and contextual perspective guiding this research, the self-reported group mean on the ideal self for each of the three dimensions was calculated and taken as the anchor point. These group ideals do not differ significantly from those reported by a local sample of college students (Maton, Note 1). Each person's score is obtained by subtracting the group ideal from the actual score obtained from the peer ratings. This score represents each person's deviation from the group ideal on Dominance-submission, Hostility-caring, and Giving-and-open, as perceived by member and non-member peers, for both the pre-joining-the-fellowship past and the present.

Interpersonal behavior criteria—self report. The pre-fellowship and present scores on the sixteen Leary scales were subjected to separate principal components analyses with varimax rotation. Based on eigenvalue and consistency with peer rating consider- ations, a three component structure was retained. The component congruence scores were .99, .92, and .83 for the past and present solutions. The two time period scale scores were then combined and components analysis with orthogonal rotation again applied. The resulting three components have factor congruence scores of .92, .96, and .95 with the peer components counterparts. Given the similarity, the peer components solution was applied to the self- report scales. The group ideal scores were again used to obtain deviation scores on each dimension.

Reliability and validity of criteria measures. Intraclass reliability coefficients on the three retrospective past interpersonal scales of Dominance-submission, Hostility-caring, and Giving-and-open were .85, .70, and .59 respectively for member peer ratings, and .81, .82, and .88 for non-member peers. The comparable interrater reliabilities for present scales are .78, .72, and .68 for member peers and .88, .75, and .86 for nonmember peers. There are no sig- nificant correlations between member peer (self-report) scores on social desirability and their ratings of other members on past or present interpersonal scales.

There are significant positive correlations between member scores on social desirability and their self-ratings of present Dominance-submission and Hostility-caring. Available evidence suggests an interpretation of these correlations as providing support for the validity of the Hostility-caring measure but raising questions about the validity of the Dominance-submission scale (Maton, Note 1). Since, however, the evidence is far from definitive the self- report Dominance-submission measure is retained along with the other two interpersonal self-report criteria.

Interrater reliabilities on ratings of pre-fellowship esteem were .36 and .44 for member and nonmember peers respectively. For present ratings of self-esteem the reliabilities were .36 for member peers and .55 for nonmember peers. These self-esteem reliabilities are at the borderline of acceptability.

Member and nonmember peer ratings on the interpersonal behav- ior and self-esteem criteria measures were summed and averaged separately to obtain final scores for members from each source. Second order components analysis was not performed since member peer, nonmember peer and self-report perceptions of interpersonal behavior are each viewed as distinct phenomena.

Summary. Preliminary analyses resulted in the generation of eight predictor measures, three sets of three interpersonal behavior measures from separate criteria sources, and a self-esteem measure from two criteria sources. Commitment, God not man, Consistency, Guidance and Instrumental orientation are predictor variables which represent a convergence of self-report, member peer, and nonmember peer measures. The other three predictor measures are Life crisis and Encounter religious history (interviewer scales), and Living situation. The three past and present interpersonal behavior criteria of Dominance-submission, Hostility-caring, and Giving-and-open are available for member peer, nonmember peer, and self-report sources. A one item measure of self-esteem from member peers and nonmember peers are the other criteria measures. Table 6 presents brief descriptions of each of the predictor and criteria variables.

Primary Analyses

The primary intent of this study is to test for a relationship between psychological-religious predictor variables and perceptions of change on interpersonal empowerment criteria. Separate analyses are performed for each of three criteria sources: member peers, nonmember peers and self-report. First, an analysis of overall perceived change for the sample as a whole is presented. Next, univariate partial correlation analyses of each predictor with each criterion measure are reported. Finally, in order to assess the joint contribution of predictor variables to explaining variance in the criteria, canonical correlation analyses are presented.

Overall perceived change. Within group *t*-tests of perceived change on the Leary scales yield significant results on eight of the nine tests across the three criteria sources (Table 7). Only perceived change on Giving-and-open for nonmember peers does not achieve significance. These findings indicate a consistent perception of change by member peers, nonmember peers and self-report in the direction of fellowship ideals on the interpersonal behavior dimensions. In addition, *t*-tests of perceived change in self-esteem are significant for both member and nonmember peer sources.

Predictors of perceived change. The major task of this analysis is to explain variation in the perceived interpersonal change noted

TABLE 6

Final Set of Variables

Predictors	Description	Source
1. Commitment	Commitment to intimate relationship with (a) God and (b) congregation	Self; Member peers; Interviewer
2. God not man	A perception of God as influencing the outcome of events in one's life rather than complex perceptions of human (i.e., self, others) factors in control	Self; Interviewer
3. Consistency	Consistency in attempting to apply religious beliefs to life situations	Self
4. Guidance	Guidance provided by religious models in one's quest for meaning	Self
5. Instrumental	Instrumental orientation to religion as a means to personal goals	Self
6. Life Crisis	Life crises rather than childhood religion leading to a personal relationship with God	Interviewer
7. Encounter	Spiritual encounter rather than cognitive considerations as the basis of conversion	Interviewer
8. Living Situation	Living situation includes one or more members of the congregation	Self
Criteria		
Dominance-submission	Congregational ideal of appropriate combination of assertiveness and responsiveness to others in interpersonal behavior	Member peers; Nonmember peers; Self-report
Giving-and-open	Congregational ideal of appropriate combination of giving and openness in interpersonal behavior	Member peers; Nonmember peers; Self-report
Hostility-caring	Congregational ideal of appropriate combination of directness and caring in interpersonal behavior	Member peers; Nonmember peers; Self-report
Self-esteem	Positive feelings about oneself	Member and nonmember peers

above, using the eight predictor variables. Since individuals differ on their pre-joining-the-fellowship scores on interpersonal scales and on the length of the past to present assessment period, analyses of differential individual development must statistically partial out these two factors. Age, sex, and level of education completed do not achieve nor approach statistical significance in correlations with perceived change, or present level, on the interpersonal criteria and are not controlled for. Univariate partial correlation and multivariate canonical correlation analyses relating the predictor and criteria measures represent the major data analytic techniques.

TABLE 7

T-Tests of Perceived Change

Source Measure	Past Mean	S.D.	Present Mean	S.D.	t	p
Member Peers (N=74)						
Dominance-submission[a]	-8.5	6.6	-4.7	4.0	6.5	.000
Giving-and-open[a]	-5.2	4.5	-4.2	2.9	2.3	.025
Hostility-caring[a]	-7.5	5.9	-5.1	4.4	4.9	.000
Nonmember Peers (N=49)						
Dominance-submission[a]	-6.6	6.1	-4.8	4.9	3.0	.004
Giving-and-open[a]	-5.2	4.4	-5.1	4.0	0.4	.697
Hostility-caring[a]	-6.4	6.9	-3.5	4.2	3.9	.000
Self-report (N=60)						
Dominance-submission[a]	-8.3	6.5	-5.0	4.1	4.6	.000
Giving-and-open[a]	-6.1	6.2	-4.0	3.2	2.6	.010
Hostility-caring[a]	-9.1	5.3	-7.0	3.9	3.2	.002
Member Peers (N=70)						
Self-esteem[b]	2.7	0.9	3.4	1.0	5.1	.000
Nonmember Peers (N=45)						
Self-esteem[b]	3.0	1.0	3.3	0.9	2.2	.037

[a]The mean represents the mean deviation from the ideal, keyed in such a way that zero is the ideal. The farther away from zero (in a negative direction) the farther from the mean ideal.

[b]The mean represents the mean on a scale from 1 to 5, in which 1 represents low and 5 represents high self-esteem.

Univariate analyses. Univariate partial correlation analyses with the pre-score and length of assessment period partialled were performed for all predictor and criteria variables (Table 8). The results reveal that Commitment, God not man, and Life crisis predictors have reasonably consistent patterns of relationship with Hostility-caring, Giving-and-open, and Dominance-submission both within and across criteria sources. Four other predictors, Consistency, Guidance, Instrumental orientation, and Living situation, have more modest patterns of relationship with criteria. The eighth predictor, Encounter, does not have any significant correlations with the interpersonal criteria. The pattern of partial correlations with the one-

TABLE 8

Partial Correlations of Predictors with Perceived Change
(pre-score and length of retrospective pre-post period partialled)

Source Criteria / Predictors	Member Peers D-S	Member Peers G-O	Member Peers H-C	Nonmember Peers D-S	Nonmember Peers G-O	Nonmember Peers H-C	Self-Report D-S	Self-Report G-O	Self-Report H-C	Member Peer S-E	Nonmember Peer S-E
Commitment	.22[d] (.34)[b] (57)	.32[b] (.31)[b] (57)	.26[c] (.39)[a] (57)	.27[d] (.41) (32)	.46[b] (.58)[a] (32)	.34[c] (.32)[c] (32)	-.24[c] (-.06) (51)	.15 (.12) (51)	.13 (.09) (51)	.23[d] (.32)[c] (52)	.02 (-.12) (27)
God not man	.04 (-.13) (57)	.17 (.21)[d] (57)	.21[d] (.23)[c] (57)	.42[b] (-.19) (32)	.39[c] (.26)[d] (32)	.54[a] (.54)[a] (32)	-.06 (-.07) (51)	.26[c] (.27)[c] (51)	.03 (.08) (51)	-.14 (-.03) (52)	.22 (.05) (27)
Consistency	-.03 (-.07) (57)	.15 (.17)[d] (57)	.31[b] (.34)[b] (57)	.17 (.22) (32)	.19 (.25)[d] (32)	.20 (.18) (32)	.11 (.18) (51)	.07 (.12) (51)	.24[c] (.21)[d] (51)	.03 (.05) (52)	.18 (.13) (27)
Guidance	.31[c] (.24)[c] (57)	.04 (.16) (57)	.25[c] (.15) (57)	.13 (.04) (32)	.13 (.15) (32)	.36[c] (.14) (32)	.04 (.04) (51)	.11 (.12) (51)	-.12 (-.07) (51)	-.10 (-.17) (52)	.19 (.04) (27)
Instrumental	-.18 (-.14) (57)	-.01 (.05) (57)	-.27[c] (-.27)[c] (57)	.14 (.06) (32)	-.02 (-.07) (32)	.09 (-.04) (32)	.28[c] (.20)[d] (51)	.03 (.01) (51)	-.20[d] (-.23)[d] (51)	-.01 (-.02) (52)	.28[d] (.24) (27)
Life Crisis	.13 (-.03) (57)	.05 (.23)[c] (57)	.25[c] (.15) (57)	.19 (-.32)[c] (32)	.22 (-.05) (32)	.30[d] (.21) (32)	.20[d] (.10) (51)	.26[c] (.33)[c] (51)	.29[c] (.24)[c] (51)	-.31[c] (-.38)[b] (52)	-.16 (-.29)[d] (27)
Encounter	-.17 (-.06) (57)	.03 (.13) (57)	.01 (.17) (57)	-.07 (-.05) (32)	-.06 (-.05) (32)	-.03 (.14) (32)	-.16 (.03) (51)	.09 (.12) (51)	-.08 (-.05) (51)	.00 (.12) (52)	.05 (.30)[d] (27)
Living situation	.19[d] (.19)[d] (57)	.18[d] (.14) (57)	.12 (.19)[d] (57)	.20 (-.01) (32)	.16 (.21) (32)	.48[b] (.44)[b] (32)	.02 (.08) (51)	-.01 (-.00) (51)	.06 (.11) (51)	.10 (.14) (52)	-.05 (-.05) (27)

Notes: The number in the parentheses immediately below the partial correlation is the zero order correlation of the predictor with the present criteria measure. The number in parentheses below that indicates the number of individuals whose scores are included in the analysis.
[a] p < .001; [b] p < .01; [c] p < .05; [d] p < .10

item self-esteem ratings is inconsistent. The pattern of univariate partial correlations is unaffected when social desirability is partialled out along with the pre-score and length of assessment period.

Multivariate analyses. The univariate analyses reveal that Commitment, God not man, and Life crisis have reasonably consistent patterns of relationship with interpersonal criteria within and across criteria sources. The remaining predictors, with the exception of Encounter, have some, but limited, patterns of relationship with the criteria. The question remains which linear combination of predictor variables is optimally related to which linear combination of interpersonal scales within each source, and consistently across sources. Canonical correlation analysis is the method of choice for addressing this question. For each criteria source, the canonical model which incorporates the maximal number of predictors to significantly explain variance in all three interpersonal behavior scales is first obtained. Then, where possible, an additional model for each source which adds from the remaining predictors the variable(s) which make a substantial contribution to variance explained in two, or one, of the interpersonal scales is developed. The comparison of the canonical models across source reveals the subset of predictors and criteria which have consistent patterns of multivariate relationship.

The canonical model which explains the maximal amount of variance for all three member peer interpersonal criteria ($R = .54$, $p = .016$) contains one significant canonical variate composed of four predictors (Table 9). Commitment has the highest loading (.64), followed by Life crisis (.40), Guidance (.38), and Consistency (.32). The highest loading on the criteria side is perceived change in Hostility-caring (.57), followed by Giving-and-open (.40) and Dominance-submission (.32). Although statisticians have not yet developed statistical tests for canonical loadings comparable to those for beta weights in multiple regression, a widely used rule of thumb is that loadings greater than or equal to one-half of the largest loading on each side of the equation make non-trivial contributions to the variance explained. As confirmation of this rule of thumb, the 12.5% of variance added by the three variables with lower loadings to that contributed by Commitment alone achieves statistical significance (F $(3,49) = 2.9$, $p < .05$).

Of the remaining variables not yet in the equation, Instrumental orientation adds the next greatest percentage of variance to the model, 5.4%. Although all loadings on the predictor side remain

TABLE 9

Canonical Correlations of Predictors with Perceived Change Scores

(pre-score and length of retrospective pre-post period partialled from both sets of measures)

Criterion Source	Member Peers #1	Member Peers #2	Nonmember Peers #1	Nonmember Peers #2	Self-Report
Model					
			Statistical Results		
$R=$	.54	.59	.70	.73	.61
$R^2=$	.29	.35	.49	.53	.37
$X^2=$	24.75	29.85	20.54	24.44	31.76
$df=$	12	15	9	12	15
$p=$	.02	.01	.01	.02	.01
$N=$	57	57	32	32	51
Predictors			Weights		
Commitment	.64	.51	.45	.31	.51
God not man			.63	.54	.35
Consistency	.32	.31			
Guidance	.38	.37			
Instrumental		-.41			-.46
Life crisis	.40	.36	.36	.33	-.59
Encounter					.52
Living situation				.35	
Perceived Change Criteria					
Dominance-submission	.32	.42	.30	.27[δ]	-.68
Giving-and-open	.40	.19[δ]	.41	.31[δ]	.44
Hostility-caring	.57	.76	.55	.69	.88

[δ]The loading is below the cut-off (one-half of the size of the largest loading). The perceived change criteria does not contribute a substantial percentage of the variance explained by the model.

greater than one-half the size of the largest, on the criteria side the weight for Giving-and-open drops to .22, far below half of the .78 loading for Hostility-caring. Taken as a group, the four variables with the lowest weights together add 18.0% of variance to that contributed by Commitment alone ($F(4,48)=3.30$, $p<.05$). None of the remaining predictors add substantially to the equation. This five predictor model includes all variables which achieved significance in the univariate analysis.

For the nonmember peer criteria, the optimal model contains one significant canonical variate ($R=.70$, $p=.015$) composed of three predictor variables. The model again includes positive loadings for Commitment (.45) and Life crisis (.36), but the highest loading is a positive one for God not man (.63). The ordering of loadings for the interpersonal scales is once again Hostility-caring (.56), Giving-and-open (.41), and Dominance-submission (.30). Together, Commitment and Life crisis add 11.9% of variance to that contributed by God not man ($F(2,25)=2.9$, $p<.10$). The next highest contributor, Living situation, explains another 3.9% of variance, and all predictor variables retain loadings greater than one-half of that for God not man. However, on the criteria side the loadings for Giving-and-open (.31) and Dominance-submission (.27) drop somewhat below half of the loading for Hostility-caring (.69). In this model the three variables with lowest weights together add 15.7% of variance explained to that contributed by God not man ($F(3,24)=.68$, $p<.10$). This solution excludes one variable which achieved significance at the univariate level, Guidance. This variable adds only .3% to the variance explained, indicating that the two predictor variables with which it is correlated, God not man ($r=.37$) and Life crisis ($r=.33$), have already accounted for most of its relationship with the criteria.

The canonical model which explains the maximal amount of variance for all three self-report interpersonal criteria ($R=.61$, $p=.007$) contains one significant canonical variate composed of five predictor variables. Instrumental orientation has the highest loading ($-.59$), followed by Life crisis (.52), Commitment (.51), Guidance (.46), and God not man (.35). The highest loading on the criteria side is perceived change in Hostility-caring (.88), followed by a negative loading for Dominance-submission ($-.68$) and a positive one for Giving-and-open (.44). Taken as a group, the four predictors with the lowest weights add 20.1% to the variance explained by Instrumental orientation alone ($F(4,42)=3.4$, $p<.05$). None of the remaining predictors add substantially to the model.

This model includes a relationship between Dominance-submission and all of the predictors except Guidance which is in the opposite direction from that expected and obtained for member and nonmember peers, as well as a relationship in an unexpected, reversed direction between Guidance and Hostility-caring and Giving-and-open. Furthermore, it excludes a variable, Consistency, which has a significant univariate correlation, while including a variable, Guidance, whose largest univariate partial correlation is .12. Although the self-report model contains a majority of relationships consistent with those obtained in both peer sources, it is not fully satisfactory.

Across sources, the multivariate models reveal that Commitment, Life crisis, and God not man are the subset of predictors with the most consistent joint contributions to explaining variance in interpersonal criteria. Commitment and Life crisis make joint, substantial contributions to explaining variance in all three of the interpersonal scales across all three sources. In eight of nine possible cases the two predictors are positively related to perceived interpersonal change, with a single negative relationship with self-reported Dominance-submission. God not man is part of canonical models which explain variance in all three interpersonal scales across two of three sources. In five of six possible cases the predictor is positively related to perceived interpersonal change, with a single negative relationship with self-reported Dominance-submission.

Guidance, Instrumental orientation, Consistency, and Living situation have less consistent patterns of relationship with the interpersonal criteria. Although Guidance and Instrumental orientation each load on two canonical models, Guidance has inconsistent relationships in two of six loadings, and Instrumental orientation has an inconsistent loading on self-reported Dominance-submission and does not contribute to variance explained for Giving-and-open on model number two for the peer member criteria. Consistency is part of a canonical model only for the member peer source, and Living situation explains variance only in Hostility-caring on model number two for nonmember peers. Encounter, the eighth predictor, does not have loadings on any of the canonical models.

In all of the models Hostility-caring has the highest loadings, with Dominance-submission and Giving-and-open alternating between second highest and lowest loadings.

Follow-up data. After the individual differences data reported above were collected, follow-up data became available on a sub-sample of thirty interviewees as part of an ongoing research project (Maton, Note 2). These data reveal a significant $r = .50$, $p < .01$) correlation between individual predictor scores on Commitment and a self-reported life satisfaction measure taken three years later.

DISCUSSION: INDIVIDUAL AND SETTING VARIABLES

These results provide a reasonably consistent picture of the relationship between three psychological-religious variables and perceived interpersonal change in a particular setting. Fellowship members perceived to have changed most are more likely to be seen by themselves and others as having a strong commitment to a personal relationship with both God and other people in the setting, report a life crisis leading to a relationship with Jesus as an adult, and report perceptions of God as influencing the outcome of personal life events. The findings represent change in a desirable and adaptive direction as perceived by members, that is change toward the group ideals of Hostility-caring, Dominance-submission, and Giving-and-open. Furthermore, since the group ideals do not differ significantly from those reported by a sample of college students, it appears that change is also in the direction of societal ideals. The results are consistent with previous research in the area of intrinsic religious motivation (Entner, 1977; Kahoe, 1974; McClain, 1978; Pargament, Tyler, & Steele, 1979), in which a positive relationship between "embracing" one's religious values and adaptive psychological attributes has been reported.

Confidence in the individual differences results is enhanced by a unique feature of the study—the convergence of findings across multiple sources of predictor and criteria variables. In multivariate analyses Commitment, composed of self-report, member peer, and interviewer ratings, demonstrates relationships with member peer rated and self-report interpersonal behavior criteria, as well as with nonmember peer rated criteria. This same variable significantly predicts to a measure of life satisfaction taken three years later.

God not man, composed of self-report and interviewer scales, relates within source to the self-report criteria and across source to the nonmember peer criteria. Life crisis, an interviewer scale, establishes across source multivariate relationships with all three criteria sources.

The consistent pattern of relationship of the three predictors with the independently rated nonmember peer criteria is especially noteworthy since that source is least likely to be influenced by conscious or non-conscious desires to have more committed members, or to have the setting appear in a favorable light. Furthermore, the reasonably high peer interrater reliabilities across member and nonmember peer sources for both past and present ratings enhances credibility for the retrospective, perceived change criteria. The interrater reliabilities and convergence of findings across multiple sources makes plausible the inference that the perceived interpersonal behavior change is "real."

The findings suggest that those who are perceived by both themselves and others to have become empowered in the direction of desired interpersonal behavior change are those who are also described by themselves and others as deeply committed to God and to the particular local setting of which they are a part. In more general language they might be viewed as those with a "psychological sense of community" (Sarason, 1974). In addition, those most empowered in this setting tend to have had a life crisis which led them to their new found orientation and to perceive God as the most important influence on the events of their life. It is reasonable to hypothesize that the development of a psychological sense of community, measured appropriately for other individuals in other settings, is one variable which may be important for the development of empowerment.

As noted at the outset, there are a variety of limitations imposed by the nature of the study. It tells us some things and not others. We selected variables only after an intimate knowledge of the setting and the members. We are relying on a comparison of retrospective and present perceptions of empowerment which are subjective reports, subject to all the possibilities of distortion that any subjective report must entail. On the other hand, it must be emphasized, once again, that we are not claiming that this setting is necessarily better at creating empowerment than any other, but rather that for those people who do appear to be empowered in such a setting (in the sense of experiencing a change in their interpersonal behavior which is consistent with their ideals), we have isolated a consistent pattern which describes the process as it is seen by them and by those who know them well.

While the above relationship among the variables seems to be well established, there are a variety of plausible explanations to account for it. Direct observation, over time, led us to note a variety of setting characteristics consistent with the principles of many psychological theories of behavior change (Table 10). These behavior change theories encompass diverse motivational (Allport, 1968; Thibaut & Kelley, 1959), reduction of psychological obstacles (Frankl, 1962; Rogers, 1959, 1961; Rotter, 1954; Sullivan, 1953), skills development (Bandura, 1976; McFall, 1976) and situational (Dohrenwend, 1978; Dohrenwend & Dohrenwend, 1974; Endler & Magnusson, 1976) orientations (see Maton, Note 1, for a more complete discussion).

Although our participant-observation data are merely descriptive and hypothesis generating we found much of what we observed to be interpretable in the context of psychological theory (Table 10). The characteristics of the activities which we observed include: (1) Many members reported the experience of God's love, forgiveness and expectancies of positive outcomes for future life events, in the context of private, small group and large group prayer, worship and Bible study. (2) Reports and observation of personal affirmation from one member to another were common. (3) Meaningful responsibilities were offered to most members in the setting; (4) explicit and implicit group expectations to develop interpersonal attributes like Jesus' were frequent. (5) Emotional and material support was offered during times of stress in dyadic, small group and large group contexts. (6) Exposure to models of appropriate interpersonal behavior was frequent, and (7) opportunities for self-disclosure, guidance, and emotional insight about personal problems or limitations in "sheparding" or counseling, small group and teaching (i.e., "sermons") contexts were ongoing (Maton, Note 1).

These activities and experiences which we observed occurred in the context of explicit setting goals for spiritual development, shared community life, interpersonal development, and outreach to the poor. Leadership qualities distributed among the elders and others of service-orientation, dependence on God, vision, sensitivity, and wariness of inflexible structures represent a second potentially important characteristic. A decentralization of authority and responsibility, a setting climate of sincerity, friendliness, and excitement, and a balance between community and freedom, facilitated in part by a diversity of theological subgroupings (all sharing a common belief in God's/Jesus' activeness and in the Bible), seem to us to be important. Finally, the distinctiveness and range of previous experiences of members, along with the young age of the setting and

TABLE 10

Theoretical Explanations of the Relationship Between Commitment, God Not Man,
Life Crisis and Perceived Interpersonal Behavior Change

Theory of Behavior Change	Fellowship Activities/Experience

I. Motivational
  A. Intrinsic motivation toward values, or self ideals, provided by religion (Allport, 1968) (Thibaut & Kelley, 1959)
  B. Desire not to violate group norms and expectations (Thibaut & Kelley, 1959)
  C. Experience of Emotional pain/motivation great enough to abandon familiar coping patterns in favor of new ones
	Strong attraction to alternative self-ideal of becoming more like Jesus (Commitment)
	Desire not to disappoint values others' expectations to develop more like Jesus (Commitment)
	Capability to adopt new beliefs and interpersonal patterns more consistent with Jesus (Life crisis)

II. Reduction of Psychological Obstacles
  A. Low self-acceptance; necessity for experience of unconditional positive regard (Rogers, 1959, 1961)
  B. Maladaptive role of "self-system" in warding off anxiety; necessity of emotional insight (Sullivan, 1953)
  C. Low cognitive expectances of positive outcomes of behavior (Rotter, 1954)
  D. Lack of personal identity and meaning (Frankl, 1962)
	Experience of love and affirmation in personal relationships with God and setting members (Commitment; God not man)
	Openness to psychological feedback offered in the context of ongoing small group, "sheparding," "teachings," and via meditation and prayer (Commitment, God not man)
	Acceptance on a "gut" level of God's promise that one's personal future is secure (Commitment; Got not man)
	Secure identity based on Christian world view and meaningful roles in setting activities (Commitment)

III. Skills Development
  A. Vicarious learning from observation of appropriate models (Bandura, 1976)
  B. Specific information, guidance and feedback about skills (McFall, 1976)
	Frequent and focused observation of Fellowship models across diverse situations (Commitment)
	Direct advice and feedback received in the context of ongoing small group, "sheparding," friendship and marital relationships among members (Commitment)

IV. Situational
  A. Decreased incidence of and/or increased support during stressful life events (Dohrenwend, 1978; Dohrenwend & Dohrenwend, 1974)
  B. Change in the types of situations in which individuals are regularly involved (Endler & Magnusson, 1976)
	Prayer, emotional and financial support in the context of ongoing, intimate relationships; faith in God's capability to bring good out of difficult situations: personal development leading to decreased incidence (Commitment)
	Increased proportion of time in interactions with other committed members where shared perspectives, interpersonal acceptance and joint goals characterize situations, and elicit adaptive behavior; new behaviors influence and generalize to other situations (Commitment)

69

the sense of being part of the creation of an important setting, also appear to contribute to the adaptive attributes and impacts of the setting (Maton, Note 1).

These observations are consistent with McGaw's (1979) analysis of the potential of "charasmatic" religious settings (i.e., churches which emphasize God's spiritual activeness) as a locus for the psychological empowerment of members, although it must be emphasized that this is not a study of the efficacy of this setting, but rather a study of individual differences within such a setting. As such, these observations are offered to provide a context for understanding the individual changes reported.

Future research is necessary to replicate the present findings, to explore the generalizability of findings in related and differing setting contexts, and to directly examine the plausibility of several alternative interpretations of the findings. Ideally, longitudinal research should be conducted. In such research it is important to maintain a balance between the imposition of theoretical constructs and grounding constructs (and items) in the phenomenology of those studied. Also, in keeping with an ecological perspective, it is important to maintain a simultaneous focus on individual and setting levels of analysis, and on historical and present variables. Such a perspective will facilitate informed interpretation of findings and contribute to theory generation connecting sets of findings across settings and populations.

The participant-observation research role used in this investigation represents one useful method facilitating access to a diversity of qualitative and quantitative evidence. Obviously, cross-setting comparisons of setting level variables would lend much to our understanding, as would the more systematic observation of setting variables by more than two observers.

The research has implications for action and policy from an empowerment perspective in the area of natural support settings (Berger & Neuhaus, 1977; Rappaport, 1981). The particular religious setting studied appears to provide an adaptive niche for members, one which provides meaning, identity, opportunities for interpersonal development, and access to a network of support and resources. As research focused on empowerment in other natural settings emerges, it will presumably reveal some key processes common across settings (perhaps, for example, the "psychological sense of community") as well as empowerment criteria and processes unique to the culture and contexts of different settings. Efforts to collaborate with members in the empowerment of their natural settings thus will need to be based both on an understanding and appreciation of their particular criteria and contexts and a breadth of knowledge about efficacious processes in related settings. This research is hopefully a step in the direction of such understanding.

REFERENCE NOTES

1. Maton, K. I. *Empowerment in a religious setting: An exploratory study*. Master's thesis, University of Illinois at Urbana-Champaign, 1981.
2. Maton, K. I. *Economic sharing among church members: Psychological correlates and evaluation of an Economic Barter-Sharing Service*. University of Illinois at Urbana-Champaign, 1984.

REFERENCES

Allport, G. W. *The person in psychology: Selected essays*. Boston: Beacon Press, 1968.

Allport, G. W., & Ross, J. M. Personal religious orientation and prejudice. *Journal of Personality and Social Psychology*, 1967, *5*(4), 432-443.

Argyle, M. *Religious behavior*. Glencoe, Ill.: Free Press, 1959.

Bandura, A. Social learning theory. In J. T. Spence, R. C. Carson, & J. W. Thibaut (Eds.), *Behavioral approaches to therapy*. Morristown, N.J.: General Learning Press, 1976.

Batson, C. D. Religion as prosocial: Agent or double agent. *Journal for the Scientific Study of Religion*, 1976 *15*(1), 29-45.

Berger, P., & Neuhaus, R. J. *To empower people: The role of mediating structures in public policy*. Washington, D.C.: American Enterprise Institute for Public Policy, 1977.

Briar, S., & Bieri, I. A factor analytic and trait inference study of the Leary interpersonal check list. *Journal of Clinical Psychology*, 1963, *19*, 193-198.

Crowne, D. P., & Marlow, D. C. *The approval motive*. New York: John Wiley, 1964.

Dittes, J. Religion, prejudice and personality In M. Strommen (Ed.), *Research on religious development*. New York: Hawthorn Books, 1971.

Dohrenwend, B. S. Social stress and community psychology. *American Journal of Community Psychology*, 1978, *6*(1), 1-14.

Dohrenwend, B. S., & Dohrenwend, B. P. (Eds.). *Conference on stressful life events: Their nature and effects*. New York: Wiley, 1974.

Donaldson, W. (Ed). *Research in mental health and religious behavior*. Atlanta: Psychological Studies Institute, 1976.

Endler, N. S., & Magnusson, D. Toward an interactional psychology of personality. *Psychological Bulletin*, 1976, *83*, 956-974.

Entner, P. D. Religious orientation and mental health. *Dissertation Abstracts International*, 1977, *38*(4)-B, 1949.

Frankl, V. E. *Man's search for meaning: An introduction to logotherapy*. Boston: Beacon Press, 1962.

Glock, C. Y., & Stark, R. *Religion and society in tension*. Chicago: Randy McNally, 1965.

Golding, S. L., & Knudson, R. M. Multivariable-multimethod convergence in the domain of interpersonal behavior. *Multivariate Behavioral Research*, 1975, *10*(4), 425-448.

Golding, S. L., & Seidman, E. Analysis of multitrait-multimethod matrices: A two-step principal components procedure. *Multivariate Behavioral Research*, 1974, *9*, 479-496.

Harman, H. H. *Modern factor analysis* (2nd ed., Rev.). Chicago: University of Chicago Press, 1967.

Jacquet, C. H. (Ed.). *Yearbook of American churches.* Nashville: Abingdon, 1972.

Kahoe, R. D. Personality and achievement correlates of intrinsic and extrinsic religious orientations. *Journal of Personality and Social Psychology,* 1974, *29*(6), 812-818.

Kieffer, C. *The emergence of empowerment: Patterns and process in the evolution of participatory competence amongst lower-income individuals.* Unpublished doctoral dissertation, University of Michigan, 1981.

King, M. Measuring the religious variable: Nine proposed dimensions. *Journal for the Scientific Study of Religion,* 1967, *6*(2), 173-190.

Kopplin, D. *Religious orientations of college students and related personality characteristics.* Paper presented at American Psychological Association, Washington, D.C., September 1976.

LaForge, R. *Using the ICL: 1976.* Mill Valley, Calif.: Rolfe LaForge, 1977.

Leary, T. *Interpersonal diagnosis of personality.* New York: Ronald Press, 1957.

Levenson, H. *Reliability and validity of the I, P, and C scales: A multi-dimensional view of locus of control.* Paper presented at American Psychological Association, Montreal, August 1973.

McClain, E. W. Personality differences between intrinsically religious and non-religious students: A factor analytic study. *Journal of Personality Assessment,* 1978, *42*(2), 159-166.

McFall, R. M. Behavioral training: A skill-acquisition approach to clinical problems. In J. Spence, R. Carson, & J. Thibaut (Eds.), *Behavioral approaches to therapy.* Morristown, N.J.: General Learning Press, 1976.

McGaw, D. B. Commitment and religious community: A comparison of a charismatic and a mainline congregation. *Journal for the Scientific Study of Religion,* 1979, *18*(2), 146-163.

National Commission on Neighborhoods. *Report to the President.* Washington, D.C.: United States Government Printing Office, 1979.

Pargament, K. I., Steele, R. E., & Tyler, F. B. Religious participation, religious motivation, and individual psychosocial competence. *Journal for the Scientific Study of Religion,* 1979, *18*(4), 412-418.

President's Commission on Mental Health. *Task panel report on natural support systems* (Vol. II). Washington, D.C.: U.S. Government Printing Office, 1978.

Rappaport, J. In praise of paradox: A social policy of empowerment over prevention. *American Journal of Community Psychology,* 1981, *9*(1), 1-25.

Rogers, C. R. A theory of therapy, personality, and interpersonal relationships, as developed in the client-centered framework. In S. Koch (Ed.), *Psychology: A study of a science* (Vol. 3). New York: McGraw-Hill, 1959.

Rogers, C. R. *On becoming a person.* Boston: Houghton Mifflin, 1961.

Rotter, J. B. *Social learning and clinical psychology.* Englewood Cliffs, N.J.: Prentice-Hall, 1954.

Sanua, V. D. Religion, mental health, and personality: A review of empirical studies. *American Journal of Psychiatry,* 1969, *125*(9), 1203-1213.

Sarason, S. B. *The psychological sense of community.* San Francisco, Calif: Jossey-Bass, 1974.

Stark, R. Psychopathology and religious commitment. *Review of Religious Research,* 1971, *12*(3), 165-176.

Sullivan, H. S. *The interpersonal theory of psychiatry.* New York: Norton, 1953.

Thibaut, J. W., & Kelley, H. W. *The social psychology of groups.* New York: John Wiley, 1959.

Wiggins, J. S. *Personality and prediction: Principles of personality assessment.* Reading, Mass.: Addison-Wesley, 1973.

The Fort McDowell Yavapai:
From Pawns to Powerbrokers

Michael J. O'Sullivan
Natalie Waugh
Wendy Espeland

ABSTRACT. Faced with the loss of their homeland due to a proposed dam, a small American Indian community initially seemed powerless to prevent their relocation. This threat was associated with substantial detrimental impacts on the physical, psychological, and economic functioning of the community and its members. While the proposed dam initially was stopped in 1976, it was resurrected by local political and public pressure following two years of devastating floods affecting a nearby metropolitan area. A federally funded and highly visible study was then commissioned to investigate the impacts of and alternatives to the proposed dam. An independent investigation collected data assessing the psychological impact on the Yavapai community caused by the threat of relocation. As a result of the visibility and attention the Yavapai gained from this study, their role as a politically active pressure group, and their shrewd use of the leverage they gained, the tribal community succeeded in eliminating the proposed dam and the accompanying threat of relocation. The present case illustrates both the process of empowerment as well as the efficacy of a large and thorough scientific study of alternatives for finding a viable option for such divergent interest groups. The political and mental health ramifications of these realities are discussed.

In our cultural folklore, "Friday the 13th" more often than not has been associated with back luck. On Friday, November 13, 1981, Secretary of the Interior James Watt announced his decision

Michael J. O'Sullivan is in the Department of Psychology, Saint Louis University, Natalie Waugh is with Dames & Moore, Phoenix, Arizona, and Wendy Espeland is in the Department of Sociology, University of Chicago.

Requests for reprints should be sent to Michael J. O'Sullivan, Department of Psychology, Saint Louis University, 221 North Grand Boulevard, Saint Louis, MO 63103.

to select a water control plan for central Arizona which would *not* include a dam at the confluence of the Verde and Salt Rivers. Depending on whom one talks to, that decision could be viewed as good or bad—but "luck" had very little to do with it. For the Yavapai Indians living at Fort McDowell, that decision was very good. With that one decision the very likely death of a culture and the concomitant psychological devastation of a tribal people were prevented. The key to this story of prevention was that the people "at risk" came to realize the power they possessed and learned to use it effectively to forge their own survival and growth.

In the present paper an attempt is made to portray some of the events, processes, and data that contributed to that decision. The authors are not members of the Fort McDowell community and consequently are not familiar with the various negotiations and processes which occurred within the tribe and/or between the tribe and other interested parties. Whether or not such information ever becomes public remains the perogative of the tribe. However the authors were involved both in studying the impacts various water control plans would have on the Fort McDowell people, and in entering that data into the decision-making process. As a result they gained familiarity with some of the important ingredients involved in that decision. In the following discussion they are limited both to what is public knowledge and, of course, by their own interpretations of what happened.

FORT McDOWELL AND THE CENTRAL ARIZONA PROJECT (CAP)

The Fort McDowell Indian Community is located approximately 25 miles northeast of Phoenix, Arizona. Its land is bordered by the Salt River Pima-Maricopa Indian Community on the south, the affluent planned community of Fountain Hills on the west, and the Tonto National Forest on the north and east. The reservation is among the nation's smallest: a parallelogram covering 24,630 acres, it extends approximately 10 miles north-south and 4 miles east-west. The Verde River runs north-south through the middle of the reservation and converges with the Salt River approximately 1.5 miles from the reservation's southernmost border.

According to the 1980 national census there are approximately 350 Indian people residing at Fort McDowell, 75% of whom identify themselves as members of the Yavapai tribe (O'Sullivan, Note 1). The Yavapai people twice experienced compulsory relocation at the hands of the United States government in the 1870s. After more than 25 years of being forced to live with their traditional enemies, the Apaches, the Yavapai were allowed to return to their original homeland and settle on the Fort McDowell reservation in 1903. Since that time there have been repeated attempts to relocate them from the Fort McDowell environs—beginning with an early effort by the federal government to resettle them with their own traditional foes, the Pimas.

A dam at the confluence of the Salt and Verde Rivers in central Arizona was proposed by the U.S. Army Corps of Engineers in a study conducted in 1945-1947. The proposal for the dam languished until 1961 when the U.S. Bureau of Reclamation (within the Department of the Interior) began preliminary studies for a dam to store Colorado River water that would be imported into central Arizona via the proposed Central Arizona Project (CAP).

The CAP had been a dream of some Arizonans for decades. The project involved diverting water from the Colorado River at Lake Havasu and conveying it across 350 miles of desert in an open canal to the cities, farms, and mines of central Arizona. The CAP would be more reliable and Arizona could take more of the water to which it was entitled if the water could be stored at a location in Arizona during times when water was plentiful and taken out of storage later when the water was needed. The projected dam at the confluence of the Salt and Verde Rivers was to provide this so-called regulatory storage.

Such a confluence dam also would control the flows of the Salt and Verde Rivers. Historically there have been major floods along these rivers, with the damage occurring downstream below the confluence of the two rivers where the Salt River winds through downtown Phoenix. Most of the time the Salt River is totally dry in the Phoenix area because of water storage dams which were built upstream on both the Salt and the Verde. However, when there is heavy rainfall, especially during the late winter after the snow in the surrounding mountains begins to melt, floods occur of sufficient magnitudes that the various dams pass the flow to the valley below. The dam at the confluence of the Salt and Verde was to provide the flood control that downstream Phoenix needed, as well as the regulatory storage of CAP water the Bureau of Reclamation wanted.

From its beginning CAP had massive support from business, agriculture, and the political leadership of Arizona. Support in Congress was shored up by Arizona's congressional delegation as well as most other Arizona leaders who had been working for it since the 1940s. By 1961, the Bureau of Reclamation was beginning to evaluate the feasibility of building the aqueducts, pumping plants, and dams that would comprise the overall project. In that year, the Bureau approached the Fort McDowell community to ask for permission to enter the reservation for purposes of surveying the proposed reservoir.

PRELIMINARY NEGOTIATIONS

The engineers from the Bureau who wrote asking for an entrance permit received a gracious response from the Fort McDowell Tribal Council. If the council had known that the engineers were just the vanguard of wave after wave of surveyors, assessors, planners, government officials, sociologists, anthropologists, community psychologists, reporters, and ever more engineers, they probably would have turned down that request for entry.

In anticipation of authorization and appropriation of money for the project, the Bureau of Reclamation continued to meet with both the Fort McDowell community and their downstream neighbors, the Salt River Indian Community. The proposed dam, called Maxwell Dam until the mid-1960s and Orme Dam thereafter, was to be built on the land of the Salt River Indian Community. The reservoir behind the dam was designed to flood the Verde River valley that bisects the Fort McDowell community's lands, and tribal members who lived in that area would have to relocate. As the proposal became more definite, the full dimensions of the relocation became apparent. Virtually all of the community's then 300 members would have to relocate. Most of the community's facilities would be subject to flooding on an annual, or less than annual, basis. All in all, about 14,000 of Fort McDowell's 25,000 acres of land would be required for the Orme project as it was envisioned in the 1960s and 1970s, although not all of the acquired land would be under water.

In 1967 and 1968 while the CAP legislation was in preparation, then Secretary of the Interior Stewart Udall recognized the extent of the loss of resources to the Fort McDowell Indian Community. At that time, the National Environmental Policy Act (NEPA) was not in existence and therefore there was no requirement to prepare an environmental impact statement. Nor did anyone consider the psychological and social impact of relocation. Secretary Udall seems to have acted on behalf of the tribe only from an economic standpoint. The policy for land acquisitions was to negotiate monetary compensation for landowners. If owners refused to negotiate, the land could be condemned and taken. In the interests of the Fort McDowell people, Secretary Udall asked Congress to include additional compensation: 2,500 acres of nearby U.S. Forest Service land would be given to the tribe, and the tribe would be permitted to derive recreational benefits from the Orme reservoir. Monetary compensation would include payment for the assessed value of the land and buildings, plus additional money for the indirect costs of moving. This was considered by the House Interior Committee as very generous and in keeping with special consideration frequently given to Indian tribes when dams are located on their lands.

With the passage of the Colorado River Basin Act of 1968 (PL 90-537) the Bureau of Reclamation moved ahead to negotiate a monetary settlement with the Fort McDowell community. The tribe had *not* participated in the agreement worked into the provisions of the act and did not think that the compensation was adequate. As time passed, the tribe became more and more articulate in expressing the view that no compensation ever would be adequate to repay them for the loss of their land (Casserly, 1981). Nevertheless, the tribe initially listened to the government's proposals, asked questions, requested clarifications, and attempted whenever possible to gain some leverage. In order to compensate more fully for the loss of 14,000 acres of high-quality land in the Verde River valley, the tribe's efforts in the late 1960s and early 1970s were focused on obtaining a lease of up to 14,000 acres of Forest Service land, in addition to the initial grant of 2,500 acres. After considerable discussion and negotiation between the tribe and the Bureau of Reclamation, this proposition was denied since the CAP authorizing legislation did not permit any additional land beyond the 2,500 acres originally made available.

When attempts to obtain additional leased land collapsed in late 1972, the tribe's position began to harden. They seemed to understand more fully how much they stood to lose from relocation: essentially everything. No provision was made, for example, to compensate or transfer the tribe's water rights. The "replacement" land offered by the government was in no way equal in value to the land lost. The tribe even came to contest the government's appraisal of the land and the amount of monetary compensation offered to them. As the negative effects of the Orme project became clearer, resistance stiffened. The question became whether their opposition to the dam would be efficacious.

On the surface, the tribe had little or no power. As a community they were small (less than 400 members even to this day), poor, inexperienced and seemingly not adept in political maneuvering (Casserly, 1981). For example, when the CAP legislation was in hearing before the House Interior Committee in 1968, the Salt River Indian Community had representatives on hand to present a prepared statement. Fort McDowell was *not* represented. As late as 1968, Fort McDowell did not have a lawyer to represent the community in matters related to CAP.

Externally, there appeared to be little chance that relocation would not be forced on the tribe. The government's position was exceptionally strong. If the tribe did not negotiate, the government could condemn and acquire the land. If the tribe did negotiate, the government could pay only up to the appropriations ceiling already requested by the Department of the Interior and approved by the Congress of the United States. Moreover, all of Arizona's congressional delegation was not only behind CAP, but fervently advocating that it be built. State leaders saw CAP as the solution to the state's water problems, and city leaders in Phoenix and in bordering communities saw the Orme Dam portion of CAP as salvation from any future flooding problems. In short, the existing business and governmental power establishment was firmly in support of building Orme Dam at the expense of the Fort McDowell Yavapai community. The community itself had few resources to protect itself from being expropriated and relocated to a new piece of land a tenth the size of their original reservation.

CHANGES IN THE POWER RELATIONSHIP

Correspondence and records of meetings between the tribe and the Bureau of Reclamation indicate that the attempts to make the best of a foreordained conclusion gradually gave way to increased resistance and finally to a determination that the tribe would not acquiesce. The story that unfolds from 1972 to 1981 shows the changing power relationship between the tribe and the supporters of Orme Dam.

After the collapse of negotiations over leased land in late 1972, the tribe could see more clearly than before that they would not be able to negotiate for more than what was included in the CAP authorizing legislation. The government's main argument was that the tribe would be wealthy from the monetary compensation that would be provided for the 14,000 acres of land acquired for the dam and reservoir. In addition, the tribe could operate and benefit from the recreation facilities that would be built on the Verde River arm of the Orme Reservoir. From the perspective of the tribe, however, the loss of 14,000 acres of land to which the Yavapai people were intensely attached spiritually, psychologically, politically, and economically could not be compensated by a monetary settlement and the right to operate a marina (Blundell, 1981; Elling, 1981; Lessner, 1981; Perry, 1981a).

The government and the Phoenix media did not see it the Yavapai's way. From the time Orme Dam became a cause celebre in the mid-1970s, the Fort McDowell Indian Community was consistently pictured as a small group of obstructionists who would not give way for the community good. Business leaders in Phoenix often described the Orme project as the "best thing that could happen to the Indians." The two major Phoenix newspapers ran editorials that called for Orme and castigated the Indians who would not relocate even though they would be given enough money to make them millionaires (Hardt, 1981). In the face of this kind of acrimony and divisiveness, the tribe became increasingly united in the fight against Orme. Events and trends conspired to help the tribe.

Although CAP was authorized before the passage of the National Environmental Policy Act in 1970, a comprehensive Environmental Impact Statement (EIS) on CAP was prepared by the Bureau of Reclamation in 1972. This EIS committed the Bureau to preparing an EIS on each of the features of the CAP as they reached the appropriate design stage. One by one, the features such as aqueducts, pumping plants, and dams would come up for environmental review and public comment. In 1976 the Bureau filed a draft EIS on the Orme Dam and heard a storm of comments from environmental groups, recreationists, and supporters of the Fort McDowell Indian Community. The Orme reservoir would have flooded out a rich area for wildlife including the endangered bald eagle, wiped out a segment of the Salt River that was used intensively for river floating, and required the relocation of the Yavapai of Fort McDowell.

The coalition of interest groups against Orme included a mix of environmentalists, religious leaders, anti-government advocates, pro-Indian supporters, and river recreationists. If they did not have a line to the power establishment, they did get noticed because of their vociferous dedication to defeating Orme. They wrote letters, organized protests, packed public hearings, and generally made life miserable for the Bureau of Reclamation officials who were attempting to move the Orme project forward. These officials recognized that the project was in deep trouble after the draft EIS was filed and public hearings were conducted. The anti-Orme coalition promised to sue on a number of issues, not the least of which was the inadequacy of the EIS in evaluating a less than complete range of alternatives to the confluence dam (Hardt, 1981).

Whereas in an earlier time the government might have had little trouble condemning and taking land for a public project, with the advent of NEPA in 1970 that type of process was opened to public scrutiny. There were new requirements for public comment on the EIS and the need to evaluate the impacts of the Orme project on the human environment. The Orme project now was open to viewing not only by the local community but also by the national media. The tribe began to realize that appeals to a broader audience than the hostile Phoenix community could be made. Furthermore, the tribe was no longer alone. The anti-Orme coalition provided an alliance of interests that gave more hope of defeating Orme than the tribe ever could have had on its own.

In 1976, after the draft EIS was filed, the tribe was embattled but not without hope. The tribe had taken a firm stance that their land was not for sale. A referendum on Orme had been held within the Fort McDowell tribal community, and the offer to negotiate a monetary settlement with the federal government was voted down by a 3-1 margin. However this vote was seen by pro-Orme supporters as a soft spot in the united front presented by tribal leaders, for it seemed that some members of the tribe wanted to negotiate. Many government officials believed that the tribe actually had not changed its position but essentially was "holding out," refusing to negotiate in order to drive up the monetary compensation for lost land. When a concrete offer of sufficient size was made, these officials believed, then the tribe would accept it and relocate without resistance.

The Fort McDowell people had no such ideas. They feared that the government, in an authoritarian position, could eventually seize the land and force the community to relocate. Clearly, the CAP authorizing legislation gave the government license to do just that if the tribe refused to negotiate a settlement. What prevented the government from going ahead and condemning the land was the fear of litigation and the intense scrutiny of the public. The government continued to hold out hopes for a monetary settlement and an uneventful relocation because the alternative was so fraught with uncertainty. It was not known if the Indians and/or the environmentalists would sue, nor was it known if their case would be substantial enough to win in court. Likewise no one knew how long Orme could be tied up in court (Blundell, 1981; Casserly, 1981).

While there was this uncertainty within the government, most officials involved with the project in the mid-1970s believed that Orme would prevail. It was such a perfect engineering solution to the twin problems of CAP regulatory storage and Salt River flood control that the thought of other alternatives was almost absurd. There just was no other location where one dam could be built and provide all the functions of Orme. No other alternative would be nearly as cost effective, because two dams instead of one would have to be built and the performance would not be nearly as good as Orme's. It was absolute belief in the superiority of Orme that caused many government officials and supporters in Phoenix to become wedded to Orme (Perry, 1981b).

As a result, there was a highly polarized community in central Arizona: the Indians and their supporters on one side, the political and business leaders of Arizona on the other side. The national election of 1976 intervened. Jimmy Carter was elected President, and during his first months in office reviewed all the major federal water projects being planned. He particularly focused on the Bureau of Reclamation's western water projects, of which CAP was the most well known. In 1977 President Carter eliminated CAP from the administration's funding request to congress. When the organized clout of the Arizona congressional delegation and other western states' delegations was brought to bear, Carter backed off, keeping CAP but deleting Orme Dam. He deleted Orme because of environmental concerns and the relocation of the Fort McDowell Yavapai community. Orme Dam was dead. The Fort McDowell people rejoiced but remained skeptical—as they had come to know too well white people and their ways of getting what they want.

It was a short respite for Fort McDowell. The first of three major floods hit the Phoenix area in March 1978, resulting in a renewed cry for Orme Dam. If Orme had been in place, virtually all flood damage would have been prevented. The major newspaper in

Phoenix, *The Arizona Republic*, in an editorial on March 4, 1978 summarized the position of the Orme supporters: "the basic question is whether a few Indians and bald eagles should be inconvenienced, or whether hundreds of thousands of Valley residents should be inconvenienced." By March 9, 1978, the ban on Orme studies was lifted, and the Bureau of Reclamation embarked on a renewed evaluation of Orme and its alternatives.

CENTRAL ARIZONA WATER CONTROL STUDY (CAWCS)

This new study would take four years and focus on a thorough and detailed evaluation of all reasonable options for flood control and CAP regulatory storage, including a dam at the confluence of the Salt and Verde Rivers. The Bureau of Reclamation would lead the study, with help from the U.S. Army Corps of Engineers. The environmental, social, and economic evaluation of the various alternatives would be performed by a consultant hired by the Bureau for this purpose. The consultant also would conduct the highly visible public participation program. The award of the consulting contract was made in April 1979, and the study—called the Central Arizona Water Control Study (CAWCS)—was not in high gear until the summer of 1979. Two of the present authors were involved with CAWCS: Waugh was the project manager for the consultant, and Espeland was the sociologist who served as the principal author of the CAWCS section dealing with the social impacts of relocation on the various communities affected by the different options studied.

CAWCS was heavily supported by all of the interested parties. The pro-Orme advocates supported it because they felt sure that Orme would prove to be the only alternative that would provide all the functions that were needed and be the most cost-competitive. The study, they hoped, would lay to rest all the questions raised by the tribe and the anti-Orme coalition: were there any reasonable alternatives to Orme, what impact would Orme have on the eagles and the Indians, would Orme be safe, and were both flood control and CAP regulatory storage really needed?

The anti-Orme coalition, on the other hand, felt that if these questions were answered fairly, Orme could not survive. They questioned the basic need for the dam, advocating that floods caused damage because people had built homes and located businesses in the floodplain without legal right. They also questioned the need to store CAP water in Arizona and wanted to see the cost/benefit analysis for this function. They disbelieved the optimistic picture of impacts to the Fort McDowell people painted in the Orme EIS of 1976. That EIS had portrayed the Fort McDowell Yavapai as people who had endured hardship and had survived relocations in the past; accordingly, they would be able to survive this relocation and thrive because of the monetary compensation (Natelson, Note 2; Pearson, Note 3). However, that study was plagued by serious conceptual and methodological flaws, given the complexity of the issue. It also failed to note that the cost of the tribe's survival of past relocations included the wiping out of whole bands and families, and the death of over half the total Yavapai population (Brandt, Note 4). Anthropologists argued that the conclusions in that EIS flew in the face of other studies of rural relocations and Indian relocations; and that, in fact, the Yavapai culture would be in peril if the relocation occurred. The anthropologists, the tribe, and the anti-Orme supporters all wanted a very thorough examination of the impacts of relocation. This was one of the the most important jobs that would have to be done in CAWCS.

Another important job was to conduct the public participation program. There was intense interest in the findings of CAWCS and a strong desire by all groups to influence the decision-making process. The public participation program was the communication conduit for those on the outside of the study to make their voices heard, and it was the vehicle for disseminating information to the public. As part of the program, Governor Bruce Babbitt of Arizona appointed a Governor's Advisory Committee (GAC) made up of 29 representatives from the cities, organizations, interest groups, and affected entities who had a stake in the outcome of the study. The Fort McDowell Indian Community was represented on GAC, along with *The Arizona Republic*, business development interests, environmental interests, water development and control interests, and general citizens' interests. Babbitt purposely put significant competing interests on this one advisory committee, and admonished it to make a recommendation to him at the end of the study that would represent a consensus.

CAWCS, then, was supposed to find a water control solution that everyone in Arizona could support. The study was done in stages, going from an evaluation of a large number of potential alternatives down to a small number, from which the best alternative would be picked to be implemented. The alternative of " no action" was included in the evaluation, as well as numerous combinations of "action" alternatives. At certain points in the study, decisions were made to drop alternatives from further evaluation. The alternatives that remained were studied in depth and re-evaluated. At the beginning of the final stage of the study, in 1981, there were some nine "elements" that could be combined into water control "plans." The elements were individual dams or nonstructural actions that could provide for flood control or regulatory storage. The plans were combinations of elements that could meet both of the project objectives.

As the Bureau of Reclamation began putting together the final plans, they found that they had to include another project purpose: safety of the existing dams on the Salt and Verde Rivers. A concurrent study of dam safety had been going on, reviewing many of the same elements under study by CAWCS. The Bureau found that the two studies were hopelessly intertwined and could not be completed separately in the time allocated. Therefore, dam safety was incorporated into CAWCS. This had a profound effect on the alternatives and ultimately on the outcome of the study.

Before dam safety became a core issue, when considering the various alternative plans developed by CAWCS to accomplish both CAP regulatory storage and Salt River flood control, the alternatives which included a so-called confluence dam (Orme Dam) had an advantage because Orme could do everything with one dam. However, in order to insure the safety of existing dams, all the alternatives had to include the construction of at least two additional dams (one on the Salt River and one on the Verde) which would prevent the existing dams on the rivers from failing if there were a massive flood. When the final alternatives were developed, there were eight different plans, three of which included Orme-like dams. But each of the Orme plans now also mandated the construction of additional dams to insure the safety of the Salt and Verde system of dams. The engineering and economic advantage the original Orme concept had of accomplishing all goals with one dam was now lost.

Meanwhile, CAWCS studies of impacts were going on. Federal regulations designed to protect the data collection efforts of the approaching 1980 national census would not permit CAWCS personnel to collect "hard" empirical data via surveys or other numerically oriented instruments. Burdened with this federally imposed methodological handicap, CAWCS proceeded with studies at Fort McDowell focused on interviewing community members to determine the existing conditions in terms of variables that were important to predicting impacts. The interviews were taped and transcribed. An extensive review of the literature was conducted and existing or ongoing studies that were pertinent to relocation of Fort McDowell residents were incorporated into the analysis (CAWCS, Note 5).

PSYCHOLOGICAL IMPACTS OF THE THREAT OF RELOCATION

Previous research on the effects of relocation would suggest that the compulsory relocation of the Fort McDowell community from their homeland would have a very detrimental psychological impact on members of the community (O'Sullivan & Handal, Note 6). Much of the research on relocation has occurred within the past 20 years and generally has demonstrated that relocation, whether voluntary or compulsory, functions as a significant stressor and disrupts social support networks (Finsterbusch, 1980; Kantor, 1969; Scudder, 1973, Note 7). Compared to voluntary relocation, the effects of compulsory relocation appear to be significantly more negative in terms of the subsequent social support disruption and psychological distress (Butler, McAllister, & Kaiser, 1973; Scudder, 1973). Research on compulsory relocation has revealed that the poor, elderly, long-time residents, minority groups, and community-oriented cultural groups are high risk populations in which the effects of compulsory relocation are particularly negative in terms of psychological adjustment and social networks (Finsterbusch, 1980; Scudder, 1973; Watson, 1980; Scudder, Note 7). Additional effects of compulsory relocation have been demonstrated by increased morbidity and mortality rates (Finsterbusch, 1980; Fried, 1963; Kowalski, 1978; Scudder, 1973; Thomas, 1979; Watson, 1980; Scudder, Note 7) and increased utilization of medical facilities (Topper & Johnson, 1980; Scudder, Note 7).

Another negative effect of compulsory relocation that appears to be applicable to American Indians is the experience of a cultural identity crisis, a resistance to innovation, and increased dependency upon the national government which is responsible for the relocation (Colson, 1971; Kiste, 1972; Scudder, 1973, Note 7).

When relocation is of a compulsory/involuntary nature, it is evident that power is a major issue. Those being relocated have been forced to surrender control over a central dimension of their lives.

The decision is out of their hands and belongs to an outside authority. The psychological evidence illustrating the importance for people of the felt sense of control over their personal and communal lives is well-known (Lefcourt, 1982; Phares, 1973; Rotter, 1975; Seaman, 1972). The dependency that seems to develop in involuntarily relocated community-oriented cultural groups who place such psychological significance on their homelands seems to correspond well with the psychological research on learned helplessness (Seligman, 1975; Seligman & Maier, 1967; Sue & Zane, 1980).

For nearly all American Indian and Alaskan Native tribes their homeland is of immense significance psychologically—touching many dimensions of their lives as well as their cultural identity as a people (Sutton, 1975; Task Panel Report on Mental Health of American Indians and Alaskan Natives, 1978). For the Yavapai, the land at Fort McDowell has a profound psychological significance for their cultural and tribal identity as it is quite sacred as well as being their homeland (O'Sullivan, Note 1; Brandt, Note 4). The profound meaning and importance of the land for the Navajo greatly compounded the difficulties and negative impacts of their compulsory relocation (Scudder, Note 7).

After reviewing much of the literature on the relationship between stressful life events and psychopathology, Dohrenwend (1979) hypothesizes that there is a triad of stressors whose impact surpasses internal and external mediating factors, neutralizes mechanisms of adaptation, and leads directly to psychopathology in previously normal persons. That pathogenic triad of stressors includes fateful loss events, physical illness and/or injury, and disruption of social supports. The relocation literature indicates that all of those stressors are normally expected consequences of compulsory relocation.

In the summer of 1980 one of the authors, O'Sullivan, began investigating possibilities for his doctoral dissertation in clinical psychology. Suggestions for possible Indian-related dissertation topics were sought from several Indian people and Indian Health Service (IHS) mental health professionals in Arizona. Among these people the consensus seemed to be that it would be beneficial to the Fort McDowell Yavapai if an attempt were made to document the effect of the relocation issue on the community's psychological well-being, as well as the expected consequences to their mental health, if they were resettled.

Through a clinical psychologist under an IHS contract to provide mental health services to the Fort McDowell community, the tribal council at Fort McDowell was approached with a proposal to conduct the dissertation study. Many of the tribal council meetings are open to all members of the Fort McDowell Indian community which is small and very close knit. Consequently great care was taken never to mention relocation and/or Orme Dam in the proposal given to the tribal council. The intent was to avoid possible biasing of responses if the people at Fort McDowell had prior knowledge that the study was related directly to the controversial dam and/or its effects on the people. The proposal presented to the council discussed the study in general terms as an attempt to assess the psychological effects on the tribal community of the considerable amount of controversy and stress regarding its future—and that such information would be useful to the council as it planned for the future. The study was proposed to the tribal council of a second reservation both in terms of serving as a needs assessment/planning study for that community and as a comparison group with the data collected at Fort McDowell. Permission to conduct the study was given by the tribal councils of both reservations.

Even though it was conducted independently of CAWCS, O'Sullivan's study (O'Sullivan, Note 1) soon was found to complement the social assessment efforts of CAWCS in presenting a more complete picture—both of how the tribe currently was being affected by the ongoing threat of compulsory relocation, and the expected consequences if the community was forced to move. The Social Assessment Team of CAWCS collected their primary data through use of three techniques: (1) recording of case histories, (2) discussions with key informants, and (3) unobtrusive field observing. Members of the Social Assessment Team attended community meetings, social events, protest meetings, and public forums in order to gather data (CAWCS, Note 5).

Using a community-wide epidemiological approach, O'Sullivan assessed the psychological impact of the threat of compulsory relocation on the Fort McDowell community (O'Sullivan, Note 1). Instruments used were the Langner 22-Item Screening Scale (Langner, 1962), Rotter Internal-External Control Scale (Rotter, 1966), and aggregate medical facility utilization statistics. The community's feelings about the dam as well as their estimation of its potential effects were assessed through a number of specific questions employing a Likert-type rating scale. The data were collected both on the Fort McDowell reservation and on a culturally similar reservation located in central Arizona approximately 100 miles upstream from Fort McDowell. Since this latter population had not been and would not be affected directly by the construction of the proposed dam, it served as a comparison or nonequivalent control group in a quasi-experimental "static-group comparison" design (Cook & Campbell, 1979). An ancillary study calibrated the Langner scale for the population under study.

While the details of this study are available elsewhere (O'Sullivan, Note 1), a review of the major findings is pertinent to the present discussion. The data from both the psychiatric screening scale (Langner) and the aggregate medical statistics indicated a rather high level of psychological distress at Fort McDowell, but the Rotter scale indicated an internal locus of control. Since there were significantly higher rates of both severe distress and medical service utilization at Fort McDowell than at the comparison reservation, the evidence suggested that some specific environmental stressor(s) was responsible for the higher distress at Fort McDowell. The responses to the questions regarding the proposed dam clearly defined the construction of this dam as a powerful stressor in the lives of this community. They experienced it to be as distressing as the death of a loved one. They perceived the proposed dam as causing the death of the tribe and culture. It is not unlikely that the association of this socio-political stressor with the death of such an essential dimension of their lives most likely generated an exacerbated level of psychological distress and medical utilization.

Two factors interacted so as to produce a level of severe psychological distress that far exceeded what would be expected just from their additive effects alone. The people at Fort McDowell are American Indians living on a reservation and were being threatened with compulsory relocation from their homeland. Compared with national norms, American Indian communities have exacerbated levels of psychological distress (Dohrenwend, Dohrenwend, Gould, Link, Neugeberger, & Wunsch-Hitzig, 1980; Manson & Shore, 1981; Martin, Sutker, Leon, & Hales, 1968; Roy, Choudhuri, & Irvine, 1970; Sampath, 1974; Shore, Kinzie, Hampson, & Pattison, 1973). This most likely reflects the pathogenic impact of the dominant political and socioeconomic structures under which these people live (Task Panel Report on Mental Health of American Indians & Alaskan Natives, 1978). The Fort McDowell community's mean score on the Langner identified them as a population at high risk for psychological dysfunction (Dohrenwend & Dohrenwend, 1969; Manson & Shore, 1981) which would make the severe distress of compulsory relocation even more deleterious (Lasry, 1975). Such psychological hazards have been observed to begin with the initial rumors of the possible resettlement. Expectations of impending hardship and loss cause the proposed relocation to be perceived as psychologically very threatening (Finsterbusch, 1980; Scudder, 1973).

It was thought that the data generated in the dissertation study would be useful to the Fort McDowell Yavapai in their efforts to prevent the dam and their relocation. With the tribal council's permission the data were made available to CAWCS. In assessing the social impacts and effects of the various water control plans, the CAWCS team's operative theoretical model called for first ascertaining the expected level of increased stress to be generated by the event, and then determining the ability of the target population to tolerate this stress. The difference between these two factors would provide an assessment of the event's impact and the desirability of its effects. The data from the dissertation were significant for creating the profile of the Fort McDowell residents' ability to cope with the increased stress which their relocation would produce.

It was the conclusion of both CAWCS and the dissertation study that forcing the Fort McDowell Yavapai to relocate would be quite pathogenic on the individual, interpersonal, and community levels. It was predicted that such a relocation from their homeland would result in extremely high levels of stress, substantial increases in morbidity and mortality rates, and extreme declines in the levels of personal autonomy and satisfaction with their lifestyle. There would be serious disruptions of familial as well as informal support networks leading to substantial increases in the incidence of family problems such as divorce, family violence, and drug and alcohol abuse. Community cohesion which had solidified during this time of crisis would be decimated—resulting in many members moving away from the community. Isolation would become a major problem. Likewise an extreme decrease in community viability could be expected, accompanied by widespread unemployment, increased dependence on the federal government, minimal resident participation in community activities, and the undermining of the authority of and respect for tribal government and leadership. The survival of the Yavapai culture itself was in question.

EMPOWERMENT

The decision on the "preferred alternative" was scheduled to take place in the fall of 1981. Findings were to be released in September for the public and the Governor's Committee to review. The GAC was to make a recommendation by October and the Secretary of the Interior would make his recommendation by mid-November. Because of the high interest in the findings relating to relocation, public officials were briefed on the predicted impacts. As outlined above, these findings were based on the best available information on the effect of relocations of Indian communities and the extensive data on the Fort McDowell Yavapai that had been collected by CAWCS and O'Sullivan.

At the same time that the findings were released, the tribe engaged in an effective, consistent, and intensive media campaign, culminating in a three-day march from the reservation to the state capitol on September 24, 25, and 26. Tribal leaders presented Governor Babbitt's representative with a signed petition from all members of the tribe backing an alternative: "Plan 6." While eliminating the need for a confluence dam, this plan would provide the functional equivalent of the best of the Orme plans by calling for: (1) regulatory storage to be achieved by the construction of a dam on the Agua Fria River to the west and north of Phoenix; and (2) flood control storage, new conservation space, and the safety of existing dams would be accomplished both by reconstruction on two existing dams on the Salt River to the east of Fort McDowell and by construction of a new dam on the Verde River far north of the Fort McDowell reservation.

The political processes involved in the tribe's strategy and decision to endorse "Plan 6" remain within the custody of the tribe and are not public knowledge. However, in backing one of the so-called "action" plans, the tribe essentially announced a break from the rest of the anti-Orme coalition, who were solidly behind the "no action" plan. The tribe also entered more fully into the political arena by supporting one of the action plans, in effect signaling other participants in the conflict that they were taking a position for doing something about the water control problems in the valley, and not merely opposing Orme Dam.

In other ways the tribe had moved closer to recognizing that they had power and using it. When Secretary of the Interior Watt visited Arizona in mid-September, he made a special and well-publicized visit to Fort McDowell. Pictures of Watt, visibly moved by speeches of the elders, emblazoned the front pages of the daily newspapers. The embattled Watt, who was picketed at other appearances in Phoenix, told the community that "no decision will be made on my part until I weigh the commitment you have made from the heart. . . (for) what has been said today will weigh heavily on my decision" ("Watt vows," 1981, pp. A1-2). Stories about Fort McDowell and Orme appeared in the *Christian Science Monitor* and the *Wall Street Journal*. Rumors circulated that the CBS network's "60 Minutes" would do a story if an Orme plan were selected.

To make the decision-makers aware of the probability of legal action, the tribe formed a legal defense fund and hired lawyers. Ecumenical prayer services were held on behalf of the Fort McDowell people's cause. All major church organizations came out in opposition to relocation of the tribe. In CAWCS interviews and other published interviews, some members of the tribe vowed to resist Orme even if it meant civil disobedience. Elders spoke eloquently of never leaving the land. Younger tribal members became ardent in support of Yavapai culture, including the Yavapai language and traditions, and spoke at rallies of the next generation's dedication to implacable opposition to the dam.

In short, the tribe publicly demonstrated opposition to the Orme alternatives that was *forceful, skillful*, and *credible*. To use Bell's (1975) lexicon of political linguistics, the Fort McDowell tribal community entered a power position by communicating to their opponents that they could and would tie up Orme for so long that it could not be built in the foreseeable future. With the advent of Ronald Reagan's administration and the tightening federal budget, all the actors were aware that funding of such a mammoth water project could be a problem. Funding was more problematic for the Orme alternatives because of the likelihood of litigation, delaying project initiation and moving the appropriations date further and further into the future. It was assumed that funds would become harder to obtain as time went by. The tribe, in the end, controlled the most important resource in the CAWCS deliberations—the relative feasibility of implementing a plan—and hence they came to be, in an important sense, powerbrokers.

The power of the tribe was based on their ability to convince other groups that they had power—power to influence the relative "costs" of the dam. Nothing objective changed in their situation; they were still poor, still relatively inexperienced politicians, and they retained the same values. What changed was their definition of themselves which in turn changed their relationship with the other groups. They began to see themselves not as powerless victims but as powerful participants. They came to realize that they could make a difference in the decision-making process if they presented a united front, organized their opposition, utilized their legal resources, and generated public support. The effectiveness of their resistance and the political leverage it generated had not been anticipated by pro-Orme supporters. Whereas a confluence dam initially seemed to be the most expedient and feasible way to accomplish the needs of CAP, alternatives now had to be found as it became clear that the tribe could forestall the construction of such a dam for years to come. Feasibility was the piece of the "power pie" which the tribe had had all along. They had learned how to use it and they convinced others that they could use it well.

On October 2, 1981, the Governor's Advisory Committee voted 19-1 to recommend "Plan 6" to the Governor. The one dissenting vote was not for an Orme plan, but was for "no action," and it was cast by one of the environmentalists. The CAWCS study team forwarded three alternative plans to Secretary Watt for the final decision—one of which was an Orme plan. Watt announced that "Plan 6" would be implemented because of its strong public support and relatively moderate environmental and social impact, and because it would not require the relocation of the Fort McDowell Indian Community.

EFFECTS OF EMPOWERMENT

Following Secretary Watt's decision, the reactions of the Fort McDowell community were paradoxical: while there was great rejoicing that the dam had been defeated and that they had played such an important role in defeating it, their joy and relief were moderated by a sense that "the outside powers will be back again sooner or later either with this dam or with something else that necessitates our moving from our homeland" (Blundell, 1981). If history is a reliable predictor of the future, the Yavapai are probably right. The difference now is that they have attained power and political respect and have learned how to effectively counter such threats to their individual and communal existence.

If it is true that the several psycholoigical distress evidenced in the

Yavapai community strongly correlated with their felt sense of powerlessness in the face of a strong socio-political stressor, then it would seem reasonable to expect that the process of empowerment which enabled them to overcome this stressor would be correlated with increasingly healthy psychological functioning. Time and appropriate follow-up studies will be needed to substantiate this contention.

While the long, drawn-out dispute between the Yavapai and the Orme supporters took its toll on the community as evidenced in the measured level of psychological distress, it resulted in some positive changes for the tribal community. The conflict over their differing values forced many residents, especially the younger people, to re-examine their Yavapai identity. As a result, many expressed a renewed interest in learning the history and culture of the tribe, and in learning to speak Yavapai. Their victory dramatically increased both the self-confidence of the residents and their trust in their leadership. As one elder stated "it was the first time the Yavapai had ever won a battle with the government, and we beat the white man at his own game." Their success did much to mitigate their old feelings of powerlessness.

So too outside of Fort McDowell, the respect for the tribe skyrocketed. Before the Orme Dam controversy became well-known, most people in Phoenix had never heard of the Yavapai people. Now when the tribe has an election, it is front page news.

LESSONS TO BE LEARNED

In terms of community empowerment, the Fort McDowell case is quite illustrative. It is questionable how many of its specific elements are replicable for other people in other situations. Nevertheless there is much to be learned about the process.

Bell (1975) provides a useful way of understanding power relationships in terms of political linguistics using three related concepts—power, influence, and authority. Prior to the mid-1970s, the Fort McDowell community tried to assert influence in the Orme controversy both by advising against Orme because of the questionable safety of such a dam, and by trying to persuade decision-makers through rational as well as spiritual appeals. They appealed to conscience by stressing the adverse impacts they would incur as a result of relocation. With the advent of federal legislation both on environmental policy and on the safety of dams, the decision criteria for the construction of the Orme Dam changed. Now there was greater emphasis on the relative expedience of actually implementing a decision to build the dam. The power of the Yavapai rested both in their realization that they controlled how soon and how easily the dam could be built, and in their success in convincing the other interest groups that implementation hinged on their endorsement.

Another key component in their success was that over the course of the controversy the Fort McDowell Yavapai accomplished a profound unification of the tribe and a total community commitment to opposing Orme. They remained steadfast in their values and priorities—one which government officials, social planners, and people in the private sector had difficulty comprehending. These latter groups, with good intentions, thought they knew what "the Indians" *needed*.

A significant lesson and source of encouragement for social scientists is that a large, open, objective, and adequately funded study like CAWCS actually achieved its purpose. It was to evaluate the full range of alternatives and indeed did develop a viable alternative to Orme Dam and thereby avoided all its damaging social, psychological, and environmental impacts. Key to this study's usefulness was not only the collection of quality scientific data pertinent for the decision-making process, but also the forum for a public participation program that gave all affected parties an opportunity to be involved in the decision. The very existence of this open and objective source of data enabled those in authority (Governor Babbitt directly and Secretary Watt indirectly) to require that competing interests must arrive at a consensus. CAWCS, the development of a viable alternative to Orme, the participation of the public, and the governor's committee mandated to reach consensus were all crucial to the Yavapai's process of empowerment. They provided the visibility and political leverage the Yavapai needed to move, in Bell's terminology, from the position of influence to that of power.

As social scientists we can learn from the Fort McDowell Yavapai's experience that people who are seemingly powerless do have power. With time, persistence, and much energy and effort that power can be brought into focus and utilized not just to prevent social and psychological damage but to facilitate growth and well-being. Uniting the tribe around this survival issue and organizing their opposition to the dam not only bought the tribe some time, it also enabled them to enter into coalitions with other groups and establish beneficial links with a wide variety of resources. As a result, the tribe was enabled to capitalize on the opportunities to enhance their power base—opportunities presented by the legislative developments and changing circumstances over the course of the prolonged struggle. Certainly many people, circumstances, and CAWCS itself helped the Yavapai in their efforts. But it is important to note that power was not given to the Yavapai, rather they took the components of the situation and used them to empower themselves.

It was a mistake to think that outsiders knew what the Yavapai needed—American Indians have been fighting that kind of paternalism for centuries. Indeed when all the interested parties were involved in the decision-making process, there occurred a reciprocal process in which everyone became aware of one another's real needs and were responsive to the needs of others. The result was a solution that all parties could live with and from which all would benefit.

Community organizers have known for years about the importance of unifying communities around their concerns and facilitating empowerment. Community psychologists can apply social scientific methodologies directly to such community socio-political issues. They cannot only generate data but also use those data in the decision-making process so as to facilitate the efforts of people to gain control over their own lives and collective destiny. The alternative is to deal with the psychological debris left in the wake of paternalistic policies. Empowerment prevents paternalism.

REFERENCE NOTES

1. O'Sullivan, M. J. *The psychological impact of the threat of relocation on the Fort McDowell Indian community.* Unpublished doctoral dissertation, Saint Louis University, 1982.

2. Natelson Company, Inc. *Socioeconomic study of the Fort McDowell Indian Reservation and community with and without development of Orme Dam and reservoir.* Prepared for the United States Department of the Interior Bureau of Reclamation—Arizona Project Office, 1976.

3. Pearson, K. L. *Attitudinal Survey: Summary and analysis. A research report concerning the Fort McDowell Tribe.* The Natelson Company, Los Angeles, 1975.

4. Brandt, E. Yavapai culture and history and their relationship to proposed relocation. In Central Arizona Water Control Study, *Final report: Social impacts and effects of CAWCS plans.* (Dames & Moore: Contract #9-07-30-V0053). Prepared for the Bureau of Reclamation, U.S. Department of the Interior, 1982.

5. Central Arizona Water Control Study. *Final report: Social impacts and effects of CAWCS plans.* (Dames & Moore: Contract #9-07-30-V0053). Prepared for the Bureau of Reclamation, U.S. Department of the Interior, 1982.

6. O'Sullivan, M. J., & Handal, P. J. *The stresses of relocation: Strategies for preventive interventions.* Manuscript submitted for publication, 1982.

7. Scudder, T. *Expected impact of compulsory relocation on Navajos with special emphasis on relocation from the former Joint Use Area required by Public Law 93-531.* Report submitted to the Navajo Nation by the Institute for Development Anthropology. 1979.

REFERENCES

Bell, D. V. *Power influence, and authority: And essay in political linguistics.* New York: Oxford University Press, 1975.

Blundell, W. E. Arizona Indians win victory over U.S.: Refuse $33 million. *The Wall Street Journal,* December 17, 1981, pp. 1, 14.

Butler, E. W., McAllister, R. J., & Kaiser, E. J. The effects of voluntary and involuntary residential mobility on females and males. *Journal of Marriage and the Family,* 1973, *35,* 219-227.

Casserly, J. J. Different drummers: The Indians and Orme Dam. *The Arizona Republic,* May 22, 1981, p. A7.

Colson, E. *The social consequences of resettlement: The impact of the Karibe resettlement upon the Gwembe Tonga.* Manchester: University of Manchester Press, 1971.

Cook, T. D., & Campbell, D. T. *Quasi-experimentation: Design and analysis issues for field settings.* Chicago: Rand McNally College Publishing Company, 1979.

Dohrenwend, B. P. Stressful life events and psychopathology: Some issues of theory and method. In J. E. Barrett (Ed.), *Stress and mental disorder.* New York: Raven Press, 1979.

Dohrenwend, B. P., & Dohrenwend, B. S. *Social status and psychological disorder: A causal inquiry.* New York: John Wiley & Sons, 1969.

Dohrenwend, B. P., and Dohrenwend, B. S., Gould, M. S., Link, B., Neugebauer, R., & Wunsch-Hitzig, R. *Mental illness in the United States: Epidemiological estimates.* New York: Praeger Publishers, 1980.

Elling, K. High noon at Fort McDowell. *The Scottsdale Daily Progress: Saturday Magazine,* April 11, 1981, pp. 3-5.

Finsterbusch, K. *Understanding social impacts: Assessing the effects of public projects.* Beverly Hills, California: Sage Publications, Inc., 1980.

Fried, M. Grieving for a lost home. In L. J. Duhl (Ed.), *The urban condition.* New York: Basic Books, 1963.

Hardt, A. Orme is just a four-letter word. *New Times,* October 14, 1981, pp. 13-17.

Kantor, N. Internal migration and mental illness. In S. G. Plog & R. B. Edgerton (Eds.), *Changing perspectives in mental illness.* New York: Holt, Rinehart and Winston, 1969.

Kiste, R. Relocation and technological change in Micronesia. In H. R. Bernard & P. Pelto (Eds.), *Technology and social change.* New York: Macmillan, 1972.

Kowalski, N. C. Fire at a home for the aged: A study of short-term mortality following dislocation of elderly residents. *Journal of Gerontology,* 1978, *33,* 601-602.

Langner, T. S. A twenty-two item screening score of psychiatric symptoms indicating impairment. *Journal of Health and Human Behavior,* 1962, *3,* 269-276.

Lasry, J. C. Multi-cultural comparisons of a mental health scale. In J. W. Berry & W. J. Lonner (Eds.), *Applied cross-cultural psychology: Selected papers from the Second International Conference of the International Association for Cross-Cultural Psychology.* Amsterdam: Swets and Zeitlinger, 1975.

Lefcourt, H. M. *Locus of control: Current trends in theory and research.* Hillsdale, New Jersey: Lawrence Erlbaum Associates, 1976.

Lessner, R. Yavapai faith snared in Orme Dam's web of problems. *The Arizona Republic,* September 12, 1981, pp. F1-2.

Manson, S. M., & Shore, J. H. Psychiatric epidemiological research among American Indians and Alaskan Natives: Methodological issues. *White Cloud Journal*, 1981, *2*, 48-56.

Martin, H. W., Sutker, S. S., Leon, R. L., & Hales, W. M. Mental health of eastern Oklahoma Indians: An exploration. *Human Organization*, 1968, *27*, 308-315.

Perry, M. A. M. Yavapais fear Orme Dam would wash away ties to land. *The Arizona Republic*, September 13, 1981, p. C3. (a)

Perry, M. A. M. Orme Dam loses longtime support of water director. *The Arizona Republic*, October 2, 1981, pp. A1-2. (b)

Phares, E. J. *Locus of control in personality*. Morristown, New Jersey: General Learning Press, 1976.

Rotter, J. B. Generalized expectancies for internal versus external control of reinforcement. *Psychological Monographs*, 1966, *80*(1), Whole No. 609.

Rotter, J. B. Some problems and misconceptions related to the construct of internal vs. external control of reinforcement. *Journal of Consulting and Clinical Psychology*, 1975, *48*, 56-67.

Roy, C., Choudhuri, A., & Irvine, D. The prevalence of mental disorders among Saskatchewan Indians. *Journal of Cross-Cultural Psychology*, 1970, *1*, 383-392.

Sampath, H. M. Prevalence of psychiatric disorders in a Southern Baffin Island Eskimo settlement. *Canadian Psychiatric Association Journal*, 1974, *19*, 363-367.

Scudder, T. The human ecology of big projects: River basin development and resettlement. *Annual Review of Anthropology*, 1973, *2*, 45-61.

Seaman, M. Social learning theory and the theory of mass society. In J. B. Rotter, J. Chance, & E. J. Phares, *Applications of a social learning theory of personality*. New York: Holt, Rinehart & Winston, 1972.

Seligman, M. E. P. *Helplessness: On depression, development and death*. San Francisco: W. H. Freeman, 1975.

Seligman, M. E. P., & Maier, S. F. Failure to escape traumatic shock. *Journal of Experimental Psychology*, 1967, *74*, 1-9.

Shore, J. H., Kinzie, J. D., Hampson, J. L., & Pattison, E. M. Psychiatric epidemiology of an Indian village. *Psychiatry*, 1973, *36*, 70-81.

Sue, S., & Zane, N. Learned helplessness theory and community psychology. In M. S. Gibbs, J. R. Lachenmeyer, & J. Sigal (Eds.), *Community psychology: Theoretical and empirical approaches*. New York: Gardner, 1980.

Sutton, I. *Indian land tenure: An annotated bibliography*. New York: Clearwater Press, 1975.

Task Panel Report on Mental Health of American Indians and Alaska Natives. Submitted to the President's Commission on Mental Health, 1978, Volume 3.

Thomas, E. G. Morbidity patterns among recently relocated elderly. In *American Nurses' Association, Clinical and scientific sessions, 1979*. Kansas City, Missouri: American Nurses' Association, 1979.

Topper, M. D., & Johnson, L. Effects of forced relocation on Navajo mental patients from the former Navajo-Hopi Joint Use Area. *White Cloud Journal*, 1980, *2*, 3-7.

Watson, W. H. *Stress and old age: A case study of black aging and transplantation shock*. New Brunswick: Transaction Books, 1980.

Watt vows to study Indian objections to Orme Dam site. *The Phoenix Gazette*, September 15, 1981, pp. A1-2.

Vehicles for Empowerment: The Case of Feminist Movement Organizations

Stephanie Riger

ABSTRACT. This paper considers organizations that empower by examining feminist movement groups. The contemporary feminist movement has generated a wide variety of organizations which provide social services to women and act as vehicles for social change. Yet many of these organizations are short-lived. Factors that affect the structure and goals of feminist movement organizations are examined in order to develop a theoretically-based understanding of why some organizations thrive while others disintegrate. The contingencies under which feminist movement organizations maintain themselves, transform into other sorts of organizations, or decline and dissolve are described, and strategies for managing conflict are discussed. In particular, the paper emphasizes the organizational consequences of ideology, and concludes with a consideration of the role of organizations within a social movement.

Grassroots organizations that enable people to obtain access to resources and develop skills and self-esteem can be important vehicles for empowerment. The contemporary feminist movement has been particularly successful in creating such organizations. Rape crisis centers, battered women's shelters, services for displaced homemakers, and multi-purpose women's centers emerged initially

An earlier version of this paper was presented in the symposium "Feminist Issues in Urban Communities" at the American Psychological Association Convention, Los Angeles, August 1981. The author is grateful to Cindy Patterson for suggestions and research assistance, and to Pauline Bart, Howard Becker, Christopher Keys, Jean Hardisty, Dan A. Lewis, Jane Mansbridge, Mary Rogel, and Rebecca Sive-Tomashevsky for comments on an earlier draft. Address correspondence to the author at: Lake Forest College, Lake Forest, IL 60045.

99

as part of the feminist movement. These organizations share many values—such as a belief in participatory structures—with other grassroots groups. Examining the problems and possibilities of feminist groups, therefore, can be useful for understanding a wide variety of empowerment organizations.

One of the major problems of feminist organizations has been survival. Some feminist movement organizations (FMOs) manage to survive and even grow, expanding their domain by incorporating additional services. Others are absorbed by larger or more traditional social service agencies. But many groups simply fade away, leaving behind a residue of guilt and bitter feelings among former staff, as well as fewer organizations which serve women. This paper examines the factors that account for the demise, institutionalization, or transformation of FMOs. In particular, I consider how feminist ideology affects the work that FMOs do (i.e., organizational goals) and the strategies employed to get that work done (i.e., organizational structure).

Previous research on feminist movement organizations consists predominantly of histories of the women's liberation movement (e.g., Deckard, 1980; Evans, 1980; Freeman, 1975), catalogues of women's services and client characteristics (e.g., Brodyaga, Gates, Singer, Tucker, & White, 1975; O'Sullivan, 1978; The Women and Mental Health Project, 1976; Sweeney, Note 1), and enumerations of problems and strengths of women's groups (Batchelder & Marks, 1979; Galper & Washburne, 1976; Weisstein & Booth, 1975). While these studies provide a valuable glimpse of a social movement in action, most lack a theoretical perspective which would permit analysis as well as description. The study of feminist organizations which is analytical in nature, Freeman's critical assessment of the dynamics of unstructured feminist groups, appeared in 1973, before publication of much of the relevant research on participatory organizations (Kanter & Zurcher, 1973; Mansbridge, 1973; Rothschild-Whitt, 1976). Since many feminist groups employ participatory processes, the findings of this research provide useful insights into organizational dynamics.

This discussion analyzes FMOs from the perspective of research on social movement organizations (e.g., Gittell, 1980; Piven & Cloward, 1977; Rothschild-Whitt, 1976; Zald & Ash, 1966). Studies using this approach typically examine the relationship between organizational goals and structure and identify pressures from both the external environment and from the internal dynamics of the organization to change those goals (Zald, 1969). The central question examined is whether social movement organizations can meet survival needs while retaining goals and an ideology that call for social change (Breines, 1980).

The classic analysis of social movement organizations rooted in the work of Weber (1946) and Michels (1962) asserts that as a movement organization attains a base in society, it inevitably becomes more bureaucratic and develops more conservative goals as a means of maintaining itself. Piven and Cloward (1977) confirmed this analysis in their study of poor people's movements. They suggest that organizations survive by abandoning their oppositional stance so that they can obtain resources to sustain the organization. Yet some researchers argue that this process is not inevitable (Jenkins, 1977; Zald & Ash, 1966).

The transformation of a social movement organization may be due to factors within the organization itself or pressures from the larger environment in which the organization operates. Such external factors as a lack of funding sources, hostility from other local institutions, or a scarcity of workers can threaten the survival of an FMO. However, as Weisstein and Booth (1975) assert in their assessment of feminist organizations, "Our organizations and our alternate institutions die from internal bleeding long before they succumb to external pressure" (p.3). Therefore, I emphasize here the way internal processes affect goals and structures, and consider a number of factors which potentially explain the life course of an FMO.

POTENTIAL EXPLANATORY FACTORS

Organizational Structure

Schein (1970) defines an organization as "the rational coordination of the activities of a number of people for the achievement of some common, explicit purpose or goal, through division of labor and function, and through a hierarchy of authority and responsibility" (p.9). In a typical rape crisis center, for instance, counselors must be recruited and trained, contacts made with local hospitals and police, and funds obtained to support the organization. The crisis center's organization structure determines how these activities are accomplished. The distribution of decision-making power varies from bureaucratic hierarchy to collectively (Rothschild-Whitt, 1979).[1] The centralization of power and rational division of labor in bureaucracies are supposed to ensure that a particular task is done in the most efficient way (Weber, 1946). But the impersonal and often rigid, rule-bound nature of bureaucratic structures may be a weakness rather than a strength, and even their alleged superior efficiency has been questioned (Argyris, 1973; Bennis & Slater, 1968). FMOs (or other grassroots groups) using hierarchical organizational structures may find the inequality of power incongruent with their values.

In order to democratize and humanize their organizations in accordance with feminist ideology, some FMOs adopt a collective structure that takes into account the individual worker's needs and potential for growth while sharing power equally. Some collectives share tasks or rotate jobs to develop skills among all members; others divide labor but share power in decision-making. Women in Transition, Inc., a program providing emotional support and legal services to separated and divorced women, used an organizational model in which some work responsibilities were divided but major policy decisions were made by the whole group. Administrative tasks "from writing proposals and speaking in public to typing and taking out the trash" were shared by everyone (Galper & Washburne, 1976, p. 48).

Collectivity may foster a sense of belonging and a spirit of community and may facilitate individual growth. But the problems associated with collectivity are "time, emotion and inequality" (Mansbridge, 1973 p. 351). Nonhierarchical groups take more time to make decisions since everyone is involved in the decision-making process. Interaction can be emotionally intense, and there is pressure to make decisions on the basis of feelings rather than reason. Since many FMOs do not have a formal authority structure, especially when they are first organized, power may be distributed on the basis of friendship groups or inequalities in skills (e.g., verbal fluency). Yet the lack of formal authority inhibits establishing procedures for determining individual accountability. Freeman (1973) called this "tyranny of structurelessness."

The problems associated with collectivity may be exacerbated in

---

[1]While the continuum of bureaucratic-hierarchy to collectivity characterizes most FMOs, other innovative structures, such as a matrix (Galbraith, 1971) or parallel organizational design (Stein & Kanter, 1980) are possible.

some FMOs by the expectation that they will be exemplars of feminist organizational functioning. Since many feminists perceive hierarchy and leadership as oppressive, they may conclude that "the only good structure is no structure at all" (Deckard, 1979, p. 462). However, lack of structure can make it difficult, if not impossible, to achieve group goals. Girard (Note 2) found that, when asked to report their associations to the words "power" and "leadership," feminists responded with negative associations such as "oppression, authoritarian,. . . controlling, forceful, rational, and linked to domination over others. . . the opposite of what feminists are striving for" (p. 3). Indeed, one of the reasons for employing a collective organizational structure is to eliminate leaders or "stars" (Bunch, 1980). Members expecting equality in feminist groups assume that equality will be manifest in similarity of influence and power among members, though such similarity is difficult to realize because members differ in skills, ability, and effort. Failure to fulfill this expectation of equal influence leads to tension and conflict. Bunch (1980) suggests that the antileadership stance in collective organizations does not mean that there are no leaders, but rather that leadership has to be hidden, preventing accountability. She proposes a new understanding of power—"seen as the ability to act, to get something done"—rather than as manipulation or control (p. 48). Leadership in this sense becomes facilitative rather than dominating.

Organizational structure may determine the goals of the FMO as well as how decisions are made. For many grassroots groups, participation in decision-making becomes the goal of the group, rather than simply a means to achieving a goal (Kanter & Zurcher, 1973). Weisstein and Booth (1975) have observed this phenomenon in feminist organizations: "We become obsessed with process, group dynamics, making everybody happy rather than getting a concrete job done" (p.3). However, FMOs exist not simply as alternatives to bureaucratic structures, but also to bring about change in society. The efficiency needed to take effective social action may be difficult to achieve in collective organizations (Mansbridge, 1973). Serving clients or lobbying legislators may be difficult if staff time and concern are focused inward on group processes.

The collective structure has advantages as well as problems. Its high degree of interpersonal interaction facilitates the development of close relationships, which then act as a "solidary" incentive to participate in the FMO. Other incentives an organization can use to encourage participation are "material" (remuneration) or "purposive" (value fulfillment) in nature (Zald & Ash, 1966). Rothschild-Whitt (1976) suggest that alternative institutions need to emphasize purposive incentives because staff attracted by high pay scales will not be fully committed to the purposes of the organization. Yet low (or no) pay conflicts with feminists' ideological disapproval of the volunteer syndrome; it excludes working class and poor women from participating in the organization; and it contributes to high attrition among members because the organization is staffed by people in time left over from other jobs. Members with professional training may resent the gap between their low (or nonexistent) salaries and those of colleagues in established agencies (Galper & Washburne, 1976).

The level of commitment to a FMO can be quite deep, since members may be seeking not only a work setting or a vehicle for social change, but also an experience of "sisterhood" and personal acceptance (Blanton, Note 3). Yet the need for high levels of commitment on the part of active members and the intensity of interaction in a collective leads to a high rate of "burn-out" among those most involved, a typical problem of feminist groups. A recent study of campus-based women's centers found that 75% of the groups surveyed identified the tendency of staff to overcommit time and energy as a problem (Source, Note 4). Staff members of Women in Transition, Inc., report feeling that "there was no time that we were not on call, either to write a proposal overnight or deal with an emergency situation. We never left the job at the office. . ." (Galper & Washburne, 1976, p. 51).

The intense interpersonal interaction found in collectives is typical of small or newly formed organizations. During the initial stages of organization life, communication among members tends to be frequent and informal. Creativity is needed to solve the problems of developing services provided by the new organization and establishing a market for those services. As organizations age and grow, the increasing numbers of employees and clients require greater efficiency in management, and role definitions and communication patterns become more formal, routinized, and impersonal (Greiner, 1972; Kanter, 1977; Salter, 1970; Schein, 1980). For example, memos may replace face-to-face conversations. Research findings indicate that first-generation members of organization tend to be more satisfied with their relationship to the organization, while second-generation staff experience a wider gap between their expectations and reality (Johnston, 1976). Kasarda (1974) suggests that communication is the most critical problem that emerges with increasing organizational size. For those seeking close personal ties, the bureaucratization of an FMO can be dispiriting.

All new organizations face similar problems of obtaining resources, defining goals, attracting members, and finding a market for their products or services. Yet FMOs differ from other organizations because of their orientation to a social movement. Social movement organizations, which thrive on the intensity of interaction among members, are likely to consider the increasing bureaucratization that comes with age and growth to be a threat to the values of the organization. Consequently, a willingness to remain limited in size facilitates the maintenance of a collectivist organizational structure (Rothschild-Whitt, 1976).

Feminist ideology, therefore, affects the organizational structures, both formal and informal, used to allocate resources and tasks within an FMO. The feminist ideology which gives rise to the creation of many FMOs is likely to result in a collectivist organizational structure. Yet that type of structure will, in turn, present certain organizational dilemmas for FMOs: slowness of decision-making procedures, emotional intensity of interactions, inequitable influence processes within groups that value equality, difficulty in holding members accountable, and the demands of growth. Some organizations can tolerate the tensions resulting from these organizational dilemmas. Others disintegrate or adopt hierarchical bureaucratic structures in order to reduce tension. The research reviewed above suggests the following:

Proposition 1: FMOs are more likely to remain a collective organizational structure if:

1. skills and knowledge are distributed fairly equally throughout the FMO;
2. the FMO is small in size;
3. the FMO is financially dependent on its members for support;
4. procedures are developed which permit efficient responses to external demands;
5. members expect and value participation over organizational efficiency;
6. members receive solidary or purposive rewards as incentives for participation; and/or
7. networks of friendship, expertise, and support are not over-

lapping, preventing the centralization of informal sources of power.

Proposition 2: FMOs are more likely to develop a hierarchical organizational structure if:

1. expertise is distributed inequitably throughout the group;
2. the FMO is large (i.e., the woman-power available exceeds that needed for the jobs at hand);
3. an independent source of funding is used (e.g., foundation or government grants)
4. rewards for organizational participation are primarily remunerative, rather than solidary or purposive in nature;
5. members value organizational efficiency over participation; and/or
6. networks of friendship, expertise, and support are overlapping, resulting in the centralization of informal power.

Proposition 3: FMOs are more likely to decay and disintegrate if:

1. some members value efficiency while others value participation;
2. the conditions facilitating a hierarchical organizational structure (outlined in Proposition 2 above) prevail but the FMO uses collectivist practices; and/or
3. the conditions conducive to collectivity (outlined in Proposition 1 above) prevail but the FMO uses hierarchical practices.

Organizational Goals

FMOs can adopt a variety of goals. A rape crisis center may provide counseling services to rape victims, attempt to change community and institutional responses to victims, or try to alter the fundamental processes of socialization which result in societal attitudes conducive to rape. These goals range from being remedial in nature, aiming to reduce the impact of the problem once it has occurred and adopting individuals as the target of change efforts, to being concerned with primary prevention and aiming at change in institutions and society (Caplan, 1964). Organizations are torn between demands for direct services and other priorities (O'Sullivan, 1978). However, social service and social change, though opposites, need not negate each other. Reissman (1976) suggests that they are complementary: social action creates a demand for services, while the provision of services increases the supply available to those in need. Yet organizations striving for social change, by definition, maintain a certain degree of opposition to the status quo that is not required for organizations dedicated to providing social services. The critical distinction may not be that of changing individuals versus changing social conditions, but whether the intervention accepts or repudiates established standards of behavior (Rein, 1973).

Tension among those with different goal orientations or priorities has surfaced both within individual FMOs and within national feminist coalitions. Describing problems occurring at the National Coalition Against Sexual Assault (NCASA) meeting in August, 1979, Kelly reports that:

> Many of the problems from the NCASA conference seem to me to reflect tensions between two parallel developments in the anti-rape movement: those people primarily concentrating on providing services to rape victims, coordinating with other agencies, and performing advocacy work, and those groups doing more outreach work such as communication, direct action, prevention, and community organizing. Members of the latter group often hold a set of values somewhat more radical than those of the service-oriented groups. They deal with rape as part of an overall analysis of sexist society and are often more sensitive to questions such as propriety of funding. More service-oriented people are sometimes impatient with questions of political correctness and more interested in running their specific projects effectively. (p.11)

Organizational goals change because of both internal and external pressures. For instance, the structure of the organization affects the goals it can achieve. As discussed above, collectivity can result in a focus on participation as an end in itself, rather than a means to an end (Kanter & Zurcher, 1979), and a tendency toward oligarchy may mean that the goals favored by the elite will prevail (Jenkins, 1977). In addition, the desire to keep the organization alive may require compromising oppositional goals for more conservative ones (Michels, 1962; Piven & Cloward, 1977; Weber, 1946). Galper and Washburne (1976) compare their organization (which used a collective structure and didn't charge fees for services) with others in their area which were hierarchically organized and charged fees: "They saw themselves as feminist, political, and committed to social change. We saw them as not being as pure as we. They still exist, and we don't" (p. 46).

The transformation of goals in a conservative direction is closely linked to the availability of resources with which to sustain the organization. In a study of citizen's organizations aimed at educational reform, Gittell (1980) found that those which relied on membership resources for organizational maintenance could adopt a social change orientation, while those which relied on external sources of funds adopted either service delivery or advisory strategies. Organizations with middle class membership could rely on internal sources of funds while lower income organizations had to obtain funding externally. Thus a social change orientation was limited to middle-class groups. Blanton (Note 3) identified a tendency among FMOs to adopt vague and grandiose goals while resources remain small or nonexistent. It is not unusual, for example, for a group with no budget to adopt the goal of ending societal oppression based on race, sex, or social class. Burnout, frustration, and despair can result from the disparity between goals and resources.

Some funding from public and private sources is available for groups which seek to provide services, but such funds are seldom available for activities designed to advocate social change. Some groups refuse to accept available funds because of ideological conflicts with the funding source (e.g., Playboy Foundation; see "Funding from Pornography: An Open Forum," 1980) or because funding requirements may dictate program content (O'Sullivan, 1978). The infusion of funds can alter decision-making procedures and the distribution of work (Friedman, 1977). In a funded shelter for battered women, paid staff did more work and so became more knowledgeable about the organization's actual operations and needs than volunteers (Aherns, 1980). Thus, paid staff ended up making more of the day-to-day decisions, exacerbating possible differences between paid and non-paid workers (or between those heavily involved and those less active in the organization). Organizations with outside funding may find that the board focuses on fiscal accountability, while the staff are primarily concerned with client's needs. These different areas of responsibility may push the board in a more conservative direction while the staff becomes more radical (Hardisty, Note 5).

Members oriented toward the social movement, rather than committed to the organization per se, can resist the conservative shift in goals more easily. As Rothschild-Whitt (1976) says, "Becoming oriented to the organization per se seems to lead to a narrowing of one's sights toward providing a good service vis-à-vis other organizations in the same profession, but entails a loss of the larger vision of social-historical change out of which the organization was born" (p. 80). Consequently, FMO members who are oriented toward the movement may dissolve the organization or drop out of it in favor of other women's movement activities rather than accept more conservative goals. FMOs oriented toward the women's movement have to retain a social change orientation in order to compete with other movement activities for members' time, energy, and resources. On the other hand, FMOs oriented toward service delivery and whose members emphasize professional growth and development have to compete with other service agencies for member's resources.

FMO members' orientation toward the women's movement can influence organizational goals and activities. Recent analyses have identified at least four different ideological stances within feminism (Jaggar & Struhl, 1978):

1. *Liberalism* attributes the roots of women's oppression to the lack of equal civil rights and educational opportunities for women. Many liberals seek to create services in order to fill the gaps left by traditional institutions which ignore women's needs.
2. *Traditional Marxism* locates the origins of women's oppression in a system of social organization based on the ownership of private property. Sexism is viewed as a secondary phenomenon, a symptom of a more fundamental form of oppression based on capitalism.
3. *Radical feminism* insists that the oppression of women is fundamental and must be attacked directly. Many radical feminists seek to create alternative social service institutions which meet women's needs in ways distinct from the sexist practices which prevail in mainstream society.
4. *Socialist feminism* enriches the traditional Marxist analyses by arguing that sexism is at least as fundamental as economic oppression. In this view, capitalism and sexism reinforce each other.

These differences in philosophy lead to sharp disagreements about practice. For instance, liberals may accept the participation of men in the operations of the FMO while radical feminists find it abhorrent.[2] Socialist feminists may see cooperation with local law enforcement agencies as anathema to their political principles, while liberals see it as an essential means of getting better treatment for rape victims or battered wives.

The differences among various feminist positions in attitudes toward other groups and institutions in society affects the goals of an FMO. Many rape crisis centers seek to bring about more sympathetic responses on the part of local hospitals, police, and courts servicing rape victims. Rape crisis centers may see these institutions as benign and cooperative, simply needing education to rectify their past errors, or may take a fundamentally oppositional stance toward them. An oppositional stance may strengthen the internal cohesiveness of the FMO while the introduction of reforms in traditional institutions may weaken the solidarity of the FMO by removing some of the justification for its existence (Rothschild-Whitt, 1976). The very success of the FMO in changing traditional institutions may spell the demise of the FMO itself. Many mental health centers now provide services for rape victims and battered women, reducing the need for separate feminist organizations serving these groups.

FMOs may shift their emphasis from social change to the provision of social services in response to the overwhelming demand for services (Hardisty, Note 4), or when they recognize the difficulty of achieving social change goals and the relative availability of funding for service provision. Members' commitment to feminism and the solidarity produced by an oppositional stance counters these pressures toward goal change. The contradictory tendencies exerted on organizational goals will lead to tensions and conflicts. The choices made to reduce or manage those conflicts, and the factors determining those choices, determine the life course of the FMO. In summary, the research discussed above suggests that:

Proposition 4: FMOs are more likely to emphasize social change over social service if:

1. their members are more committed to the women's movement than to the organization itself;

---

[2]Research by Aries (1977) suggests that the presence of men in FMOs can affect both the dynamics of interpersonal interaction and the content of group discussions.

2. the FMO holds an oppositional stance toward other local institutions;
3. the FMO depends on internal sources for funding;
4. their members adhere to traditional Marxist or socialist feminist philosophies; and/or
5. their members value social change over professional growth.

Proposition 5: FMOs are more likely to emphasize social service over social change activities if:

1. their members are more committed to the organization itself than to the women's movement;
2. the FMO holds a collaborative stance toward other local institutions;
3. the organization depends on external sources of funding (e.g., government or foundation grants);
4. their members adhere to liberal or radical feminist philosophies; and/or
5. their members value professional growth over social change.

Proposition 6: FMOs are more likely to decay and disintegrate if:

1. some members are primarily committed to social change while others are more committed to the provision of social services;
2. their members differ sharply in feminist ideologies;
3. the conditions conducive to social change activities (outlined in Propositon 4) prevail but the organization focuses on the provision of social services; and/or
4. the conditions conducive to the provision of social services (outlined in Proposition 5 above) prevail but the organization emphasizes social change activities.

STRATEGIES FOR COPING WITH CONFLICT

This discussion has identified a number of sources of conflict within feminist organizations. If unchecked, these conflicts can result in an intolerable level of tension that can destroy an organization or transform it in ways that are unacceptable to many of its members. However, decay and transformation are not the only available options. While FMOs may contain a level of conflict that is difficult for members to tolerate, conflict-management strategies can enable the organization to survive and even flourish. Indeed, in this respect FMOs are no different than other organizations. That is, all organizations, be they families, schools, factories, or feminist collectives, inevitably contain some degree of conflict. The traditional view that such conflict is the result of destructive personality clashes has been replaced in recent years with the assumption that conflict is an inevitable result of the complexities of contemporary organizational life (e.g., Coser, 1956). If managed in creative ways, conflict can stimulate growth and innovations that benefit the organization. The substance of conflict in FMOs may differ from that in non-ideological organizations. Yet the presence of conflict itself is a problem common to all organizations. The question remains how to deal with that conflict in constructive ways.

One obstacle to conflict resolution within FMOs is the belief that only a collective organizational structure in which power is shared equally is "truly" feminist. A collective structure is suitable under certain circumstances (as outlined above), but in other situations the inappropriate match between a collective structure and the goals and resources of the organization will create considerable strain. For example, a collective might work well with a small homogenous group. A large, heterogenous group in which skills, values, or resources differ might find that a collective structure prevents resolution or even acknowledgement of these differences. Decay and disintegration of the organization seem especially likely if there are discrepancies between (1) the values and goals of some of the members, and (2) the organization's overt and covert structure and mission. In order to match the design of the organization with its goals and resources, feminists (and other grassroots groups) must be willing to consider forms other than the egalitarian collective.

Feminists emphasize the necessity of an equal distribution of power in order to achieve internal democracy and thereby protect the interests of the workers within the organization. This view is posited on a model of democracy that is adversarial in nature, that is, on the assumption that people have different and opposing interests. Yet equal power is not necessary in all circumstances. In a book which attempts to move "Beyond Adversary Democracy," Jane Mansbridge (1980) suggests that there are only three purposes for which we desire equality. Such equality is a means to equal protection of interests, equal respect, and personal growth. If members of a group share a common long-run interest, if respect derives from sources other than power, and if many opportunities for personal growth are available, then equal power may not be necessary to ensure these ends. The implications for FMOs are many. If there are problems in operating as absolute equals, then feminist organizations should establish mechanisms to deal with factors that divide the common interest of groups members, such as class or race differences; they should emphasize diverse bases of respect other than simply power (so that all members can be respected equally even if unequal in power); and they should maximize opportunities for growth. Under these conditions, the ends that political equality is intended to realize can be achieved by means other than absolutely equal power. FMOs then would be free to use structures other than collectivity if conditions required yet still would ensure that their basic egalitarian values are protected and promoted in the functioning of the organization. Accomplishing this requires considerable creativity in organizational design. We need case studies of successful feminist organizations in order to identify and promote existing models which can be adapted elsewhere.

Beyond modifying the entire structure of the organization, other strategies exist for managing the dysfunctional aspects of conflict. Non-ideological organizations use a variety of problem-solving techniques to manage conflict; these techniques could be employed by feminist groups as well. Strategies for resolving conflict can be classified into three categories: avoidance, defusion, and confrontation (Ivancevich, Szilagyi, & Wallace, 1977). Avoidance of conflict can mean simply ignoring it or structuring situations in such a way that conflict is not permitted to surface, e.g., by physically separating warring parties or limiting their interaction. Defusion strategies aim to ''cool out'' the conflict or buy time until it becomes less crucial or intense. One technique is to play down the differences between warring parties or goals, or to compromise so that everyone wins at least something. However, the belief that conflict can be a source of growth and creativity in organizations has led in recent years to the development of strategies that permit open identification of sources of problems and the creation of solutions to those problems.

Strategies based on confronting conflict begin by emphasizing the overarching purposes of the organization in order to promote allegiance to the organization as a whole rather than to one faction or goal. Such techniques involve articulating the common interests of opposing groups or goals, or holding discussions in which opposing groups present their views on the sources of the problem and possible solutions without assigning blame (see, e.g., Black & Mouton, 1964). For example, if some members of a FMO are interested in advocating for social change while others want to provide services, the first step in resolving this conflict is to openly identify these differences in goals. A variety of solutions may be possible, e.g., dividing tasks among group members, or assigning priority to different goals at different points in time. Mansbridge (1980) suggests a "consociational" system in which subgroups share power in proportion to their numerical strength. That is, instead of majority rule, proportional strength could determine outcomes. Groups could take turns setting goals on the basis of their numbers in the organization.

The danger in confronting conflict directly is that not all conflicts permit consensual resolution. Openly identifying sources of tension may exacerbate clashes within a group and make explicit differences that are irreconcilable. A group may splinter or disintegrate when this occurs. While the thrust of this discussion has been on strategies for survival of feminist organizations, the death of a FMO may not always be a cause for mourning. We value feminist institutions because they offer much-needed services to women, because they are vehicles for social change, and because they provide a means of realizing and perpetuating feminist values. Yet survival of these organizations may not necessarily insure that these ends are achieved, and may not be the only means of achieving them. Indeed, the survival of an organization may require that it abandon its oppositional politics (Piven & Cloward, 1977), thereby losing the feminist values that gave it a reason for existing in the first place. Those who have participated in the creation of FMOs may view this perspective with dismay, since they know full well the time and effort required to bring an organization to maturity. I do not advocate the destruction of organizations simply to prevent them from becoming less "pure" on a scale of feminist orthodoxy. Rather, we must carefully consider the reasons for desiring the perpetuation of FMOs. Charlotte Bunch offers five criteria for evaluating reforms. These criteria seem appropriate for assessing the impact of an FMO as well.

1. Does it materially improve the lives of women and if so, which women and how many?
2. Does the reform build an individual woman's self-respect, strength, and confidence?
3. Does working for the reform give women a sense of power,

strength, and imagination as a group and help build structures for further change?

4. Does the struggle for reform educate women politically, enhancing our ability to criticize and challenge the system in the future?
5. Does the reform weaken patriarchal control of society's institutions and help women gain power over them? (1979, pp. 31-32)

If some of the answers to these questions are affirmative, then the FMO is worth saving.

Feminist movement organizations have played a valuable role by educating society about the inequities faced by women and the consequences of those inequities and by providing innovative services to women. Yet the short lifespan of many FMOs has costs both to women deprived of much-needed services and to staff members who view the demise of their organizations with dismay and are reluctant to involve themselves again in organized efforts to meet women's needs. This discussion provides an analysis of some of the contingencies which determine the life cycle of FMOs; suggests some strategies for enhancing the effectiveness and likelihood of survival of these organizations; and raises the fundamental question of the role of organizations in a feminist movement. While preventing the dismantling and decline of FMOs is a key priority for those concerned with sex equity and social change (Wekerle, 1980), the ultimate goal is not survival of organizations, but rather the success of the social movement.

Some of the problems faced by FMOs are the result of feminist ideology, and therefore are unique to these organizations. Yet many of their concerns—such as the emphasis on participation and the need to maintain oppositional values and goals—are shared by a wide variety of grassroots groups. Thus the factors that account for the life course of feminist groups operate to varying degrees in other organizations as well. All political organizations must strike a balance between survival needs and the mission of the organization. Organizations that seek to empower face the added difficulty of striking that balance in environments that are often hostile to their mission. Understanding problems which result from the organizational consequences of ideology may help ensure the survival of these groups, and may enhance their ability to promote empowerment.

REFERENCE NOTES

1. Sweeney, J. L. *Women's centers: Organizational and institutional constraints on meeting educational needs.* Paper presented at the meeting of the American Educational Research Association, Toronto, March 1978.
2. Girard, K. L. *Power, leadership and equality in feminist groups: The confusions, contradictions and patterns beneath our rhetoric.* Paper presented at the meeting of the Association for Women in Psychology, Dallas, March 1979.
3. Blanton, J. *Women consulting with women: Feminist ideology and organizational structure and process.* Paper presented at the annual meeting of the American Psychological Association, Los Angeles, August 1981.
4. Sorce, P. *Identified needs of women's centers as feminist organizations.* Paper presented at the meeting of the Association for Women in Psychology, Dallas, March 1979.
5. Hardisty, J. *The liberation of women in a socialist transformation.* Unpublished manuscript, Evanston, IL, 1979.

REFERENCES

Aherns, L. Battered women's refuges: Feminist cooperatives vs. social service institutions. *Radical America*, 1980, *14*, 41-47.

Argyris, C. Some limits of rational man organization theory. *Public Administration Review*, 1973, *33*, 253-267.

Aries, E. Male-female interpersonal styles in all male, all female, and mixed-sex groups. In Sargent, A. G. *Beyond sex roles.* St. Paul, MN: West, 1977.

Batchelder, E., & Marks, L. Creating alternatives: A survey of women's projects. *Heresies*, 1979, *2*(3), 97-127.

Bennis, W., & Slater, P. *The temporary society.* New York: Harper & Row, 1968.

Blake, R., & Mouton, J. *Managing intergroup conflict in industry.* Houston: Gulf Publishing Co., 1964.

Breines, W. Community and organization: The new left and Michel's "iron law." *Social Problems*, 1980, *27*, 419-429.

Brodyaga, L., Gates, M., Singer, S., Tucker, M., & White, R. *Rape and its victims: A report for citizens, health facilities, and criminal justice agencies.* Washington, D.C.: U.S. Government Printing Office, 1975.

Bunch, C. The reform tool kit. *Aegis: Magazine on Ending Violence against Women.* 1979, (July/August), pp. 25-34.

Caplan, G. *Principles of preventive psychiatry.* New York: Basic Books, 1964.

Coser, L. A. *The functions of social conflict.* New York: Free Press, 1956.

Deckard, B. S. *The women's movement: Political, socioeconomic, and psychological issues.* New York: Harper & Row, 1979.

Evans, S. *Personal politics: The roots of women's liberation in the civil rights movement and the new left.* New York: Vintage Books, 1980.

Freeman, J. The tyranny of structurelessness. In A. Koedt, E. Levine, A. Rapone (Eds.), *Radical feminism.* New York: Quadrangle, 1973.

Freeman, J. *The politics of women's liberation.* New York: David McKay, 1975.

Friedman, D. Structuring a rape crisis center. *Feminist Alliance Against Rape News*, 1977 (Sept./Oct.), 8-10.

Funding from pornography: An open forum. *Aegis: Magazine on Ending Violence against Women*, 1980, (Winter/Spring), pp. 60-80.

Galbraith, J. R. Matrix organizational design: How to combine functional and project forms. *Business Horizons*, 1971, *14*, 29-40.

Galper, M., & Washburne, C. K. A women's self-help program in action. *Social Policy*, 1976, *6*(5), 46-52.

Gittell, M. *Limits to citizen participation: The decline of community organizations.* Beverly Hills, CA: Sage, 1980.

Greiner, L. E. Evolution and revolution as organizations grow. *Harvard Business Review,* 1972, *51,* 37-46.

Ivancevich, J. M., Szilagyi, A. D., Jr., & Wallace, J. M., Jr. *Organizational behavior and performance.* Santa Monica: Goodyear, 1977.

Jaggar, A. M., & Struhl, P. R. *Feminist frameworks: Alternative theoretical accounts of the relations between women and men.* New York: McGraw-Hill, 1978.

Jenkins, J. C. Radical transformation of organizational goals. *Administrative Science Quarterly,* 1977, *22,* 568-586.

Johnston, H. R. Interactions between individual predispositions, environmental factors, and organization design. In R. H. Kilmann, L. R. Pondy, & D. P. Slevin (Eds.), *The management of organizational design: research and methodology.* New York: Elsevier North-Holland, Inc. 1976.

Kanter, R. M. *Men and women of the corporation.* New York: Basic Books, 1977.

Kanter, T. M., & Zurcher, L. Concluding statement evaluating alternatives and alternative valuing. *Journal of Applied Behavioral Science,* 1973, *9,* 381-397.

Kasarda, J. D. The structural implications of social system size: A three-level analysis. *American Sociological Review,* 1974, *39,* 19-28.

Kelly, J. Anti-rape coalition. *Off Our Backs,* 1979, *9* (Oct), p. 11.

Mansbridge, J. J. Time, emotion, and inequality: Three problems of participatory groups. *The Journal of Applied Behavioral Science,* 1973, *9,* 351-368.

Mansbridge, J. J. *Beyond adversary democracy.* New York: Basic Books, 1980.

Michels, R. *Political parties.* New York: Collier Books, 1962.

O'Sullivan, E. What has happened to rape crisis centers? A look at their structures, members, and funding. *Victimology: An International Journal,* 1978, *3,* 45-62.

Piven, F. F., & Cloward, R. A. *Poor people's movements: Why they succeed, how they fail.* New York: Pantheon Books, 1977.

Rein, M. Social work in search of a radical profession. In B. Denner & R. H. Price (Eds.), *Community mental health: Social action and reaction.* Holt, Rinehart & Winston, 1973.

Reissman, F. A neighborhood-based mental health approach. In E. L. Cowen, E. A. Gardner, & M. Zax (Eds.), *Emergent approaches to mental health problems.* New York: Appleton Century Crofts, 1976.

Rothschild-Whitt, J. Conditions facilitating participatory-democratic organizations. *Sociological Inquiry,* 1976, *46*(2), 75-86.

Rothschild-Whitt, J. The collectivist organization: An alternative to rational-bureaucratic models. *American Sociological Review,* 1979, *44,* 509-527.

Salter, M. Stages of corporate development. *Journal of Business Policy,* 1970, *1,* 23-37.

Schein, E. *Organizational psychology* (2nd ed.). Englewood Cliffs, NJ: Prentice-Hall, 1970.

Stein, B. A., & Kanter, R. M. Building the parallel organization: Creating mechanisms for permanent quality of work life. *Journal of Applied Behavioral Science,* 1980, *16,* 371-386.

The Women and Mental Health Project. Women-to-women services. *Social Policy,* 1976, (Sept/Oct), 21-27.

Weber, M. Politics as a vocation. In H. Gerth & G. W. Mils, (Eds.), *From Max Weber.* New York: Oxford University Press, 1946.

Weisstein, N., & Booth, H. Will the women's movement survive? *Sister,* 1975, *4,* 1-6.

Wekerle, G. Women in the urban environment. *Signs,* 1980, *5* (Supp.), pp. 188, 214.

Zald, M. N. Organizations as polities: An analysis of community organization agencies. In R. M. Kramer & H. Specht (Eds.) *Readings in community organization practice.* Englewood Cliffs, NJ: Prentice-Hall, 1969.

Zald, M. N., & Ash, R. Social movement organizations: Growth, decay and change. *Social Forces,* 1966, *44,* 327-341.

Help Seeking and Receiving in Urban Ethnic Neighborhoods: Strategies for Empowerment

David E. Biegel

ABSTRACT. This paper presents findings from a National Institute of Mental Health funded research and demonstration effort aimed at addressing impediments to seeking and receiving help in two white ethnic communities. A community mental health empowerment model was developed and implemented in the target communities over a four year period. This model succeeded in building upon the strengths of individuals and neighborhoods to help overcome help seeking and receiving obstacles. Mechanisms were developed through a variety of means to enhance the ability of lay and professional helpers to interact and work with each other.

Several years ago, a college in the New England area opened up a new campus. Instead of the architects and planners placing cement walkways to interconnect the buildings, the entire campus was planted with sod. One year after the campus was opened, the areas where the sod was worn away from walking were dug up and cement walkways put in their place.

Human service professionals have much to learn from this experience. Why should we force clients to fit their problems into the frameworks professionals have created to meet their needs? Rather, we should discover how clients naturally solve their problems and meet their needs and then graft professional interventions onto this natural process. For such professional interventions to be most successful, empowerment of community residents is a necessity.

This research was supported in part by Grant #MH 26503 from the Mental Health Services Development Branch, National Institute of Mental Health. Reprints may be obtained from David E. Biegel, School of Social Work, University of Pittsburgh, 2206 C.L., Pittsburgh, PA 15260.

119

Unfortunately, interventions of this nature are not easy to develop. In order for service delivery systems to be more effective, a fuller understanding is needed of the processes by which people in urban neighborhoods define problems, obtain access, and utilize informal and professional support systems. Yet, despite abundant evidence documenting the important roles that social networks and community support systems play in help-seeking and receiving behavior (Caplan, 1974; Collins & Pancoast, 1967; President, 1978), professional services have operated, by and large, with little understanding of the community based ties of many neighborhood residents and independently of neighborhood based informal networks. Although there has been a growing amount of research pertaining to social networks and help seeking and receiving behavior in the last several years, our knowledge of how such informal helping systems operate is still extremely limited.

Turning to an examination of mental health services,[1] we find the same problems. One of the chief shortcomings of the community mental health centers movement has been its failure to base mental health programs on the strengths, resources, and diversities existing in local communities. An examination of the Task Panel Reports on Special Populations of the President's Commission on Mental Health (1978) reveals that a number of population groups—from white ethnics to women, hispanics, elderly, and Pacific Islanders—are saying the same thing, "The mental health system doesn't understand our unique needs and therefore services that are offered are not truly accessible to us." Too often, mental health centers are seemingly "parachuted" into the local community and operate with few, if any, linkages to the informal support systems. They bypass organizational and cultural networks that have the willingness and capacity to support people in need. The community is not effectively linked with the service delivery system nor is the positive identification of community residents fully utilized as a means for overcom-

---

[1]There is no clear demarcation between mental health and human services. Mental health services focus upon the severely ill (depressed, suicidal, delusional, etc.) and the worried well (those who experience problems, stresses, and crises leading to loneliness, tension, marital discord, etc.). Though both groups can benefit from nonpsychiatric assistance, the worried well, especially, are not the exclusive concern of the mental health system. The worried well can, and should, receive assistance from a wide variety of human service agencies. They can be especially helped by community support systems. Our use of the term mental health pertains principally to the worried well, and also implicitly encompasses human services for this population group. As we shall see, to the residents in urban ethnic neighborhoods, mental health is equated primarily with the severely ill. For a further discussion of this issue, see Naparstek and Biegel, 1982.

ing personal and institutional obstacles—administrative, fiscal and legal—to seeking and receiving help.

This paper presents findings from a National Institute of Mental Health (NIMH) funded research and demonstration effort aimed at addressing obstacles to seeking and receiving help in two white ethnic communities. Through the Neighborhood and Family Services Project, a community mental health empowerment model was developed and implemented in the target communities over a four year period. This model succeeded in building upon the strengths of individuals and neighborhoods to help overcome obstacles to seeking and receiving help. Mechanisms were developed through a variety of means to enhance the ability of lay and professional helpers to interact and work with each other.

CRITICAL SERVICE DELIVERY ISSUES IN WHITE ETHNIC COMMUNITIES

Before professionals can develop linkages with informal networks, they have to understand how such systems function, and more specifically, how they function differentially for specific population groups. The importance of gaining a better appreciation and understanding of the factors affecting the help-seeking and receiving process is especially relevant and significant to urban ethnic communities for a number of reasons.

First, in urban ethnic communities there is a documented under-utilization of community mental health services in situations other than emergencies (Giordano, 1973; Giordano & Giordano, 1976; Spiro, Crocetti, Siassi, Ward, & Hansen, 1975). This may be due to a combination of personal and structural factors. Personal factors that have been identified by researchers as related to characteristics of community residents include: unwillingness/inability to ask for help; unwillingness to admit a problem exists; pressure from informal network of family, friends, and co-workers not to seek professional help; pride; and a value differences in defining what is a problem. Structural factors cited include problems relating to: accessibility; auspices of services; sex and ethnicity of service providers; confidentiality; availability of services; fragmentation of services; and, lack of accountability of services (Biegel, 1982).

Second, urban ethnic communities do have considerable mental health needs. Such communities typically contain large proportions of aged and lower social class residents whose mental health problems tend to be more severe than other population groups (Hollingshead & Redlich, 1958; Myers & Bean, 1968; Spiro, 1975).

Third, the urban ethnic neighborhood is an important resource in the help-seeking process in two contexts. First, it provides the locus for many informal caregiving networks. Second, attachment to neighborhood (as measured by psychological identification, relationships with neighbors, activities engaged in within the neighborhood, length of residence, and degree of home ownership) plays an important role in help-seeking and receiving. Urban ethnic communities have strong systems of informal support based upon ties of kin and kith, church, ethnic, and fraternal groups. The residents also exhibit strong attachments to the local neighborhood, a high degree of homeownership, and great stability in residence, i.e., low frequency of recent moves (Biegel, 1982).

A better understanding of how individuals in ethnic communities seek and receive help can assist in designing strategies for overcoming some of the problems cited above. The existence of strong, informal support systems in these communities implies that there are a number of points in the community to which linkages between the informal and formal support systems can be made. Such linkages can reduce obstacles toward help-seeking and receiving, reach people earlier in need, and in general, improve the quality of care (Froland, 1982).

THE NEIGHBORHOOD AND FAMILY SERVICES
PROJECT—AN OVERVIEW

Philosophy

The Neighborhood and Family Service Project of the University of Southern California, Washington Public Affairs Center, developed out of dissatisfaction with the willingness and ability of the community mental health system to adequately serve white ethnic communities. New models of service delivery are needed which build upon community strengths to overcome identified obstacles to service delivery. Central to the development of these new models is the notion of empowerment. Our definition of empowerment is dependent upon two concepts: *capacity* and *equity* (Naparstek, Biegel, & Spiro, 1982).

Capacity has three components. It is an individual or group's ability to: (a) utilize power to solve problems, (b) gain access to institutions or organizations that are serving them, and (c) nurture. Power and nurturance depend on different types of resources. Power involves skills and financial resources. The skills required for the effective exercise of power include organization, leadership, management, and the technical expertise to plan, conduct research, and implement programs. The defining elements of the nurturance dimension of capacity are human and community resources. Included here are people interacting and providing social support to each other on both an individual level (family, friends, neighbors) and also on an organizational level (churches, PTAs, ethnic clubs, fraternal associations, block clubs, self-help groups, etc.). The principle of equity is defined by citizens in two ways: whether their investment (objective or subjective) is equal to their return; and whether their neighborhood organization is getting its fair share of resources as compared to other parts of the city (Naparstek & Haskell, 1977).

Purpose

A four year grant was received from the National Institute of Mental Health, Mental Health Services Development Branch, to fund the project from 1976-1980. Although the project officially terminated two years ago with the ending of the federal funding, community groups organized through the project are still functioning as are a number of intervention programs that were developed.

The goals of the project were to develop a conceptual framework and program and policy models for human service delivery which could lead to the following:

1. Reduction of negative attitudes associated with mental health services among ethnic working class populations.
2. Development of service delivery systems which were more congruent with the life-style of ethnic working class populations.
3. Determination of the necessary rearrangements of the formal service delivery systems, including the removal of obstacles to help-seeking and receiving, so as to increase utilization, and reach people in need earlier.
4. The development of policy initiatives on the national, state,

and local levels in support of neighborhood-based community mental health services.

Target Areas

The two project communities were Southeast Baltimore City, Maryland and the Southside of Milwaukee, Wisconsin. Because of limitations of space, intervention strategies in only one of the two project cities will be presented. The Milwaukee intervention was chosen because it exemplifies empowerment strategies that can be utilized in hard to reach communities.

The Milwaukee target area contains approximately 66,000 persons and is almost entirely a white area (99%). Over 32% of the area's population is of foreign stock. Most of the ethnic population is Polish with lesser percentages of German individuals also represented. Only 7% of the population lives in poverty; this is one-half of the national rate. There is a high percentage of population aged 65 years and older and a low percentage of recent movers (within the last five years). This latter figure is indicative of high community stability.

Organizational Process

It was planned that the project in each city would work thorough, and be directed by, a local community organization. In Milwaukee, however, there was no community organization that represented the entire community. A neighborhood organizing effort with concentration on the Catholic parishes, the area's most significant institutional resource, led to the formation of the South Community Organization (SCO). SCO had approximately twenty members on its initial steering committee, all of whom were key community leaders representing parishes, institutions, and ethnic organizations serving the Southside. The way we went about this organizing is described below.

Parallel to the community groups' organizational process, professionals on Milwaukee's Southside were engaged to serve on a professional advisory committee as a resource to the community groups. This arrangement facilitated the "empowerment" of community residents. Unlike traditional models, where consumers are brought in as advisors to existing programs, professionals were invited as advisors to a community directed process. The professionals brought legitimacy, resources, and structures for programs if needed, but more importantly, they became active participants in the evolution of a community "process" which was led and controlled by lay community residents.

Research Plan

The first year of the project focused on collecting research data and organizing the community task force and professional advisory committee. The research focused on: personal problems of community residents; where people go when they have these problems; how and when people make use of helping networks; what the obstacles are to seeking and or receiving help; and how factors of ethnicity and community attachment influence the process of defining problems and seeking help.

The research undertaken by the project consisted of three major elements:[2]

1. *Community leader and helper survey*—300 interviews of community helpers and leaders in each city, including clergy, human service agency staff, natural helpers, neighborhood leaders, pharmacists, physicians, and school personnel serving the target area
2. *Community resident survey*—250 interviews of a random sample of community residents in each city
3. *Statistical data*—utilization of mental health services, and social indicator data-crime rates, welfare, health, and educational statistics—utilized supportively.

INTERVENTION STRATEGIES

Organization of the South Community Organization

A key element of the project strategy was that the local sponsor be an organization representative of the community. The role of the sponsoring organization was to function as the grant recipient to help community residents plan, organize, and initiate programs and activities that built on community strengths and that helped over-

---

[2]For a fuller discussion of research methodology, see Naparstek, Biegel, and Spence, 1979.

come obstacles to help seeking and receiving. There was no such broadly representative organization on the entire Southside. There were church organizations, ethnic clubs, and fraternal organizations, but there was no single organization that represented the entire community. Thus our first step was to hire a local community organizer to form an organization that could act as a sponsor of the project. This was a slow and time consuming process, but one that was absolutely essential to the success of the project.

To achieve community legitimacy, it was necessary to locate key community and institutional leadership and solicit their support and endorsement for the project. The issue of legitimacy was critical since we had not been invited into the community and we didn't have a single community contact. We had originally planned to work in ethnic neighborhoods in Providence, Rhode Island and Baltimore, Maryland, in which there were already existing community organizations. However, by the time the grant was funded, the organization in Providence was no longer in existence. The Southside of Milwaukee was chosen as a substitute community because of its high ethnic concentration (one of the project's requirements) and because the research director of the project had recently relocated in Milwaukee. The organizational process of forming the sponsoring organization in Milwaukee was the most essential and critical aspect of the project. The organizing strategies will be presented in some detail to help explicate our empowerment philosophy and to present an alternative to the "parachuting" of professional interventions into the community.

The organizer hired for the project had previous experience on the East Side of Milwaukee. He was Italian, with pride in his working-class background. The combination of his community organizing experience and ethnic identification made him an ideal candidate for the difficult task of gaining entry into a community that was hostile and suspicious toward outsiders. Since we did not have any contacts in the community, we decided against hiring an indigenous organizer from the Southside. Such a move would be risky given our lack of knowledge of power relationships and possible organizational rivalries in the community. It should be added here that while we were very committed to working on the Southside, we knew that the final decision as to whether the project would be placed here would be made by the local leadership of the community and not by us. Of course, we did everything we could to facilitate a positive response.

The initial strategy in Milwaukee was to learn slowly about the Southside, with special emphasis on discovering the crucial leaders and key institutions in the community. The organizer, who was unfamiliar with the Southside community, met with people he knew who were from the area and they provided him with the names of several prominent leaders in the Polish community. Interviewing each of these people, he asked them to provide names of other Southsiders who were knowledgeable about their community and who might be interested in the project. Through this "snowballing" technique, over a three month period the worker spoke individually with some 70 persons. He gave a general description of the project to each and explained how it would incorporate and build upon the cohesion and strengths of the community. From each interview, he learned more about the leaders, the major institutions, and social networks in the area.

During this initial organizing process, a number of strategies were followed. First, not wanting to define the community as a problem area, the organizer stressed that the project would build on the strengths in the community; talk of problems initially was minimized. Of course, there indeed were strengths in the community and our strategy was one of using those strengths to address any identified problems.

Second, the matter of mental health was not initially raised. Our sensitivity to this issue was acute based upon negative experiences in trying to find a sponsoring organization for the project in the Federal Hill area of Providence, Rhode Island. Here we were told by representatives of the Italian community, "Italians don't have mental health problems." We had wanted the Federal Hill House, a 100 year old settlement house, to act as the local sponsor for the project. At a meeting of their board to discuss our request, the chairman remarked, "We're afraid that the stigma of mental illness might rub off on our organization." Thus we felt that gaining legitimacy would be difficult enough without compounding it by having to struggle with the stigma issue. The project was presented in its broader context of human services. That is, the project would try to strengthen networks in the community through which residents could receive help in addressing problems of daily living (i.e., family communications, loneliness, widowhood, divorce, etc.). As will be discussed below, after the initial three month organizing period, the specific research aims of the project were presented in detail to an assembled meeting of community leaders.

Third, the organizer, in addition to obtaining names of persons to contact, was always careful to ask respondents what they thought his reception would be by the contact person. On several occasions, the organizer was advised not to contact a particular person until he had first met with certain other individuals and gained their support. He was also advised to begin his contact with a new individual with the information that he had been referred by so and so. These suggestions were carefully adhered to and proved successful in helping to gain legitimacy and reduce potential opposition to the project.

Several characteristics of the area became apparent from these initial interviews. The clergy enjoy a great deal of respect and deference; the community is self-contained, independent, suspicious of outsiders wishing to help them, and especially leery of federal funds; and the community has tremendous strengths and resources, but is reluctant to admit that problems exist, particularly to "outsiders."

Many of those interviewed were cautious and questioned why we were there since no one from the community had invited us in. One influential local priest remarked to the organizer after hearing a description of the proposed project, "Why are you picking on the Southside Poles?" Part of this was due, we believe, to the strong stereotyping of the Polish ethnic community by civil rights leaders and white liberals in the 1960s and 1970s. If we were going to succeed, the project had to overcome much of this hostility toward outsiders.

Some of the positive factors that shape this community are pride, dignity, inner strength, and self-respect. The organizer staffing the project was able to state honestly and without being patronizing that he had been brought up in a white ethnic neighborhood like the Southside, and therefore had some personal knowledge of the pride, values, and concerns of the ethnic working class. His manner won him a great degree of respect among these community leaders. They realized we were not engaged in a "missionary" effort to change the community (as some had initially feared).

Although many community and institutional leaders were identified, they were not strongly tied with each other on an informal or formal basis. The Catholic parishes had selective, informal ties among various priests but were quite separate entities. There were a number of ethnic, civic, social, and fraternal groups, the strongest and most respected included the Milwaukee Society of the Polish National Alliance, the Pulaski Council (an umbrella organization consisting of some 20 member groups), and Polanki (a women's cultural group). There were neither block clubs nor action/issue groups in the community.

The organizer maintained contact with approximately 15 people whom others had identified as key leaders of fraternal and civic groups, local businesses, churches, and community institutions. The organizer spoke individually with these "core" leaders about the possibility of forming a coalition to sponsor and direct the project. When most of them seemed interested, a meeting was held on the Southside involving these leaders and the project staff from Milwaukee and Washington, D.C. The leaders invited to the group represented both the clergy and the laity and were all well respected, older, established community leaders. Though they had individually expressed interest in coming together for the meeting, most were still very suspicious of this "Washington controlled" effort. None of these individuals had ever worked together in a broad, neighborhood-based coalition such as we were proposing. Would this idea work, they wondered?

Invitations to the initial meeting were sent to 17 leaders; 11 came. One of the area pastors was asked to host this first meeting and to act as temporary chairman. Seven other priests were also invited, as were four civic leaders from the groups mentioned above. The administrators of a local day care center and hospital, both Felician nuns, were also invited because both these institutions, built through the nickel and dime contributions of Polish-Americans, were cited as crucial to the community. Two other agencies were asked to send representatives: Catholic Social Services, which had established an outreach program in the community two years earlier; and a life long learning institute (senior citizens school) located just north of the target area.

Five parish priests, one civic leader, and the administrators and staff of the four above mentioned agencies were present. The chairman gave an excellent introductory talk, urging the gathering to unify and support the project. The key point made at the meeting was a description of the successful Catholic Social Services parish outreach project, concrete evidence of a successful small scale professional intervention on the Southside.

Certain activities, we said, were dictated by the grant from NIMH: A detailed needs study and assessment of resources had to be completed as the first step; this would be followed by the creation of pilot projects that focused on the broad area of mental health. Beyond these two essentials, the newly formed coalition would guide the project and make all decisions as to its activities, including the selection of the projects. If the group did not feel this project was potentially beneficial to their community, then it would not be located there and a new field site would be sought. The choice was theirs. The group cautiously accepted these terms. It agreed that such work was needed in their community. Interest was expressed in learning further details about the project structure, and a second meeting was scheduled for the following month. At the next meeting, concrete plans for the project were solidified and the community leaders gave their final go ahead. The name South Community Organization (SCO) was later selected by the coalition for their group.

The sponsoring coalition gave tremendous legitimacy to the project. Each person in the group represented a series of strong helping networks that were not necessarily closely linked with the others. The monthly meetings stimulated an exchange of information about these networks and generated ideas about the linking of resources. In earlier interviews, some of the leaders would say, "We do not have any problems in our community." Now they were talking about strengthening helping networks to meet the issues and concerns, such as family communications, widowhood, and divorce, that traditional services could not always cope with. The process of determining needs and linking resources, which had begun at the first meeting of the group, continued in the ongoing dialogue.

As demonstration projects developed over the course of the project, considerable organizational time was devoted to locating and recruiting "grassroots" members for the steering committee. SCO staff spoke about the project at numerous meetings of home and school associations (PTAs), ethnic and fraternal organizations, and church groups. At each of these meetings, solicitations were made of individuals willing to become involved in and work with the project. These efforts proved successful and a number of "grassroots" members were added to the steering committee. Over time, these individuals assumed much of the leadership and direction of the SCO from the initial members. This was facilitated by an intensive leadership development process for these new members instituted by the SCO staff. The founders still supported and helped the organization, but a number of them lacked the time necessary to develop and maintain the organization over a long time period. Thus, after several years, leadership of SCO was a mixture of established community leaders and interested working people from the community who had not previously been identified as natural leaders.

Formation of the Professional Advisory Committee

During the organizing phase of SCO, agency leaders were also contacted to assess their interest in serving on a professional advisory committee (PAC). Some 30 agencies participated in the first PAC meeting. Initially, meetings were on a quarterly basis, later they became monthly. Agencies chose to participate in the project for different reasons. Some had experienced difficulty gaining entry, and therefore, clients, on the Southside. Participation in this project seemed to them a way to gain a foothold in the community. Others joined to satisfy the demands of their funding agencies for community involvement, to develop relationships with other agencies, or simply to keep abreast of a new community activity. The PAC worked actively with SCO committees as the project developed. For example, many members of the PAC also served as members of SCO committees and helped in the development and organization of demonstration programs.

The PAC was organized during the same time period that SCO was being developed. This was done because we wanted the agencies to be part of the project from the beginning. This would, we thought, help them feel that this also was their project. During the first project year, SCO and the PAC were kept apart from each other. If the empowerment of SCO was to occur, we needed sufficient time for the capacity building process to take place. Indeed by the time the two groups got together, the community leaders and helpers had successfully identified the community strengths and needs on their own with technical support from project staff. They were thus better able to interact with the professionals on a parity basis.

PAC members tended principally to be administrators and supervisors, although there were some line staff members. Membership by individuals often changed during the four years of the project, a reflection of high staff turnover.

The Data Analysis Phase

The early phase of the empowerment process provided opportunities for neighborhood leaders to gather information about community assets and issues to be addressed. The staff was concerned that the community would view this research negatively and refuse to cooperate. SCO leaders, however, spread the word around the community that they were endorsing the research, that the findings would be used to help the community, and that it was okay to be interviewed. Refusal rates were very low for six of the seven interview groups (Clergy—19%; Human Service Agencies—3%; Natural Helpers—13%; Neighborhood Leaders—15%; Pharmacists—11%; School—6%). Refusals rates for physicians were very high (70%); therefore, this data was used with caution.

SCO members analyzed census and other social indicator data as well as interview data. The members demonstrated their "expert" knowledge of their community by explaining and elaborating upon formal statistics. For instance, census data indicated a high concentration of elderly, low-income, and foreign born people in a certain neighborhood. A priest and a nun who were part of SCO and who were raised in that neighborhood explained that the statistics reflected the presence of many "displaced persons" from Poland who had settled there after World War II. Another member, who was himself a postwar immigrant, listed the various fraternal and veterans' organizations that these people belong to and provided the names of appropriate contact people. This example represents one important tenet of the project; that is, that residents are the "experts" on their neighborhood and that a truly accurate understanding of any community requires a combination of formal data and the informal knowledge of community residents.

The PAC was also actively involved in reviewing research findings. Two entire meetings were spent reviewing the findings. At the second meeting, a brainstorming session was held to discuss possible intervention strategies and projects that might stem from the data findings.

The research findings confirmed many of our original hypotheses. The participation of local leaders and agency staff in the research process helped create a sense of energy and commitment for addressing unmet needs. During the initial phase of the project, community leaders denied there were any problems on the Southside. Now, looking at interview findings based upon interviews with leaders such as themselves, they clearly recognized and stated that problems existed. Because they were defining the problems themselves, they were eager to do something about them.

Among significant findings were the following (for a fuller discussion of data findings see Biegel, 1982; Naparstek, Biegel, & Spence, 1979; Naparstek, Biegel, & Spiro, 1982).

1. The term mental health was negatively "loaded."
2. People were often unaware of available agency services and reluctant to use them because of mistrust or pride.
3. Southsiders usually turned to community helpers—family, friends, neighbors, clergy—in times of need.
4. There was extensive fragmentation *within* the lay and professional helping networks as well as *between* lay and professional helping networks.
5. Many helpers and leaders, both professional and lay, were unaware of the major problems of community residents and indicated an even greater degree of lack of awareness of the networks employed by community residents to meet these needs.
6. Poor family communications (especially between parents and teens) and the problems of single parent families and the elderly were often cited.

Development of Demonstration Programs

Intervention programs were developed and implemented during the second through fourth project years. After reviewing data findings and listening to suggestions from the PAC, SCO decided that its first priority was to help inform Southside residents of existing agency services. A one-page *Referral Directory* was developed that has since had three printings and has spun off a 60 page directory of services for the elderly. Other projects included: a series of family communication workshops; support groups for the divorced, widowed, and agoraphobics; a "wellness" project cosponsored by three private social service agencies and funded by the United Way; clergy agency luncheons; and a community helpers newsletter (Naparstek, Biegel, & Spiro, 1982).

THE OUTCOMES OF EMPOWERMENT

Based upon our experience, there are a number of advantages, as follows, to empowering community residents and to enhancing neighborhood and professional support systems:

(1) A neighborhood support systems approach can reach populations who are in need of assistance but unwilling or unable to seek professional help. Through the research process, it was determined that there were large numbers of ethnic, working-class women on the Southside who were living alone. Many were divorced or

widowed and considered at high risk for developing mental health problems. There is documented underutilization of mental health services by working-class women. They do not usually seek help from mental health centers or participate in organized self-help groups. This is a population that many mental health programs have difficulty reaching. As a result, they have remained largely under-served, except during psychiatric emergencies.

When this project began, there were no support groups for the divorced or widowed in the Southside target area. The data established that a need existed. We were not sure how to begin serving this population. Mental health professionals were eager to assist us, but we were concerned that a support group organized inside a mental health center would "label" participants as sick or crazy and would therefore not work on the Southside. A group for young widowed persons with dependent children arose spontaneously when one woman initiated the idea with the project staff. Then a local pastor from the area approached our organizer and stated that he knew of a number of older widowed women in his parish who could also use a group. He gave the organizer several names. The widows were approached by the community organizer individually and were queried about their needs and interests in a support group. Each expressed reluctance or indifference. The organizer called the pastor and explained what had happened. The pastor said that he would contact the women himself. When the women found out that the pastor was supporting the program, they changed their minds and came to a meeting. Through interaction of staff and community, two ongoing support groups for widows were developed involving a total of over 50 women—one for older widows, the other for widows with children. Over time, staff involvement with both groups decreased. The community organizers gradually became consultants to the two groups as each developed strong indigenous leadership.

Thus, as a result of efforts by networks of community clergy and neighborhood organizations, ethnic working-class women were drawn into self-help efforts sponsored under the aegis of the community. The organization of these groups reflects their own particular social and educational needs and interests. Initially, the widows were wary about involving professionals in their meetings. Over time, as group members developed rapport with one another and the groups coalesced, professionals were invited to speak and to serve as consultants on leadership development. In a reversal of what has been the "traditional" professional role, professionals served as advisors to this community-directed process. To be most effective for this population group, the initial organizing effort had to come from the community, not the professional sector.

(2) A neighborhood support systems approach is built upon the strengths, not the weaknesses, of the community; it utilizes and enhances the neighborhood's preexisting systems of informal support, thus increasing the community's sense of competency and power. On the Southside, a federally funded community mental health center had for several years been aware of family communications problems in the neighborhood. Social workers from the center had broached with the clergy the idea of communications seminars as a means of addressing this issue. Failing to get a favorable response, and aware of the fact that the Southside is a proud, tightly knit community that is unwilling to let a professional agency define its problems for it, the initial effort was abandoned. The mental health professionals had recognized and defined family communications as a problem, but the community and its leadership had not yet done so. As a result, the social workers from the mental health center could not gain access to the population, and their efforts ended in frustration.

SCO undertook a different approach to the same problem, this time with positive results. As stated above, community residents received assistance in developing a process to collect and analyze data on community strengths and needs. The emphasis was upon strengths and how those strengths could be employed to address unmet community needs. Community residents and staff worked closely together to decide which people to talk to, what information to collect, and how to analyze the findings.

Once the data was collected, a workshop to review the findings was held for community leaders and helpers. Many community helpers were surprised to find the extent to which family communications appeared to be a major problem. There was little reluctance to admit this, however, because they were interpreting and summarizing the results of raw data that they themselves had helped obtain from local community leaders and helpers. The definition of the problem clearly came from the community, not from "outside" professionals.

When the problem was recognized, people wanted to do something about it. A decision was made to employ the strength of existing neighborhood helpers. A committee of community helpers was organized, and "brainstorming" meetings were held with project staff to discuss possible interventions. The residents decided to ask agency professionals for their suggestions, inviting several agency representatives to the meetings. Once again, the professionals acted as advisors to the community-directed planning process.

The expanded committee decided to hold a four-part workshop on family communications. Community members took responsibility for getting people to the workshop by means of brochures, through bulletin announcements, and perhaps most importantly, through the informal communication channels of the community helpers. Professionals agreed to serve as staff coordinators at the workshop, following a plan devised by the entire committee. This first workshop was very successful; over 40 people participated, and a follow-up session was held for those who asked for more time to develop their communication skills. The first workshop led to a dozen more, with a total of over 350 people participating. Over time, community helpers have taken on a larger role in staffing the workshops, including the teaching of communication skills.

(3) A neighborhood support systems approach builds upon the unique ability of neighborhood residents to know what will work in their communities. Data findings from the project showed that many community residents did not know where to go for help. A committee of residents and agency professionals, which was formed to discuss this problem, quickly agreed that a referral directory for use by community residents was needed. Considerable disagreement, however, arose over what form this directory should take.

Agency professionals favored a comprehensive directory for Southsiders with a complete listing and program description of all agencies serving the area. It would be a smaller version, about 20 pages, of the Directory of Agencies published in Milwaukee by United Way. The community residents listened, then responded: "That sounds interesting—but Southsiders won't use it." They then suggested a one-page directory with listings by problem or population group (alcoholism, problems of the elderly, health care, emotional distress, etc.). They felt it should contain only the most essential services. The professionals were concerned about leaving some agencies out. They did not want to be accused by other professionals of being biased or unfair. In the end, the professionals acceded to the wishes of the community residents. A two-sided, one-page directory listing 45 agencies in 17 service categories was developed. It was printed on heavy folded stock to be posted near the telephone (another suggestion of residents). Printing costs were covered through grants from several Milwaukee foundations. The directory, now in its third edition, has been widely distributed— over 30,000 copies—through churches, neighborhood stores, community groups, ethnic clubs, and agencies. Specific directories for elderly and youth services have also been developed as a result of this small initial effort.

(4) Creating linkages between neighborhood support systems and mental health and human service programs can reduce fragmentation of services and provide help in a more effective manner. In Milwaukee, the organization of a professional advisory committee of agencies serving the Southside substantially reduced the fragmentation of services. Representatives of some 30 agencies met on a regular basis over a three-year period to discuss ways to coordinate their efforts, thus simplifying the process of seeking and receiving help for Southside residents. This was the first organized, ongoing group of Southside agencies in a decade or more. Initial efforts focused on information-sharing among agency representatives. A looseleaf directory of Southside agency services, featuring one-page descriptions of each agency's programs and services, was developed for use by agency staff. It provided much greater detail than the "red book" of community agencies for the entire metropolitan area. Other specialty directories, such as one on alcohol and drug abuse, followed. Many agency representatives have found these directories invaluable for aiding multi-problem clients requiring the services of several agencies.

Another effort of the PAC was a four-day Southside spring fair with workshops for children, teens, adults and the elderly. Brochures on individual Southside agencies, as well as copies of a central agency directory, were circulated. Several hundred persons attended. Community residents and agency representatives were pleased with results. An indirect byproduct of the advisory committee was the fostering of informal relationships and linkages among service providers, which resulted in an increase of beneficial referrals.

The success of the PAC of Southside agencies led to similar spin-off groups of agencies focusing on particular population groups. The Southside Youth Committee and a half dozen youth, for example, assisted representatives of almost every agency working with Southside youth. They shared information on problems and sponsored two successful teen workshops, the first for teens and their parents, the second for teens only. Over 30 persons attended each workshop. Evaluations were very positive. A teen rap group was formed because teens asked for an ongoing support mechanism. The committee and the PAC also published a directory of Southside youth services.

CONCLUSION

The above vignettes are examples of both programs and process, ends and means. The overriding objective of our effort was to strengthen networks, lay and professional, and to remove impediments to partnerships between community helpers and leaders and agency professionals. Development of each intervention program served as a "means" as well as an "end." The end was achieved because intervention programs—whether they were self-help groups, family communication seminars, or referral directories—addressed a specific need that had been identified by the community organization in collaboration with the professional advisory committee. The means—namely, the planning and development process—achieved the end of enhancing the capacity of lay people, first to work together and then to work in concert with professionals as full partners.

The objectives of the empowerment model described above can be summarized as follows: (1) to create an awareness by residents of neighborhood strengths and needs; (2) to strengthen the neighborhood lay helping network; (3) to strengthen the professional helping network; (4) to form linkages between the lay and professional helping networks; and, (5) to link the lay and professional helping networks to the macrosystem, i.e., city, state, and federal agencies, organizations, and funding bodies (see Naparstek et al., 1982 for a fuller explication of these objectives).

Evaluation of Empowerment Strategies

The project achieved considerable success in its goal of empowering community residents. Utilizing the concepts of empowerment presented earlier, these accomplishments will be briefly reviewed below.

Capacity

Utilizing power to solve problems. Utilizing power requires organization, leadership, and management skills as well as technical expertise in planning, conducting research, and implementing programs. SCO's power can be seen in a number of ways. It was the first neighborhood wide organization that was broadly representative of the community. It brought together in one organization a variety of leaders, each of whom had their own power base yet who were able to coalesce and interact together for the benefit of the entire community. Although the federal funding for this project ended over three years ago, SCO is still very strong and functioning well. It has been able to secure local funding to continue its programs. This is one indication that the community residents have secured some power.

The technical expertise of SCO can be seen by the fact that the community invited agency professionals to assist them in developing programs and the professionals agreed. This in itself is one recognition of community expertise and power. Even more important, however, is the fact that over time community residents have taken increasing leadership of the demonstration programs from the professionals. For example, the first family communications seminars, though planned by both community residents and professionals, were run by professionals. Over a one year period, community residents gradually assumed greater responsibility for the staffing of these workshops, such that the professional role became a very minor one. In the case of the self-help groups for the widowed, the SCO organizer initially took a very active role in getting the groups started and in facilitating group meetings. Gradually, group members assumed leadership roles and the staff role became one of backup and technical support. Another example of community power is the fact that the community residents demonstrated expertise in knowing what would work in their community and in developing successful interventions where professionals had tried but had previously failed. For example, community residents exhibited great success in organizing prevention programs, such as family communication seminars. Professionals had tried to do this earlier but had been unsuccessful.

Gaining access to institutions and organizations. Before the project began, there was an underutilization of professional mental health and human service agencies on the Southside. Most of these agencies had difficulty gaining entry into the community. SCO was able to gain access to these agencies in a variety of ways. First, through the organization of a professional advisory committee, SCO developed ongoing relationships with over thirty agencies, most of whom had little previous involvement in the community. A number of representatives from these agencies participated as members of SCO committees and gave significant input into the development of demonstration programs. SCO gained access to several family service agencies through the development of an innovative program called the Wellness Project. SCO secured a grant from the United Way which provided funding for a consortium of family service agencies (Catholic Social Services, Family Service Society, and Lutheran Social Services) under the leadership of SCO. The purpose of this program was to develop prevention programs such as self-help groups, workshops, seminars, etc., for high risk population groups. The major premise was that professional agencies did not have expertise in knowing how to successfully gain entry and develop programs in hard to reach communities. SCO provided community legitimacy and community organization skills; the family service agencies provided workers with clinical expertise.

Nurture. Much of the project was focused on enhancing systems of social support in the community. This occurred on two levels. On an individual level, social support systems for high risk individuals were enhanced (i.e., self-help groups for widowed, divorced, and agoraphobics, and family communication seminars). On an organizational level, support systems of informal and formal service providers were strengthened through interventions aimed at reducing the fragmentation among service providers. Examples of this include the formation of the professional advisory committee, the involvement of agency professionals on SCO committees, and the development of referral directories for service providers.

Equity

Is one's investment equal to one's return? Does the neighborhood organization receive its fair share of resources compared to other parts of the city? In some communities, residents feel disenfranchised, they do not think that they are getting a fair break as compared to other communities. Southside residents did not express strong feelings of disenchantment despite some question as to whether the community was indeed receiving its fair share of public and private resources. Part of the reason for this is the respect of Southsiders for established leadership. Residents on the Southside traditionally have looked to their church, fraternal, and political leadership to protect their interests. Unlike many other urban ethnic communities, the Southside never formed a "grassroots" organization to address civic concerns. SCO was thus the first Southside group to organize the community residents for civic action and to press "equity" demands upon policy makers.

Several years after SCO was formed, residents expressed concern for the unmet needs of the aged in the community. A senior citizens committee was formed to study the needs of the elderly and to recommend programmatic interventions. Residents wanted to obtain a senior citizens center in the community. The local government had funds available for this purpose. However, it soon became apparent that the Southside would not receive any of these resources despite earlier indications to the contrary. A community meeting was held to which local politicians representing the Southside were invited. The turnout was large, the residents were demanding, and the politicians were impressed. This was the first time in recent memory that grassroots residents had pressed demands on the political system. The politicians used their influence with city hall and obtained the needed resources for the Southside Senior Center.

Empowerment Model: Limitations and Dangers

As in any model, there are limitations and dangers. From an agency perspective, network building such as we have proposed requires a considerable "up front" investment of time and energy before any products (programs) begin to appear. Thus mental health agencies that need a quick product, such as a new program of service, perhaps to justify expenditure of consultation and education monies, may find this approach a difficult one. In fact, there is a danger that the need by agencies for quick products may circumvent the network building process and lead to an undermining of community support systems. A combination of clinical, group work, and community organization skills is required of staff for this model to work; this may mean retraining of existing staff or getting appropriate agency consultation. At the very heart of the model is the requirement that agencies form partnerships with community organizations and vice versa. Many professionals are uncomfortable with such approaches and may consciously or unconsciously try to subvert the process. This issue is a two sided one, however, in that many community leaders and helpers are also uncomfortable interacting with professionals. There are considerable obstacles which must be overcome for these partnerships to work (Biegel, 1979; Biegel & Naparstek, 1982).

Although the dangers are real and the obstacles formidable, community helpers and leaders are already working with professional mental health and human service providers in many neighborhoods and communities around the United States. What is needed are mechanisms to catalyze the neighborhood potentials and reduce the administrative, fiscal, and legal obstacles that hamper progress. Although the empowerment model is no panacea, it is, we feel, a step in the right direction.

REFERENCES

Biegel, D. *Neighborhood support systems: People helping themselves.* Keynote address at the Pittsburgh Conference on Neighborhood Support Systems, Pittsburgh, PA, 1979.

Biegel, D. *Help seeking and receiving in urban ethnic neighborhoods.* Doctoral dissertation, University of Maryland, School of Social Work, 1982.

Biegel, D., & Naparstek, A. The neighborhood and family services project: An empowerment model linking clergy, agency professionals and community residents. In A. Jeger & R. Slotnik (Eds.), *Community mental health and behavioral ecology.* New York: Plenum Press, 1982.

Caplan, G. *Support systems and community mental health.* New York: Behavioral Publications, 1974.

Collins, A., & Pancoast, D. *Natural helping networks.* Washington, D.C.: National Association of Social Workers, 1976.

Froland, C. Community support systems: All things to all people? In D. Biegel & A. Naparstek (Eds.), *Community support systems and mental health: Practice, policy and research.* New York: Springer Publishing Company, 1982.

Giordano, J. *Ethnicity and mental health.* New York: American Jewish Committee, 1973.

Giordano, J., & Giordano, G. Ethnicity and community mental health. *Community Mental Health Review,* 1976, *1*, pp. 1, 4-14.

Hollingshead, A., & Redlich, F. *Social class and mental illness: A community study.* New York: John Wiley, 1958.

Myers, J., & Bean, L. *A decade later: A follow up of social class and mental illness.* New York: John Wiley, 1968.

Naparstek, A., & Haskell, C. Neighborhood approaches to mental health services. In L. Macht, D. Scherl, & S. Scharfstein (Eds.), *Neighborhood psychiatry.* Lexington, MA: Lexington Books, 1977.

Naparstek, A., Biegel, D., & Spence, B. Community analysis data report: Volume I, First level analysis. *Catalogue of Selected Documents in Psychology,* November 1979, Manuscript #1964.

Naparstek, A., Biegel, D., & Spiro, H. *Neighborhood networks for humane mental health care.* New York: Plenum Press 1982.

Naparstek, A., & Biegel, D. Community support systems: An alternative approach to mental health service delivery. In U. Reuveni, R. Speck, & J. Speck (Eds.), *Therapeutic Intervention*. New York: Human Sciences Press, 1982.

President's Commission on Mental Health. *Report to the President* (Vols. 1-4). Washington, D.C.: U.S. Government Printing Office, 1978.

Spiro, H., Crocetti, G., Siassi, I., Ward, R., & Hansen, E. Cost financed mental health facility I. Clinical care patterns in a labor union mental health program. *Journal of Nervous and Mental Disease*, 1975, *160*, 231-240.

Creating and Using Social Technologies for Community Empowerment

Stephen B. Fawcett
Tom Seekins
Paula L. Whang
Charles Muiu
Yolanda Suarez de Balcazar

ABSTRACT. Powerlessness appears to be associated consistently with widespread problems of living. Recently, enhancing community empowerment has been suggested as an important emphasis for human service professionals. This manuscript illustrates a role for human service professionals in creating and using social technologies to facilitate empowerment. Seven case studies are presented that represent seven frequently cited goals of empowerment efforts. Finally, the ethics of the empowerment strategy are analyzed and other implications of designing and using empowerment technologies are considered.

Tocqueville (1976) noted over 150 years ago that a popular ideal in America is that each person "learns to think and act for himself without counting on the support of any outside power" (p. 489). Unfortunately, a shared conception of self-determination as an ideal does not lead necessarily to widespread empowerment or to conditions in which it may be likely. Indeed, mass movements (Piven & Cloward, 1979)—such as the unemployed workers' movement of

This research was supported, in part, by grants to the Community Technology Project at the Center for Public Affairs and the Research & Training Center on Independent Living at the University of Kansas. We are grateful to the many members of poverty organizations, low-income neighborhoods, and consumer organizations of persons with disabilities who helped shape these tools for community empowerment. In addition, we thank Curt Braukmann, Keith Miller, Julian Rappaport, and Don Stull for comments on an earlier version of this manuscript. Reprints may be obtained from the authors at either the Center for Public Affairs or the Department of Human Development, University of Kansas, Lawrence, KS 66045.

145

the 1930s, the civil rights movement of the 1950s and 1960s, and the women's movement of the past decade—suggest that the conditions under which people attempt to control their lives may be unequal. The significance of this circumstance for the human service profession was noted by Kessler and Albee (1975) who concluded that individual and group powerlessness is associated consistently with widespread problems of living.

An understanding of power and its relationship to justice, political influence, social structure, and individual and general welfare has been the subject of study in such fields as philosophy (e.g., Rawls, 1971), political science (e.g., Banfield, 1961), sociology (e.g., Warren, 1977), education (e.g., Freire, 1972), and psychology (e.g., Ryan, 1971). Further, a body of folklore on how to enhance community empowerment has emerged from such fields as community organizing (e.g., Alinsky, 1969; Kahn, 1970), public interest law (e.g., Patner, 1978), applied anthropology (e.g., Dobyns, Doughty, & Lasswell, 1964), and social welfare (e.g., Kutchins & Kutchins, 1978). However, it is widely acknowledged that efforts to enhance community power are rarely systematic, making difficult the replication of occasional successes in other communities.

Community empowerment is the process of increasing control by groups over consequences that are important to their members and to others in the broader community. For example, by forming a tenants' rights organization individual residents of a public housing project may increase their ability to redress grievances and obtain improvements in housing conditions. Empowerment may apply to several types of communities (Johnson & Tropman, 1979): a territory in which the location of turf is commonly shared (e.g., a low-income neighborhood); a subculture in which similar experiences or beliefs and values are held in common (e.g., minority groups); or an organization in which the workplace is the common connection (e.g., factory workers).

From a behavioral perspective, the ability to produce empowerment may be a function of such critical variables as *knowledge* of problems and solution alternatives and *skill* in presenting issues, leading groups, and implementing other empowerment tactics. Further, it may be related to the capacity to control consequences for critical actors in the system, including positive *consequences* (e.g., votes for elected officials) and negative ones (e.g., unfavorable newspaper reports). Finally, empowerment may be enhanced by environmental or *structural variables*, such as the opportunity to gain access to agendas of meetings of elected officials. An analysis of those with and without power might suggest the importance of similar variables in community empowerment.

Rappaport (1981) urges human service professionals to work in a variety of contexts using a diversity of techniques to enhance empowerment. The types of involvement of human service professionals in community empowerment include charismatic leadership in social action campaigns, consultation to community organizations, research examining variables affecting the acquisition and use of power, and the design of social technologies to enhance community empowerment. Perhaps by creating and using social technologies or tools for community empowerment, the effects of efforts of human service professionals and the local change agents and target participants with whom they collaborate can be amplified.

A *social technology* is a replicable set of procedures that is designed to produce an effect on socially important behaviors of relevant participants under a variety of real-life conditions. For example, a counseling training program, insofar as its effects can be repeated when used by people other than the developers, is a kind of social technology. Such technologies are particularly useful if they are designed to be inexpensive, effective, decentralized, flexible, sustainable, simple, and compatible with existing customs, beliefs, and values (Fawcett, Mathews, & Fletcher, 1980). Empowerment technologies might be designed to produce specified effects when used by human service professionals, community change agents, or targets under common conditions of individual or group action. An analysis of general empowerment tactics suggests the importance of such activities as increasing knowledge of community problems and solution alternatives, training new behaviors to increase the effectiveness of community group leaders and individual citizens, and obtaining and communicating information to influence public policies regarding the distribution of resources. Once such common tactics are identified, systematic methods for training change agents in their use can be designed. These tools can then be used by human service professionals in their collaborative consultation with a variety of community groups and organizations.

The purpose of this manuscript is to illustrate a role for human service professionals in creating and using social technologies to facilitate community empowerment. Seven case studies in the design and use of empowerment technologies are described. These brief examples illustrate the application of social technologies with seven common goals of empowerment efforts. Finally, the ethics of the empowerment strategy are considered and other implications of designing and using empowerment technologies are discussed.

EXAMPLES OF EMPOWERMENT TECHNOLOGIES

Presented below are seven examples of the design and use of social technologies to enhance control by community members over important aspects of their lives. Participants in the projects include welfare families, persons with disabilities, residents of low-income neighborhoods, community service workers, elected leaders of poverty service organizations, individual citizens, and community activists. The work was conducted by the authors and other present or former members of the Community Technology Project, a research team organized by the first author and located at the University of Kansas. The project is affiliated with the Department of Human Development, in which most of its members are doctoral students, and the Center for Public Affairs, an interdisciplinary research unit in which the first two authors serve as coordinators of the Community Development Program.

The work described in this article may be characterized as a problem-oriented, or market-driven, approach to research and development. Using the principles of learning theory and the methods of applied behavior analysis, behaviors judged to be critical to the solution of community problems or the enhancement of community strengths are identified, observed, and (if possible) modified in ways consistent with the group's goals. Where possible, experimental and quasi-experimental designs—such as interrupted time series designs—are used to determine whether observed effects on identified behaviors can be attributed to the methods used. If the procedures are judged to be effective, they are "packaged" in a form suitable for transfer to change agents in other communities (Fawcett, Fletcher, Mathews, Whang, Seekins, & Nielsen, 1982).

The examples reflect the importance of knowledge and skill in efforts to increase control by territorial, subcultural, or organizational communities over their environments. The general empowerment goals and the case studies that illustrate them follow:

1. Increasing knowledge of community problems from the perspective of those most affected by the problems (Cases 1 & 2).

2. Increasing knowledge of solution alternatives generated by those most affected by the problems (Cases 1 & 2).
3. Increasing knowledge of the possible consequences of projects proposed by persons outside the affected community (Case 3).
4. Involving consumers in the redesign of social programs to fit local needs and resources (Case 4).
5. Training new behaviors for increasing the effectiveness of leaders of community groups (Case 5).
6. Training new behaviors for increasing the effectiveness of individual citizens (Case 6).
7. Developing and communicating research information to increase the likelihood of actions taken regarding problems affecting the poor or disadvantaged (Case 7).

Case Study #1: Forming a Human Services Agenda for a City

A planning council for a city's human service agencies requested the assistance of the Community Technology Project in building an agenda for its activities. The council hoped to use input from clients of the city's human service agencies to guide its efforts to coordinate services and redirect resources to areas of greatest need.

Problem. As cutbacks in resources for human services are experienced at the local level, human service agencies may be forced to compete for scarce resources. Although the new block grant approach to intergovernmental assistance and the ''New Federalism'' assume that state and local agencies can and will expand their capacities to plan and evaluate their actions, the public agendas of agencies, organizations, and governmental units rarely reflect the involvement of a broad spectrum of their consumers. In general, agencies serving such populations as the low-income, the elderly, and the disabled lack valid and inexpensive methods for gathering information about the concerns of their consumers. Further, they often lack methods for involving their consumers in decisions about what services are offered or how they should be delivered.

The concerns report of basic needs. For the past several years the Community Technology Project has worked on a methodology to assist constituency groups in influencing the formulation of public agendas (Fawcett, Seekins, Whang, Muiu, & Suarez de Balcazar, 1982). This methodology, known as the concerns report method, is a systematic, data-based process for identifying the local concerns of consumers of public institutions and clients of human service systems. The concerns report method yields systematic information on issues of importance (both strengths and problems) and specific alternatives for improvement of the organization, service system, or community.

In this application of the method, a working group of six low-income clients selected items from an index of potential concerns. A survey was prepared and distributed to clients of 13 human service agencies in the city. The survey included questions regarding the perceived importance of and satisfaction with issues such as "safe, temporary shelter is available to those who need it."

The results of responses from 261 clients were presented to 23 clients who attended public meetings. At these meetings, clients discussed the dimensions of the major problems, (i.e., issues of high importance and low satisfaction) and strengths (i.e., issues of high importance and high satisfaction) and proposed actions that should be taken. Transcripts of these problem-solving discussions and the survey data were summarized and prepared in various report formats that were presented to the United Way Board of Directors, the city commission, and other interested decision makers.

Outcomes. The uses of the data by the United Way and the city and county commissions were monitored. The allocation of United Way and city revenue sharing monies to poverty agencies (and all other projects) was compared for this city and for a city in which information such as that provided by the concerns report was not available. This analysis suggests that the concerns report may have influenced the decisions made by those receiving presentations of the data. For example, the distribution of the allocation of funds by the United Way in the matched community showed no change between poverty and non-poverty allocations over several years. However, poverty organizations in the target community received an abrupt increase of 24% ($34,425) in the poverty services budget. This represented a 78% share of all new contributions collected and a 4% increase in the poverty services share of the total budget.

Dissemination. The procedures of the basic needs and vital services concerns report method is in preparation. The manual will be used to facilitate technical assistance to human services' planning councils and poverty advocacy organizations throughout the country. The first replication of this work, conducted in the Kansas City metropolitan area, involved over 600 low-income clients, over 20 poverty agencies, a major poverty advocacy organization in Kansas, and the United Way.

Implications. Political scientists (Cobb & Elder, 1977; Schatt-schneider, 1960; Walker, 1977) have suggested that one of the more effective ways of exerting power is through placement of items on the public agenda. Information about the priorities of poor people that is generated by them can influence the allocation of public and charitable funds and other decisions that affect their lives. Many difficulties remain in extending and refining such control. But, to the extent that a simple and inexpensive informational technology can assist change agents and their constituencies in formulating an action agenda, their power is enhanced. The concerns report method allows a constituent group to identify common problems and specify acceptable solutions. It assists the change agent by providing credible information about the opinions of constituents that may serve to exert some influence over the decisions of others.

Case Study #2: Identifying Community Concerns for Consumer Advisory Committees of Persons with Disabilities

The disabled citizens of a consumer advisory committee (CAC) for a local independent living center requested the assistance of the Community Technology Project in identifying the local community strengths and problems for residents with disabilities in the county. The CAC wanted a list of community concerns to use in forming an agenda for their advocacy activities. The project collaborated with the consumer advisory committee to adapt and implement a technology designed to identify local strengths and problems from the perspective of disabled residents.

Problem. Consumer advisory/advocacy committees are often formed within independent living centers to pursue the goal of independent living and self-help for persons with disabilities (Frieden, 1980; P.L. 95-602, 1978). Part of their function is to advocate for those aspects of independent living and self-help that are of most value or need to the larger disabled community. However, due to limited access, a lack of outreach resources, and other reasons, it is often difficult for a CAC to identify the more important concerns and the more desirable solutions from the perspective of the entire disabled community. In the absence of such community input, the CAC runs the risk of representing and advocating for issues that are of little benefit to disabled people in their efforts to live independently.

Concerns report method for disabled citizens. Similar to the project involving low-income clients described above, a concerns report was prepared to assess the strengths and problems of the county from the perspective of persons with disabilities. Five disabled citizens served as a working group to develop a survey that was returned by 45 persons with disabilities. Twenty citizens—most with disabilities—attended a public meeting in which identified concerns were discussed and possible solutions were generated. A report summarizing the data and client discussions of the results and alternatives was prepared and distributed to the CAC, the director of the independent living center, and other interested persons (Whang, Fawcett, Suarez de Balcazar, & Seekins, Note 1).

Outcomes. Ratings by citizens who developed the survey suggested that the index was helpful, representative, and complete and that they were very satisfied with the process. Those citizens who responded to the survey indicated being satisfied that their concerns were represented in the survey. The disabled citizens at the public meeting rated the discussion as being complete, useful, and satisfying. Test-retest reliability for response sets and survey items was similarly very high.

Following this implementation, the CAC used the identified concerns as an action agenda with which to plan new community advocacy activities. They addressed identified concerns such as strengthening the handicapped parking ordinance to cover commercial areas not owned by the city, increasing enforcement of ordinances regarding handicapped parking, enhancing community awareness of the strengths of persons with disabilities, and improving community advocacy skills. In addition, the CAC was able to meet and build coalitions with two other local community advocacy groups based on the identified issues.

Dissemination. The disabled citizens' concerns report method was outlined in a procedures manual for use by the research project in collaboration with CACs and independent living centers. The manual enables the Community Technology Project to provide technical assistance to independent living centers and other groups of disabled citizens throughout the country. Thus far, the method has been used in over 10 counties in Kansas and Missouri.

Implications. The concerns report method provides a systematic approach to increasing knowledge of community problems and alternative solutions from the perspective of those most affected. The consumer group maintains control over the method, the interpretation of the results, and subsequent actions for improvement without relying heavily or permanently on the assistance of outside professionals. Thus the concerns report method provides a tool for facilitating empowerment efforts by poverty organizations, groups of persons with disabilities, and others without direct access to the public agenda.

Case Study #3: Designing a Technology for Increasing Knowledge About the Possible Impacts of Proposed Roadway Projects on Neighborhoods

Several years ago, a neighborhood improvement association in a low-income area requested the assistance of the Community Technology Project in the association's efforts to block construction of a four-lane highway that was scheduled to be built through the middle of the neighborhood. We agreed to collaborate with members of the neighborhood association in designing and using a method to inform neighborhood residents about the possible consequences (both positive and negative) of the proposed highway.

Problem. Federal regulations require citizen input regarding constuction projects such as highways and shopping malls that involve the use of public funds (Francis, 1975; Kennard, 1976). However, the complexity of such projects represents an important obstacle to effective citizen input (McCoy, 1975) since it is difficult to project the likely consequences for residents of the neighborhood most affected. Further, local newspapers may not cover such stories or may cite only consequences primarily beneficial to commercial interests or to those living outside the low-income neighborhood. A practical and unbiased method for informing residents about the possible consequences of a proposed highway project might promote knowledge in those most affected and foster informed input on such decisions.

Consequence analysis method. A consequence analysis guide was designed for the education of residents who lived in the path of the roadway about the possible effects of the project. A list of 48 possible consequences was included based on a review of the social and environmental impact assessment literature (Finsterbusch & Wolf, 1977) and interviews with representatives of the neighborhood association, city planners, and other experts. Specific types of impacts (e.g., level of noise, safe access to other parts of the neighborhood) were listed under nine impact categories: economic, housing, transportation, safety, neighborhood unity and communication, recreation, community resources and services, community well-being, and environmental quality. The 10 community residents who participated examined each possible consequence and rated whether the impact would be "favorable" or "unfavorable" and "large" or "small."

Outcomes. Sanford and Fawcett (1980) used an interrupted multiple time series design—sometimes called a multiple baseline design—to examine experimentally the effects of the consequence analysis guide on residents' opinions about the favorability of the roadway project. The results showed that ratings by residents of the favorability of the proposed highway decreased for nine of ten residents by an average of one rating point (on a seven-point scale) following use of the guide. In addition, ratings by community members of the overall quality, knowledge, persuasiveness, and logic of the participants' verbal justifications of their opinions showed approximately two point rating increases (on a seven-point scale) following the intervention.

Following this study, data regarding citizen dissatisfaction with the proposed roadway and an analysis of possible negative consequences on the neighborhood were sent by the researchers to the state department of transportation that was charged with gathering information about the proposed project. Although a source of displeasure to local city officials who complained to the researchers' boss, this collaboration was judged to be a small, but significant, contribution to the neighborhood association's ultimately successful efforts to halt construction of the roadway.

Dissemination. A community impact analysis manual (Sanford & Fawcett, Note 2) was prepared, detailing how other communities might design similar guides for educating citizens about the possible consequences of projects planned for their neighborhoods. Dozens of copies have been sent to human service professionals and citizen groups in other communities and known replications have occurred in Hawaii.

Implications. This method increases knowledge among those most affected by projects proposed by persons living outside the neighborhood. As such, it may contribute to the capacities of groups of persons with limited power to control decisions affecting their lives and those of their neighbors.

Case Study #4: Extending Community Control of New Technologies Through Study Circles

In two separate instances, the Community Technology Project was asked to assist in the dissemination of educational technologies designed for use in community-based service agencies. The first involved a community living skills education program designed for use in adult education centers. The second involved a program to teach basic reading, writing, and mathematical skills designed for use in elementary schools and afterschool programs.

Problem. Each year a number of innovative programs and procedures emerge from various sources. These innovative programs are often adopted by administrators and then assigned to staff, "sold" to groups, or adopted without careful consideration. Many of these potentially useful programs are eventually rejected or fail to produce the promised results. One cause of such failures is the lack of involvement in important adoption decisions by those who must implement the program or those who are affected by it.

Study circle method. A study circle worksheet was prepared to present a sequence of prompts to be followed by potential adopters in considering innovative solutions to problems. The worksheet consists of 28 steps involved in problem analysis, program design, and evaluation. Each step describes an activity to be performed by the group considering the adoption of an innovation (e.g., defining the problem). It also provides prompts in the form of questions to be answered by the group responsible for the activity (e.g., What has been done in the past about this problem?).

During meetings of a study circle, one member acts as a proctor by reading the prompts for each step, encouraging comments from all, and recording statements that show a consensus. The innovation is considered in the context of the problem it is intended to address and in the context of other options. The outcome of the use of the study circle worksheet is a written analysis of a problem, an outline of a program designed to address it (including the innovation—perhaps in modified form), a list of actions to be taken, publicly accepted responsibilities, and standards for evaluation determined by those responsible for implementing the solution.

Outcomes. Seekins and Fawcett (in press; Note 3) used the study circle procedures in both an adult education program considering the adoption of a living skills program and in an afterschool project operated by a community center considering the adoption of a basic skills program known as the Behavior Analysis Follow Through program. In both settings the respective programs had been available for at least two years and training in their use had been provided, but neither program had been implemented. Following the study circle procedures, modified programs were initiated in both settings. However, the adult education setting directly adopted only two components from the model innovation while modifying four, rejecting eleven, and adding two completely new components. The afterschool program adopted six components directly from the Follow Through model, modified six, rejected five, and added four new components.

Dissemination. The worksheet itself has been modified and distributed to community leaders and agencies in Kansas during a series of community problem solving workshops conducted in centrally located cities. In addition, the worksheet has been used in conjunction with applications of the concerns report method described earlier.

Implications. The study circle process provides an opportunity for people to participate actively in decisions about the design and implementation of technologies that will affect them (Nelkin, 1977; 1979). In addition, it recognizes the uniqueness of their situation by providing an opportunity for individuals to use the information and skills they have acquired through their intimate familiarity with local conditions (Hinrichs, 1980; Zippo, 1980). In doing so, it may allow participants to experience self-determination (Friere, 1973). Insofar as this technology gives local groups the power to adapt social and educational innovations to their own needs and circumstances, it extends indigenous control over technology designed by people outside the community.

Cast Study #5: Training Community Members to Chair Group Meetings

Several years ago the Community Technology Project agreed to collaborate with the executive board of a low-income self-help center known as Penn House in the development and use of a training procedure for chairing meetings. The role of the chairperson at these meetings was crafted to provide an opportunity for poor people to achieve success in a position of leadership. This role rotates among the members so that each member of the executive board has an opportunity to act as chairperson.

Problem. Community boards have such purposes and responsibilities as sharing information, solving problems, and making decisions. Members of groups sometimes lack the considerable skills needed to balance the need for decision making with full and equitable participation of all members. A practical and easy method of discussion and problem solving that creates opportunities for expanded participation by all members might result in a stronger group as well as wiser, more broadly accepted decisions.

Chairperson training procedure. Based on a review of the literature (e.g., Briscoe, Hoffman, & Bailey, 1975) and discussions with individuals who had been identified as conducting good meetings, 40 specific chairperson behaviors were identified under such categories as opening and closing meetings, leading discussions, and problem solving. These behaviors were taught using a combination of behavioral specifications, examples, rationales, study guides, practice, and feedback (Seekins, Mathews, & Fawcett, in press).

Outcomes. Seekins et al. (in press) used a multiple baseline design to analyze experimentally the effects of the training procedures on the directly observed behaviors of low-income persons serving as chairperson. The results showed marked increases in appropriate chairperson activities after training to near mastery levels. In addition, the percentage of agenda items for which closure was reached increased from an average of 30% to an average of more than 85% following training. Training of new chairpersons has continued at Penn House. Successive chairs have acquired some of the chairperson skills through observation of trained members; therefore, subsequent chairpersons have learned these skills more efficiently.

Dissemination. Although dissemination of these methods will await further refinement in the procedures, a manual will be available for distribution of these chairperson training methods to other community organizations.

Implications. Insofar as these procedures increase the skills of the chairperson, they extend the community's resources for leadership. To the extent that the functioning of community groups may be improved by such social technologies, the power of such organizations to affect local conditions may be enhanced.

Case Study #6: Using Personal Opinion to Influence Public Decisions

Various advocacy groups have requested assistance from the Community Technology Project in organizing consumers of human services in support of proposals affecting their constituent groups. In response to a specific request of a consumer advisory committee for an agency serving persons with disabilities, the researchers selected for technology development two promising responses available to all citizens: writing letters to the editor of newspapers and providing personal testimony to decisionmakers.

Problem. The public expression of personal opinions can influence decisionmakers. Letters to the editors of newspapers help clarify issues and various positions to the general public and may act as a barometer of public sentiment for decisionmakers. Testimony provided directly to elected officials may also suggest the number of constituents supporting or opposing proposals and the depth of sentiment. But members of organizations of low-income or disadvantaged people often lack the skills or resources to prepare and present effective letters or personal testimony. A simple and effective method of teaching these skills to members of groups might enhance their effectiveness in influencing decisions.

Self-help guides. Self-help guides were prepared to assist members of self-help organizations and consumers of human service agencies to prepare and deliver testimony and to write letters to the editor. These guides consisted of a general description of the activity and its purpose, behavioral specifications of each response required to perform the activity successfully, and two examples of each activity (one in favor of a proposal and one opposed). In addition, each pamphlet provided space in which consumers could prepare their own testimony or letter using their own insights and experiences regarding the issue.

Outcomes. In a pilot test of the effectiveness of the letter writing guide, a consumer of services at a local agency first prepared a letter she might write to the newspaper concerning a proposed lower rate for natural gas for persons of low income. Next, she used the guide to prepare a second letter on the issue. A comparison between the two letters suggested differences in the number of responses completed and in the quality of the two letters. A similar pilot test of the testimony package was conducted with a consumer who prepared testimony for a hearing on educational regulations affecting persons with disabilities. Anecdotal comments by consumers and decisionmakers suggested that the testimony was of high quality. Formal experimental evaluations are planned for both the letter writing and personal testimony guides.

The testimony guides were distributed to five consumers of two human services agencies who volunteered to testify to the local city commission regarding the proposed lower rate for natural gas for persons of low income. Their testimony helped create early public support for the program proposal. Following this meeting, the letter writing guides were distributed to clients of three agencies, generating a number of letters sent to both the local paper and the city commissioners. No letters sent to the newspaper were published, however, the editor and publisher mounted a campaign promoting another option involving the private sector rather than local government.

Dissemination. These guides (Seekins, Note 4) are available through the Center for Public Affairs and the Research and Training Center on Independent Living at the University of Kansas. Guides for other aspects of using personal opinions to influence public decisions, including identifying important issues, writing letters to elected officials, and preparing position papers for groups, are in preparation.

Implications. Letters to the editor printed in newspapers are an important mechanism for shaping public opinion. Similarly, testimony provided to decisionmakers can influence public policy significantly. The availability of easy to use guides for preparing and delivering personal testimony extends the power of groups to influence events within their community. However, the use of these tools and the responses they help to shape takes place within a context of other actors who may use more powerful means to counteract, to punish, or to obscure these efforts. As such, these tools might be used in combination with other strategies for extending the influence of disadvantaged groups over issues that affect them.

Case Study #7: Developing and Communicating Information About the Public Acceptance of Lifeline Energy Rates for Elderly, Low-Income, and Disabled People

Recently, members of a statewide advocacy group (for utility assistance for poor families) and a representative of a local community action agency requested assistance in facilitating adoption of lifeline utility rates for poor families. "Lifeline" rates are a form of utility rate design in which lower rates are charged for targeted groups to provide for a minimum of heat for the coldest winter months. The Community Technology Project agreed to help design a survey research study to examine public support for such an action by the city commission (in Lawrence, Kansas) which had authority to set rates as part of its franchise with a local distributor of natural gas.

Problem. Increases in natural gas rates exceeding 200% in the past several years have resulted in a serious threat to the financial

security and health of many residents. For residents fortunate
enough to have their jobs, their youth, and their health, the problem
of providing adequate heat remains serious. For those who are
elderly, without means of support for their families, or with a permanent disability, the problem can be life threatening. Although the
local city commission appeared to have the authority to set reduced
utility rates for needy families, this alternative was not on the public
agenda before this study.

Policy research study. A policy research study (Fawcett, Seekins,
& Lewis, Note 5) was designed to obtain information on the perceived social importance of adequate heat in the winter months and
the perceived social acceptability of a change in rate design to provide reduced utility rates for poor families during the winter months.
A random sample of Lawrence residents was contacted by phone
and asked their opinions by volunteer interviewers from church and
community groups. The results suggested that, at the time of the
survey (September), an overwhelming majority (86%) of the city's
residents over 18 years of age supported an action by the city commission to reduce natural gas rates for persons who are elderly, low-
income, or disabled. Further, a similar number (81%) indicated a
willingness to contribute a portion of their monthly gas bill to such a
program—an average contribution of nearly three dollars per
month. The report was presented to the city commission during a
study session in October regarding utility issues. In view of these
results, the city commission requested that a detailed proposal—later called the Lawrence Lifeline Plan—be prepared by the
researchers and the representatives of the statewide utility assistance
group and a community action agency.

Lawrence lifeline plan. The Lawrence Lifeline Plan (Lewis,
Hackney, Fawcett, & Seekins, Note 6) was developed based on a
review of similar lifeline programs in other states and consultation
with the city commissioners, representatives of the gas service company, attorneys knowledgeable in law regarding utility rate reform,
and clients and providers of poverty services. The plan, as modified
during deliberations by the commissioners, called for the creation of
a new customer class that would include those households judged to
be eligible for that season based on household income guidelines
similar to federal poverty standards. Using poverty data from a recent census, it was estimated that approximately 1600 local families
could benefit.

As proposed in the plan, beneficiaries would receive a 50% reduction in rate for the first 15 mcfs (i.e., 1000 cubic feet) of gas for the billing cycles covering the two coldest months (i.e., January and February). Assuming an average consumption of 25 mcfs per month during these winter months, an eligible family's bill would be reduced from $131 per month without lifeline (more than one third of the combined household income for some families) to $91 with lifeline. The total cost of the program for the estimated 1600 beneficiaries could be recovered by an average monthly charge of $.62 per month for 12 months for the city's 16,300 ratepayers. This plan represented an estimated total public investment of $121,000 in winter utility assistance for needy families.

Outcomes. Nearly three months passed between the presentation of the Lawrence Lifeline Plan to the city commission in October and a final decision in January. During this period the designers of the plan provided technical assistance to the commissioners regarding the plan, answering questions at study sessions and at near-weekly televised meetings of the city commission. Prominent advocates of the plan included a local advisory committee composed of persons with disabilities, a local poverty organization, and representatives of a local council on community services. These and other persons wrote letters to the commissioners and to the local newspaper supporting the plan and provided expert and personal testimony at televised meetings of the city commission.

The publisher of the only commercial newspaper opposed the action, assailing it in a series of editorials as an attack on our basic economic system and as a government handout that would contribute to laziness among the poor. Several days after support for the plan by four of the five commissioners was announced, the publisher joined the head of a large local industry that has opposed lifeline plans in other states in spearheading a charitable campaign that raised $60,000 for utility bills for needy families. In two weeks of full page ads donated by the newspaper and a series of front page stories, this program ("Lawrence Warm Hearts") was characterized as a sufficient response that was consistent with the spirit of charity and volunteerism. With ample newspaper coverage and financial support from businesspeople who opposed the overall policies of some of the current commissioners, a citizen opposition group was formed. During one city commission meeting attended by nearly 100 members of this group, a petition with 2,000 signatures was presented that called for rejection of the lifeline plan. In a well-publicized news conference, this group also threatened the recall of the commissioners who supported the plan.

City commissioners modified the original proposal, reducing the proposed benefit from the first 20 mcfs to the first 10 mcfs and requiring evidence that beneficiaries attempt to reduce heat loss by using low-cost weatherization materials. The commissioners supported the plan on the first two readings with votes of 5-0 and 4-1. At a study session just 24 hours before the final vote, there appeared to be a 3-2 majority supporting the plan. However, in the final vote, only two votes of support remained, and a motion to appoint a task force to study the issue further was substituted and passed.

Dissemination. Copies of the policy study and model lifeline plan have been distributed to utility companies, energy assistance advocates, and others at local and state levels. In addition, reports have been disseminated to energy advocacy organizations at the national level, such as the National Consumer Law Center.

Implications. Decisions about what issues and alternatives are considered by policymakers are routinely made with minimum influence from the disadvantaged. Policy research studies such as this can provide timely information that increases the likelihood that actions will be taken regarding problems affecting the poor. Accordingly, such empowerment methods can enhance public influence over decisionmakers and extend the resources with which poor families attempt to control their lives. However, some objectives of empowerment efforts may lead to the active involvement of a network of actors who have previously extended major influence over the community's resources and decisions regarding their allocation. In such circumstances currently available tools to facilitate community empowerment may often be inadequate.

ETHICAL ANALYSIS OF THE EMPOWERMENT STRATEGY

Although *how* to improve community effectiveness may be enhanced by these and other empowerment technologies, questions of *what* goals should be sought and for *whom* are essentially questions of philosophy and ethics (Fawcett et al., 1980). The choice of the empowerment strategy—rather than another approach to planned change—might be informed by an analysis of ethical issues implicit in this approach. Following the framework suggested by Warwick and Kelman (1976), we will consider the empowerment strategy as it relates to the choice of goals, the selection of the targets of change, the choice of means, and the analysis of consequences for the targets, change agents, and society in general.

Choice of Goals

The choice of specific goals for an empowerment strategy represents an important standard for analyzing the ethics of empowerment activities. For example, attaining the goal of improving the skills of a chairperson (Case 5) may enhance the group's knowledge of available options (the value of freedom), the chairperson's personal sense of worth and competence (the value of self-esteem), and the fair treatment of group members in decisionmaking (the value of justice). However, this same goal may have other effects such as decreasing the variety of ways individuals may choose to contribute to debates and decisions (the value of freedom). In addition, the change agent might attempt to preserve these values by allowing disadvantaged people a greater role in choosing the problems to be selected and specification steps to be implemented (as in Cases 1 & 2). An understanding of the ideal state implicit in the choice of goals may help to inform choices designed to maximize values that may be in conflict.

Selection of Targets

The choice of target or recipient of the empowerment activity may also have ethical implications. For example, the targets of the empowerment technologies described in this manuscript were either disadvantaged individuals or community groups. The targets had minimal power to control their lives or to influence important decisions in their communities. Empowerment of these targets may reduce feelings of inadequacy (the value of self-esteem) and the discrepancy between opportunities for political and economic status for more and less empowered groups (the value of justice). However, it may simultaneously reduce the social harmony within the community (the value of security) or the amount of charitable contributions made available by more wealthy benefactors (the value of general welfare). The choice of target may have different, and sometimes opposing, effects with values held to varying degrees by different groups.

Several strategies may be helpful in mitigating the possible negative effects of selecting a target. First, the participation of targets in the empowerment effort should be ensured. For example, as with the use of the concerns report method with disabled citizens (Case 2), some portion of the targeted group was involved in defining the problem, choosing goals for action, designing and conducting the intervention, and maintaining follow-up activities. Second, protections for targets who participate should be provided, including provisions for voluntary entry and exit from the program and accountability of the researchers, human service professionals, and local change agents to public agencies. Other conditions that may ensure protection of targets include arranging negative consequences that are controlled by the targets, or conditions in which targets and change agents are similarly vulnerable to possible negative consequences of empowerment efforts. For example, sustained involvement of professionals with indigenous leaders of a low-income community or neighborhood organization may increase the chances that professionals and leaders would be similarly vulnerable to the effects of planned demonstrations or other politically sensitive activities. However, despite these protections, it remains likely that relatively powerless groups will have only modest capacities to resist becoming targets of change agents' efforts to effect increases in empowerment.

Choice of Means

Obviously, the choice of means used in the empowerment effort affects the ethics of the action. Warwick and Kelman (1976) listed five types of means: facilitation, environmental manipulation, persuasion, psychic manipulation, and coercion.

Facilitation. Facilitation is defined as "making it easier for an individual or group to implement his own choice or satisfy his own desires" (Warwick & Kelman, 1976, p. 491). Efforts to remove obstacles to action—such as providing information on community concerns (Cases 1 & 2)—are illustrative of this type of means. Facilitation efforts are consistent with the value of freedom insofar as they provide external circumstances that allow individuals and groups to act on their decisions.

Environmental manipulation. Environmental manipulation is defined as a "deliberate act of changing the structure of the alternatives in the environment" (Warwick & Kelman, 1976, p. 486).

Types of environmental manipulation include instruction, motivational procedures, and structural changes in the environment. Examples in this manuscript use instruction to increase skills in group leadership (Case 5), letter writing to public forums (Case 6), and public testimony to decision-making groups (Case 6). Insofar as this instruction increases the options of individuals and groups to affect decisions in their lives it may be consistent with the values of freedom and justice.

Persuasion. Persuasion is defined as "a form of interpersonal influence in which one person tries to change the attitudes or behavior of another by means of argument, reasoning, or, in certain cases, structured listening" (Warwick & Kelman, 1976, p. 490). Persuasion includes the use of rationales or the structured presentation of consequences (positive or negative) regarding an action. For example, the use of the consequence analysis guide to influence opinions about the proposed roadway (Case 3) may illustrate a type of persuasion campaign designed to attempt to present unbiased information. A judgment about the ethics of a particular persuasion campaign would appear to depend on the relative capacity of individuals or groups representing other viewpoints to develop counter-persuasion campaigns. In the case of the roadway project, resources of the local newspaper, the city commission, and the chamber of commerce appeared to be more than adequate to develop a campaign to persuade citizens to support the roadway.

Psychic manipulation. Psychic manipulation is defined as a "deliberate act of changing personal qualities affecting choice without the knowledge of the person involved" (Warwick & Kelman, 1976, p. 486). This issue might be raised with virtually all empowerment efforts: To what extent are the targets of empowerment efforts aware that their control over their lives will be affected? As the effectiveness of empowerment efforts is increased, issues regarding the informed consent of targets of empowerment efforts should assume greater importance.

Coercion. Coercion is defined as taking place "when one person or group forces another person or group to act or refrain from acting under the threat of severe deprivation" (Warwick & Kelman, 1976, p. 484). For example, the Lawrence Lifeline Plan (Case 7) that was adopted by the city commission included a type of coercion by requiring ratepayers to subsidize reductions in natural gas bills for low-income families. Such coercive elements of government actions would appear to be justified when there is either a clear and present danger to basic societal values (such as security or survival) or there is a need for prompt and positive action to meet an important goal.

Analysis of the Consequences

Ultimately, the ethics of a particular empowerment strategy rest on the balance of its consequences for the targets, change agent(s), and society. The consequences for each type of recipient are considered separately.

Consequences for targets. Presumably, the freedom of targets is enhanced by activities that broaden the range of choices for the targets, that increase their knowledge of the problem and its causes, that extend knowledge of choices or alternatives, that increase capacities to weigh or consider alternatives, or that remove obstacles to choosing and acting on alternatives (Warwick & Kelman, 1976). For example, the concerns report method (Cases 1 & 2)—by increasing knowledge of strengths, problems, and alternatives for action—appears to facilitate a number of positive consequences for targets of empowerment programs. However, insofar as empowerment efforts put at risk the values or resources of competing groups, they may result in aversive consequences or the loss of positive consequences for targets. For example, appearing in public to provide testimony may expose an individual to rude or derogatory comments by the opposition or may result in the loss of benefits. The change agents have a responsibility to actively seek detection of possible harmful side affects of such advocacy activities.

Consequences for the change agent. As noted by Warwick & Kelman (1976), two criteria may be particularly important. First, the targets—not the change agents—must be the primary beneficiaries of the empowerment program. Second, the target should be less (not more) dependent on the change agent as a result of the empowerment activity. The ethics of so-called "empowerment" programs should be questioned if they result in considerable monetary gain for the change agent or in increased reliance on professionals for consultation.

Consequences for society. Warwick and Kelman (1976) suggest that several consequences for society may be of special concern. First, the integrative values and norms of the subculture may be weakened or destroyed as a result of the empowerment activity. For example, by requiring all utility ratepayers to subsidize reduced rates for low-income families, voluntary charitable contributions for such groups may be decreased. Second, the empowerment activity should achieve a balance between the target group's aspirations and the opportunity for achieving them. For example, by drawing attention to longstanding social problems, the concerns report method (Case 1 & 2) might raise expectations for remediating action without increasing substantially the resources required to affect needed improvements. Finally, the empowerment effort should increase the power of the target group relative to other groups in society. For example, although the study circle procedure (Case 4) may increase the group's control over the proposed intervention, it may increase to an even greater degree the change agent's control over the target's use of the program.

Summary

This section provides a framework for analyzing several important ethical considerations: the choice of goals, the selection of targets, the choice of means, and the analysis of consequences. A consideration of these ethical issues may help to inform difficult choices in the work of empowerment. Further analytical work might yield explicit ethical guidelines that could make this analysis more systematic and subject to review by those affected by such efforts.

DISCUSSION

A prominent goal of an empowerment orientation is to discover promising empowerment methods through field research and to make these methods available to the public (Rappaport, 1981). The social technologies described in this manuscript represent an attempt to design "tools" with which human service professionals can increase the effectiveness of their collaborative efforts with local change agents and targets. Insofar as these detailed descriptions of empowerment methods facilitate their implementation in other communities, the cost and complexity of empowerment efforts may be somewhat reduced. Similarly, insofar as adopters make changes in these methods to fit local conditions, the variety of available tools for enhancing empowerment will be increased (Seekins & Fawcett, in press).

Two particularly important limitations of this work should be noted. First, considerable procedural detail has been included in each social technology to increase the chances of successful implementation by human service professionals and local change agents. However, in an effort to maximize the simplicity of these technologies, detail regarding the complexity of the context in which they might be used was omitted. Some important judgments about when such technologies might be used and how they might be adapted to fit new and changing local circumstances remains more in the area of art than technology. Perhaps subsequent attention to conditions in which systematic replications of these technologies are successful (and not successful) may increase the reliability of such judgments.

Second, the described social technologies represent neither a complete approach for any one goal nor a complete array of tools for community empowerment. For example, the chairperson training program (Case 5) represents only one of the important classes of behaviors that might increase the effectiveness of community leaders or group decision-making. Similarly, the policy research method used to promote consideration of lifeline energy rates (Case 7) reflects only a portion of the strategy and resources required to effect adoption of more fundamental changes. Like shovels and hoes, these empowerment "tools" cannot produce changes in the environment on their own. Rather, these social technologies are designed to amplify the effectiveness of change agents who will bring to bear other knowledge and competencies required to affect increases in community empowerment.

The use of a *technological* approach to empowerment appears to be self-contradictory, a kind of paradox. By adopting a social technology, the human service professional may give up some *control* over the choice of specific actions to take in a particular situation such as how to teach a leader to run an effective group meeting. However, if the social technology is functional, the new skills of the group leader may extend the group's control over decisions that affect the lives of its members. Thus, the design and use of social technologies may be quite consistent with the goal of empowerment. Indeed, empowerment may be the kind of divergent problem for which diverse and seemingly contradictory solutions may be expected and welcomed (Fawcett et al., 1980; Rappaport, 1981; Schumacher, 1977).

A second paradox implied by community empowerment is that an *individual* may have to relinquish some control in order to gain more. Each of the technologies described focuses on a group working cooperatively to achieve common ends; the strength of the individuals multiplied by their number. But when individuals join a group they may lose some control and freedom over the selection of issues addressed and solutions implemented. Thus, group participation on common problems may require short-term restrictions on individual freedom to extend control for individual members of a larger community.

A final paradox is that by increasing the power of more individuals and groups, the capacities of the entire community to take any one action may be reduced. In settings containing newly empowered individuals or groups, the increased variety of opinions may result in conflict and reduced efficiency in making decisions and taking subsequent action. As power is extended beyond a previously small network of extraordinarily influential actors, the likelihood of decisive action on any one problem may decrease. Community empowerment requires a critical balancing act between extending opportunities for control over community decisions *and* maximizing efficiency in community functioning.

Kahn (1970) ask rhetorically what the poor and powerless would say about their treatment by society:

> That I needed a home, and you gave me Food Stamps;
> That I needed a job, and you got me on the Welfare;
> That my family was sick, and you gave us your used clothes;
> That I needed my pride and dignity as a man, and you gave me surplus beans. (p. 124)

Justice requires improved opportunities for the powerless to obtain what they need to sustain their lives and to pursue happiness with a chance of success. To the extent that all of us can gain control over our needs, society's charity may be less necessary. Perhaps the design and use of empowerment technologies by human service professionals can help foster the dignity and respect that can come with self-determination.

REFERENCE NOTES

1. Whang, P. L., Fawcett, S. B., Suarez de Balcazar, Y., & Seekins, T. *A systematic method for disabled citizens to set agendas for community development.* (Available from the Center for Public Affairs or the Research and Training Center on Independent Living at the University of Kansas for the cost of reproduction and mailing.)

2. Sanford, F. L., & Fawcett, S. B. *Community impact analysis: Assessing the possible effects of planned environmental change.* (Available from the Center for Public Affairs.)

3. Seekins, T., & Fawcett, S. B. *Study circles: A method for involving local adopters in the reinvention of innovative programs.* (Available from the Center for Public Affairs.)

4. Seekins, T. *A guide to preparing and presenting brief personal testimony: The art of using your personal experiences to influence public decisions.* Seekins, T. *A guide to writing letters to the editor: Expressing your opinion to the public effectively.* (Available from the Center for Public Affairs or the Research and Training Center on Independent Living.)

5. Fawcett, S. B., Seekins, T., & Lewis, T. *Report on Lawrence (Kansas) citizens' attitudes about lifeline energy rates for persons who are elderly, low-income, disabled.* (Available from the Center for Public Affairs or the Research and Training Center on Independent Living.)

6. Lewis, T., Hackney, P., Fawcett, S. B., & Seekins, T. *Lawrence (Kansas) lifeline plan.* (Available from the Center for Public Affairs or the Research and Training Center on Independent Living.)

REFERENCES

Alinsky, S. D. *Reveille for radicals.* New York: Vintage Books, 1969.

Banfield, E. C. *Political influence.* New York: The Free Press, 1961.

Briscoe, R. V., Hoffman, D. B., & Bailey, J. S. Behavioral community psychology: Training a community board to problem-solve. *Journal of Applied Behavior Analysis,* 1975, *8,* 1957-168.

Cobb, R., & Elder, C. *Participation in American politics: The dynamics of agenda building.* Baltimore: John Hopkins University Press, 1977.

Dobyns, H. F., Doughty, P. L., & Lasswell, H. D. (Eds.). *Peasants, power and applied social change: Vicos as a model.* Beverly Hills, CA: Sage Publications, 1971.

Fawcett, S. B., Fletcher, R. K., Mathews, R. M., Whang, P. L., Seekins, T., & Nielsen, L. M. Designing behavioral technologies with community self-help organizations. In A. M. Jeger & R. S. Slotnick (Eds.), *Community mental health and behavioral-ecology: A handbook of theory, research, and practice.* New York: Plenum Press, 1982.

Fawcett, S. B., Mathews, R. M., & Fletcher, R. K. Some promising dimensions for behavioral community technology. *Journal of Applied Behavior Analysis,* 1980, *13,* 505-518.

Fawcett, S. B., Seekins, T., Whang, P. W., Muiu, C., & Suarez de Balcazar, Y. Involving consumers in decision-making. *Social Policy,* 1982, *13,* 36-41.

Finsterbusch, K., & Wolf, C. P. *Methodology of social impact assessment.* Stroudsburg, PA: Dowden, Hutchinson, & Ross, 1977.

Francis, M. Urban impact assessment and community involvement. *Environment and Behavior,* 1975, *7,* 373-404.

Friere, P. *Education for critical consciousness.* New York: Seaburg Press, 1973.

Frieden, L. Independent living models. *Rehabilitation Literature,* 1980, *41* (7, 8) 169-173.

Hinrichs, J. R. *Practical management for productivity.* New York: Van Nostrand Reinhold Company, 1978.

Johnson, H. R., & Tropman, J. E. The settings of community organization practice. In Fred M. Cox, J. L. Erlich, J. Rothman, & J. E. Tropman (Eds.), *Strategies of community organization* (3rd ed.). Itasca, IL: F. E. Peacock, 1979.

Kahn, S. *How people get power.* New York: McGraw Hill Book Company, 1970.

Kennard, B. Organization emphasis: Public's role is assessing technology. *Small Town,* 1976, *7,* 10.

Kessler, M., & Albee, G. W. Primary prevention. *Annual Review of Psychology,* 1975, *26,* 557-591.

Kutchins, H., & Kutchins, S. Advocacy and social work. In G. H. Weber & G. J. McCall (Eds.), *Social scientists as advocates.* Beverly Hills, CA: Sage Publications, 1978.

McCoy, C. R. The impact of an impact study. *Environment and Behavior,* 1975, *7,* 358-372.

Nelken, D. *Technological decisions and democracy: European experiments in public participation.* Beverly Hills, CA: Sage, 1977.

Nelken, D. Scientific knowledge, public policy, and democracy: A review essay. *Knowledge: Creation, Diffusion, Utilization,* 1979, *1*, 106-122.

Patner, M. Advocacy and the public interest lawyer. In G. H. Weber & G. J. McCall (Eds.), *Social scientists as advocates.* Beverly Hills, CA: Sage Publications, 1978.

Piven, F. F., & Cloward, R. A. *Poor people's movements.* New York: Random House Vintage Books, 1979.

Rappaport, J. In praise of paradox: A social policy of empowerment over prevention. *American Journal of Community Psychology,* 1981, *9*, 1-25.

Rawls, J. *A theory of justice.* Cambridge, MA: Harvard University Press, 1971.

Ryan, W. *Blaming the victim.* New York: Random House Vintage Books, 1971.

Sanford, F. L., & Fawcett, S. B. Consequence analysis: Its effects on verbal statements about an environmental project. *Journal of Applied Behavior Analysis,* 1980, *13*, 57-64.

Schattschneider, E. E. *The semi-sovereign people: A realist's view of democracy in America.* New York: Holt, Rinehart, & Winston, 1960.

Schumacher, E. F. *A guide for the perplexed.* New York: Harper & Row, 1977.

Seekins, T., & Fawcett, S. B. Planned diffusion of social technologies for community groups. In S. C. Paine, G. T. Bellamy, & B. Wilcox (Eds.), *Human services that work: From innovation to standard practice.* Baltimore, MD: Paul Brookes, in press.

Seekins, T., Mathews, R. M., & Fawcett, S. B. Enhancing leadership skills for community self-help organizations through behavioral instruction. *Journal of Community Psychology,* in press.

Tocqueville, A. American notes. In *Annals of America.* Chicago: Encyclopaedia Britannica, Inc., 1976, *5*, p. 489.

Walker, J. L. Setting the agenda in the U.S. Senate: A theory of problem selection. *Journal of Political Science,* 1977, *7*, 423-445.

Warren, R. L. *Social change and human purpose: Toward understanding and action.* Chicago: Rand McNally College Publishing Company, 1977.

Warwick, D. P., & Kelman, H. C. Ethical issues in social intervention. In W. G. Bennis, K. D. Benne, R. Chin, & K. E. Corey (Eds.), *The planning of change* (3rd ed.). New York: Holt, Rinehart, and Winston, 1976, Pp. 470-496.

Zippo, M. Productivity and morale sagging? Try the quality circle approach. *Personnel,* May 1980, *3*, 43-44.

The Illusion of Empowerment: Community Development Within a Colonial Context

Irma Serrano-García

ABSTRACT. This paper presents a community development experience in Puerto Rico which was guided by the goal of empowerment. It describes the socio-historical context in which the effort is embedded, its values, and its theoretical background. The intervention was carried out in a poor rural community of approximately 1,400 families. Specific strategies and tactics used to facilitate ideological and skill development among the residents are presented. The article concludes with an analysis of the achievements and limitations of the effort. Guidelines toward future conceptual and practical developments are suggested.

The community development effort presented here arises from the will of a group of people who do not understand, much less tolerate, oppression even though they live in a colonial situation. The effort arises from a group that believes in equality and freedom and in the capacity of human beings to achieve both. It arises within community psychology, a discipline with a sense of urgency and a belief in change.

As a member of that group, I write as both a Puerto Rican and a community psychologist. My work stems from a social change perspective. As a community psychologist with a commitment to the "disadvantaged" groups of society, I believe that my values should be clearly stated. I am immersed in a particular reality. Puerto Rico is an island in the Caribbean, 100 miles long and 35 miles wide, with a population of almost 3 million people. This makes it one of the most densely populated areas of the world.

The island was under Spanish colonial rule from 1493 to 1898

Reprints may be obtained from Irma Serrano-García, Department of Psychology, University of Puerto Rico, Rio Piedras, Puerto Rico 00931.

173

making our traditions mainly hispanic and our language, Spanish. The country was turned over to the United States as war booty of the Spanish American War in 1898 and at present is a "commonwealth." This means that we have powers over some aspects of our internal governmental structure. However, the following areas are still being controlled exclusively by the United States: applicability of the federal constitution, foreign trade, citizenship, jurisdiction of the federal courts, internal and external navigation, applicability of federal legislation, immigration, communications, internal relations, military service, postal services, currency, military bases, transportation, patents, bankruptcy, maritime limits, coastguard and establishment of treaties. Other areas that are controlled jointly by our government and the United States are: environmental protection, forests, monopolies, ports and airports, minerals, internal trade, quarantine laws, labor procedures and minimum wages (Berríos, 1980).

Economically at present (1) over 60% of the population has an annual income of $2,500 or less, (2) over 70% receives food stamps or current substitutes, (3) 70% of our industry is in foreign hands, (4) 90% of industrial profits leave the island, (5) 78% of our local production is spent on our external debt, (6) official unemployment is up to 22.7%, and (7) 99% of our food is imported. To top the bill, our cost of living is 15% higher than in the United States (Nieves Falcon, 1978; Colon Parrilla, Note 1; Programa del PIP, Note 2). Our reality is one of colonization and not self-determination, of hispanic not anglo-saxon traditions and of underdevelopment and not economic growth.

Taking this reality into account and being concerned with the need to change it, a community development effort directed by the quest of empowerment was begun in 1980. This paper describes the empowerment perspective and its application to this effort. It is a case study, emphasizing theoretical base, guiding values and the particular ways in which empowerment was fostered. Both successes and failures are described. Finally, the paper raises questions that are left unanswered and some thoughts on "the illusion of empowerment."

EMPOWERMENT

The empowerment perspective challenges inequality and states that it can only be overcome by altering imbalances in wealth and power (Ryan, 1971). Empowerment requires that measures be taken so that individuals are better able to control their own lives. This is achieved, in part, if they gain access to and possession of available resources (Rappaport, 1981).

The economically and socially disadvantaged lack resources, thus they lack power. Rogers (1975) defines power as "the holding of some number and quantity of attributes, circumstances or possessions that increase the ability of the holder to influence a person or group" (p. 1428). If individuals obtain greater resources they should also obtain greater control of their lives. They should be empowered.

However, our quest for empowerment is not fostered only by an ideology of equality. "Learned helplessness" (or perceived lack of power over situations) has been shown to lead to non-adaptive individual behaviors. Seligman, Greer, and Maier (1968) and Rappaport (1977) suggest that the same analysis can be applied to groups and communities, where learned helplessness is exhibited through apathy and alienation. At the community level, lack of power is related to the absence of a psychological sense of community (Sarason, 1974). At the societal level, and particularly important to the Puerto Rican situation, are the deleterious effects of national lack of power: colonialism.

Fanon (1968) and Memmi (1965) have described the individual and social decay that prolonged colonialism generates. This includes self-debasement, alienation, loss of cultural identity, dependency, and internally directed hostility.

Intertwined within these levels of analysis are the different developmental stages of empowerment. Keiffer (1982) has pointed out that empowerment at the individual level is characterized by three phases:

> (1) development of a more potent sense of self-in-relation to the world, (2) construction of more critical comprehension of the social and political forces which comprise one's daily life world and (3) cultivation of functional strategies and resources for attainment of personal or collective socio-political roles. (p. 14)

This framework points out two choice points for professionals directed by the quest for empowerment: the level of intervention and the developmental phase of empowerment. It is not a limiting choice but one of emphasis. Where are one's scarce resources best used in trying to facilitate empowerment?

My efforts have been directed at the community level and at the first two developmental stages of empowerment. The community level was selected because I believe: (1) that collective efforts are necessary to achieve control of resources, (2) that "disadvantaged" groups are usually geographically located, (3) that people need successful ventures in the environment they know best so as to risk entering larger and unknown settings, and (4) that all other intervention levels, except the macro-social, are included in community efforts in an all-encompassing manner.

I have chosen the first two developmental phases of empowerment because I believe that before strategies and tactics are selected people should identify available ones and learn to choose among them (Pargament & Myers, Note 3). Those who undertake individual or collective actions should also have the critical skills to examine their intended and unintended outcomes. In addition, the political and cultural alienation of Puerto Rican Society (Perfecto & Santiago, Note 4) requires the development of critical thinking and questioning.

In summary, this paper is written by a Puerto Rican community psychologist who has chosen community level interventions geared toward the first two phases of empowerment as those most suited to Puerto Rico's needs. The next section of this paper emphasizes the "how" of empowerment. It is to the development of creative interventions and research that most of my efforts have been devoted.

PROYECTO ESFUERZO: AN INTERVENTION WITHIN RESEARCH GUIDING VALUES AND THEORETICAL FRAMEWORK

Values

The community project described here was conducted as a practicum for the Social-Community Psychology Graduate Program at the University of Puerto Rico. It has been guided by the Intervention within Research model (Irizarry & Serrano, 1979) and one of its subsequent modifications (Serrano & Alvarez, Note 5) and is permeated by our values regarding the nature of scientific endeavors and community work.

We have a strong belief in the need for research within change efforts. The research, however, should be directed by a commitment to its participants, regardless of methodological disadvantages (Serrano, López, & Rivera, Note 6). We believe in the development of a collaborative relationship between residents and scientists. To allow for this, both groups must recognize that research efforts contain values and ideologies. Community residents have values knowledge, skills, and behaviors different from, not inferior to, scientific ones. This viewpoint requires that both groups learn and unlearn from each other (Serrano, Suárez, Alvarez, & Rosario, Note 7). It is also important for researchers to be aware of their "outsider" status and to recognize that their own needs and resources as well as those of the residents are important (Serrano, Note 8).

Our value considerations regarding community work are encompassed by (1) our belief in cultural relativity and diversity (Rappaport, 1977), (2) our commitment to the so called disadvantaged groups of society and to the just distribution of power (Martí & Serrano, Note 9), (3) our confidence in community residents' abilities to identify their needs and resources, generate a collective view of society and become responsible for their own change (Perfecto & Santiago, Note 4), and (4) the conviction that community work requires ideological analysis or consciousness-raising so as to facilitate empowerment (Serrano, Note 8).

Framework: Main Features

Intervention within Research (Irizarry & Serrano, 1979) is both a community development and a research model. Its main feature relates both aspects by conceptualizing the processes of intervention and research as simultaneous and interdependent, although distinguishable. It is assumed that all interventions have a research component (whether formal or informal) and that all researchers have an impact on the participants and the settings of their studies, willingly or not.

The conceptualization of both processes as simultaneous has important implications for social change efforts.

> A questionnaire can be administered by assuming an expertise stance from afar, without explaining its purposes or applications for participants. The same questionnaire can be administered in a manner which denotes friendship, equality and collaborativeness. Although the research components of such data collection may be identical (the same procedure, instruments

and data were used and obtained) the intervention may be radically different and thus the acceptance of the data and of whatever plans might emerge from it could be contingent on the simultaneous "intervention within research." Since this is the case, then we propose that this "intervention within research" be as carefully planned as the methodology has been. (Serrano, López, & Rivera, Note 6, p. 23)

Another main feature of the model is its commitment to participants. When carrying out formal research, the model requires the following: (1) that information, attitudes, and opinions be given as well as obtained, (2) that services be provided if requested, (3) that the study's purpose be explained, (4) that the definition of categories and terms arise from the participants, and (5) that if programs are to develop from the collected data they be planned jointly (Serrano, López, & Rivera, Note 6).

The third main feature of this model is that it should be permeated by the ideological analysis that leads to consciousness-raising. Through ideological analysis, the consciousness of the individual or group should increase from its current or "real" level to its possible capacity. Real consciousness refers to an individual's or group's current understanding of reality, while possible consciousness is the maximum understanding of reality that can be achieved at a given point in time (Goldmann, 1970). The change from one to the other signifies that "consciousness-raising includes critical judgement of situations, the search for underlying causes of problems and their consequences, and an active role in the transformation of society" (Martí & Serrano, Note 9, p. 3).

The last important feature of this model is that it requires redefinition of the role of the change agent. He or she must develop many more skills than are usually expected. These include political, administrative, community mobilization, and organizational skills (Freed, 1967; Rothman, 1974). Values must be explicitly stated and models and tools congruent with them must be developed. The most difficult task is to abandon the "expert" role, not by denying acquired knowledge, but by accepting the lack of it, and by creating collaborative strategies where decisions and actions are carried out with participants.

The Intervention within Research model that was used in Proyecto Esfuerzo is a modification of the original model (Serrano & Alvarez, Note 5). Its phases include:

1. *Familiarization with the community*—Visits to and a review of all written material about the community.
2. *Needs, resources, and expectations assessment.*
3. *Linking reality: Follow-up agency work*—Obtaining information regarding governmental agency involvement in the community.
4. *Concrete activities and resident's integration*—Residents become actively engaged as decision makers and doers in the project's activities.
5. *Transition*—Strategies that allow the interveners to leave the project.
6. *End of project*—This is achieved when the interveners leave the community.

These phases will be used as guidelines to summarize the history of Proyecto Esfuerzo. The report will show the concrete actions that embody our values and theories.

HISTORY OF PROYECTO ESFUERZO

The Community

"Esfuerzo" is a rural community of approximately 1,400 families. It is located in an area at high risk of flood. Its residents have an average monthly income of $255.73 per family, most of which is obtained from welfare and other governmental benefits.

Esfuerzo was established in 1969 and its residents have lived in the community an average of 6.7 years. They came to this location in three groups. One group was relocated by the government when they lost their homes as a result of a hurricane. Another group obtained their land in a government raffle, and the third have slowly occupied land or houses close to relatives.

The community has civic leaders who are active in trying to solve community problems and various local groups of a political, religious, and civic nature. The two main political parties on the island are represented locally as are the Catholic and Protestant religions.

The community's major difficulty is a need to be relocated, due to the risk of flooding. It is unclear when this will take place, although government authorities basically admit that it is necessary. Legislation has been drafted but approval has been delayed for a number of years. The civic leaders have fought for relocation through a variety of strategies but their efforts have been unsuccessful.

Other community needs and problems include: disastrous road conditions, lack of telephone service, erratic garbage collection, and weak water pressure. There is also an expressed need for social and community activities such as sports and recreational events, craft courses, musical events, excursions to different sites, and the like.

Creation of the project. Proyecto Esfuerzo started as the continuation of an effort initiated by the consultation and education (C & E) unit of a community mental health center (CMHC). This unit had been involved with the community during a flood in 1979 but ceased its intervention due to a lack of resources. In January 1980, a new head was appointed to the C & E unit and she requested a community development effort in Esfuerzo with joint CMHC and university (UPR) resources.

From this point on, with some variations, the project consisted of (a) a coordinating group with CMHC staff, university professors, and graduate students, and (b) undergraduate student groups. Although residents were informed of our tasks during the initial stages of our work they were not directly involved until the first phases of the intervention had taken place. Those phases are limited to gaining information about the community before actively trying to organize it.

Familiarization with the community. The informative stage was initiated in January of 1980 by reviewing a needs assessment carried out during the original CMHC intervention, by reading newspaper articles about the community, and by talking to those who had intervened there previously. We also visited the community several times. Formal entry was made in May, 1981 by distributing a leaflet to all residents informing them of the creation of the project and of our intention of working with them to solve community problems. The initial familiarization phase concluded with this effort.

Needs, resources, and expectations assessment. During the summer of 1981 our visits to the community increased and another needs assessment was carried out. Thirty (30) key persons were interviewed. These were selected by asking available residents to identify people who had one or more of the following characteristics: (a) more than 5 years living in Esfuerzo, (b) ownership or employment in local businesses, and (c) leadership of religious, political, recreational, and/or civic groups. Varied criteria were used because a previous community experience had shown us that political community leaders were control, not change, agents (Serrano, Súarez, Alvarez, & Rosario, Note 7; Alvarez, Note 10). Thus, we did not want to rely on them exclusively.

This procedure generated a list of 38 people, 30 of whom were interviewed. Some were members of the civic group and we obtained details about their efforts at relocation. We also met with workers from other social agencies that were active in Esfuerzo at the time.

A summary of the interview data was prepared and distributed to all participants. Our presentation emphasized the resources residents had identified, the activities they suggested, and the willingness that most of them expressed to work jointly toward the solution of their problems.

Linking Reality: Follow-up on Agency Work

Both our informal contacts and the needs assessment identified the issue of relocation as the residents' greatest concern. However, both also showed that information available to them was confusing, unevenly distributed, and incomplete. Most project members even had doubts about whether a flood risk really existed. These doubts made it difficult for them to take a position regarding whether to support or oppose relocation.

In order to clarify the facts for the residents and for ourselves we carried out a series of interviews with eight governmental agencies involved in Esfuerzo. The specific data obtained is not relevant here. It is sufficient to say that we were convinced of the need for relocation and of the fact that the residents were not being heard due to political maneuvering and partisan disagreements. A summary of the data collected in these interviews was returned to the agencies' staff and permission requested to provide these facts to community residents. All, except two, agreed. Residents were informed of the identity of the two agencies that refused.

By this time one and one-half years had passed. The process had been lengthened by a university strike which virtually paralyzed the project. However, in April of 1982, we were ready to integrate residents fully into Proyecto Esfuerzo.

Concrete Activities and Residents' Integration

In April, 1982 all key persons interviewed were invited to a meeting to summarize the work of the project, and to create task groups which would work on community needs that had already been identified. We also wanted to know if residents wished to collaborate in diffusing the information that had been obtained. We had a commitment to distribute the data whether they collaborated or not, but if they helped the information could more effectively reach more people. Twenty-three persons attended the meeting; half of them were members of the civic group. Others were key persons interviewed and several individuals who were invited by key persons or happened to pass by the meeting place and were invited in.

We informed the residents of our objectives and emphasized that although the relocation issue was their strongest felt need, our project was not going to work on that. The group already working on it had more information than we could ever hope to gather and had already used all the strategies we could think of to work on the problem. We also explained that it was not our role to compete with established community organizations but to foster their development through coordinated efforts. Thus, we urged all those interested in the relocation issue to work with the civic group.

Two task groups were created. One of them, called the Social Group, was to work on the social and recreational needs that had been identified. It was composed of 8-12 individuals who are not usually considered power holders in Puerto Rican communities: women, aged, and young male non-leaders. The second group, called the Propaganda Group, was formed exclusively to disseminate the interview information to the entire community. This group was composed of 5-7 male members, more than half of whom were members of the civic group. Both groups also had two graduate students and/or CMHC members as facilitators and two undergraduate students to record "verbatim" the group discussions. We sought and obtained permission to take notes.

In future meetings the Social Group established entertainment, orientation, learning, and sharing as its objectives. With these in mind, they decided to organize an all day picnic to the beach. This was preceded by a march throughout the community with the purpose of collecting funds for the activity.

From April to July the group met regularly and sponsored the march and two picnics which they evaluated as successful in meeting their specified goals.

The Propaganda Group decided that the best way to provide the interview data to the community was by organizing a general assembly. We were opposed to this idea because we felt that uniform diffusion of the information could not be achieved in this manner. However, we were overruled and the group devoted its efforts to the assembly which was held in July. Over 400 people attended and the information was provided together with other presentations by government officials regarding relocation.

The Propaganda Group also decided to stop meeting after the assembly. Although we suggested that the group turn to other propaganda tasks (i.e., a community newspaper, a bulletin board), they decided to continue their efforts within the civic group. The latter also tried to absorb the Social Group but its members opposed the move, expressing that they felt disregarded by the civic leaders.

Thus, by July, 1982, Proyecto Esfuerzo had formed two task groups (one of which ceased its work in July) which had met regularly for 4 months and organized two picnics, a funding march, and a general assembly.

In September, we evaluated the Social Groups' process, pointing out to the residents the problems we saw hindering the group's development. These included: tardiness, lack of adherence to group decisions, digressions during meetings, and more active male than female participation. They agreed with these observations and norms were generated in response to them. The need for recruitment of new members also became apparent since more than half the group members had left the group. Reasons for leaving were explored.

Various activities were planned. These included a recruitment meeting, a visit to the Ponce Museum of Art, a children's activity, and a communal Christmas party. The latter was also going to mark the end of our intervention in that group and the beginning of their independent development.

The Social Group was also consulted about the creation of another group to deal with a community newspaper. They approved the idea and elected a representative to the Newspaper Group meeting when it was formed. They also chose a representative to the civic group meetings so as to keep abreast of the relocation issue.

At this point the Social Group began its transition phase. The Newspaper Group was formed in October and is still in Phase Five. Since this group is barely starting, I will exclude it from this summary while focusing on the Social Group's development.

Transition

The transition period was to be characterized by various decisions. First of all, the process of group meetings was slowly turned over to the residents. This was done by drawing up joint agendas and having different members facilitate specific parts of the meetings. An organizational structure was identified and a resource inventory completed. Also, residents' fears regarding our departure were explored in order to deal with them. Activities continued to evidence the residents' capacities. Last but not least, an agenda of the activities that were to take place after our departure was drawn up.

The recruitment drive was essential because the group was active in only one geographical portion of the community. This facilitated the creation of a ''sense of neighborhood'' which was not spreading throughout the community. A recruitment meeting was planned to inform residents of the group's work. The meeting was to be directed solely by residents in the Social Group, who even rehearsed their parts. Much to our dismay, only two nonmembers attended. However, much to our relief, the residents were able to analyze the reasons for such an outcome and decided to continue recruitment efforts throughout their other activities. That same evening the childrens' activity was planned.

By December, 1982 the childrens' activity was celebrated as was the visit to the Ponce Museum. Both were open to all the community and approximately 60-75 members attended. The group then had to plan the Christmas party and deal with our departure.

The Christmas party was never held. Resident members of the group wanted a ''private'' party to thank us for our efforts in Esfuerzo. We wanted an open community party where they could thank us if they so wished, but could continue their recruitment of other residents. Christmas is a particularly important time in Puerto Rico as in other countries, and it seemed to us essential that they share it. Neither group budged and this resulted in paralysis. Our final meeting was devoted, instead, to the clear cut definition of the organizational structure the resident members wished to choose to continue their work. On this occasion the group selected a coordinator and a secretary to take minutes and manage the resources file. The treasurer and the two representatives to the Newspaper and civic groups retained their roles. The residents also suggested the need for an evaluator role which they decided to rotate at each meeting. A written summary of the group's history was requested.

This year will be one of trial for the Social Group and for our intervention. Although the Social Group has planned regular meetings and various activities for the future, we cannot be sure of the success of continued efforts. We will be carrying out evaluative interviews from February through June of 1983, which should provide us with more feedback. The interviews might also serve as motivators for the residents' continued work.

End of project. At the time this article was written our definite departure from the community had not taken place. We were commited to work with the Newspaper Group until March and would carry out evaluative interviews of their work in April and May. These interviews would be the final part of the transition phase.

EMPOWERMENT STRATEGIES

As previously stated our emphasis during this intervention was on the first two stages of empowerment (Keiffer, 1982). However, skill development was also stressed so that residents could link critical analysis with activities that exemplified their newly gained understanding.

Ideological Analysis

To achieve consciousness raising, the main strategy used was ideological analysis (Freire, 1974). Serrano, López, and Rosario (Note 11) have indicated that this analysis involves content and process aspects. The process aspects are characterized by three conditions. The first is a horizontal relationship between the change agent and the participants in the process. This refers to abandonment of the expert role. The second condition is the creation of genuine dialogue between those involved in the process. This requires sincere, attentive, and respectful participation, where all participation is considered legitimate even if judged to be "incorrect." The third condition is real optimism regarding change possibilities. The content aspect of this analysis includes constant questioning of the "obvious" and the provision of information regarding social, political, historical, and cultural issues that may arise. The ways in which this analysis has been carried out include modelling, explicit verbalization of values, questioning, providing information, and musical interventions.

Modelling. Our teams continuously try to model collaborative roles and engage in genuine dialogue. This is not done by downplaying our knowledge and skills, but instead by frequently verbalizing and identifying those skills that residents possess. Nor is it modelled by controlling our reactions toward behaviors or ideas that seem foreign to us; instead, we recognize their strangeness and seek to learn of their usefulness. Another way to model this role is to participate in all sorts of tasks no matter how "menial" they may seem. Thus, we cook, we clean, we prepare collection cans, we march, we carry things. In other words, we do a lot of the same things they do. Other behaviors model some of our values. Examples are: women direct most of the meetings, students play more active and directive roles than their professors, and team decisions are clearly stated as such, thus modelling our cohesiveness and discipline.

Explicit verbalization of our values. The values we emphasize include our belief in (a) the residents' capacities to perform tasks by themselves, (b) their abilities to identify their own needs and problems, (c) cultural relativity and human diversity, (d) every resident's capacity to be a leader in a specific group or for a specific situation, (e) the importance and usefulness of research, in particular, evaluation, (f) the need to organize effectively, (g) the need for shared feelings of pride in, and belonging to, the community, and (h) the importance of collective responsibility.

Questioning. One of the favorite words in our vocabulary is *why?* Why can't this be done? Why does it have to be done the usual way? Why has it always been done that way? Why doesn't everyone else think that way? Answers to our questions are not really important if a critical attitude toward the social environment is fostered.

Providing information. The following content areas have been stressed so far: socio-economic conditions of Puerto Rico, previous community development efforts, group dynamics, decision-making, processes, women's roles, alienation, leadership, political parties, relocation, and governmental agency functions. This information is provided in written summaries, meetings, and informal conversations.

Musical interventions. This mechanism was used in community picnics and the children's activity. It serves both process and content functions. It helps to group people together in a fun way and also to strengthen our ties with them. Content-wise, ideological analysis is fostered by a selection of songs that include nontraditional values, national and cultural values, and social and political criticism. This selection also considers those songs we do not want to include, because they foster the status quo.

Skill Development

Skill development has been fostered mainly during process interventions in meetings. Our task group facilitators did not consider the content of the meetings of much importance. Their role emphasized interventions which were in accordance with our goals and which promoted the development of planning, organization, and evaluation skills. These included: (a) facilitation of active participation of all residents, (b) identification of internal community resources and provision of guidelines for the creation of a resources file, (c) planning of activities ahead of time, (d) clear-cut decision making processes emphasizing problem definition, evaluation and selection of alternatives, task assignment, and follow-up, (e) refusal to carry out tasks that residents could carry out themselves, (f) development of group norms that penalized noncompletion of tasks, (g) structured evaluation time in every meeting and after every activity, and (h) promotion of a non-hierarchical organization structure where decision-making took place by consensus and most tasks were equally distributed.

As can be seen, the project had no formal training structure. We believed that course or workshop interventions would reinforce our expert role and the residents' lack of skills. This would distance us from them. We also believed there would be explicit and strong resistance to any kind of formal training. Thus, skill development was dependent on observation, trial-and-error, reinforcement, modeling, feedback, and critical analysis.

PRELIMINARY EVALUATION

The analysis that follows is based on my observations, events that took place during the project's development and an examination of a sample (the first and last five meetings) of verbatim transcripts of the Social Group meetings. At the time of this writing, a complete evaluation consisting of an analysis of transcript data and interviews was begun. Future writings will reveal these findings.

The data used for this analysis is presented in Tables 1 and 2. Events and quotations have been categorized according to the objectives and show achievement or failure. In Table 1, events have been separated into initial and final periods of the project so that a time

Table 1

Evaluation of Project's Intervention using Events

Objectives	Events			
	For		Against	
	First 4 months (May - August)	Last 4 months (September-December)	First 4 months (May - August)	Last 4 months (September-December)
Facilitate the (a) identification and development of community resources so that we could work with community residents in (b) activities or tasks that would lead to the solution of their problems as perceived by both groups.	(a) Diffusion of needs assessment results. (a) Identification of each meeting of individuals with particular knowledge skills or possessions. (b) Social group organized three activities two of which were direct responses to the needs assessment.	(a) Refusal of community to accept CMHC sports leader because they had their own. (a) Creation of resources file. (b) Social group organized five activities of which three responded to the needs assessment.	Socio political context ⟶	
(1) development or strengthening of a sense of community among residents	People who did not know each other met and worked together People from all sectors of the community attended the social group activities ⟶		Most members of the group resided in the same street Socio-political context ⟶	Most community-wide recruitment efforts were unsuccessful The final communal Xmas party was opposed by the residents
(2) facilitation of task group development	Social group met regularly - 10 times in 4 months Group members initially took over non-resident tasks like: inviting to meetings, propaganda for activities, finding places for activities; recruitment efforts.	Regular meetings continued - 14 times in 4 months During the transition phase residents directed parts of group meetings (making joint agendas, giving reports and eventually have taken over all group functions Suggestion of secretary and evaluation roles and request for summary of group's history. Decision to avoid hierarchichal structures	Resident stand-still during our vacation in August Decision-making process, particularly in evaluation of alternatives, was lengthy (average 3 meetings for one decision). ⟶ Residents did not volunteer for outside community contacts	

Table 1

Evaluation of Project's Intervention using Events

Objectives	Events			
	For		Against	
	First 4 months (May - August)	Last 4 months (September-December)	First 4 months (May - August)	Last 4 months (September-December)
		Residents volunteered for outside community contacts	Initially only a few members spoke in meetings	
		During the final meetings most members voiced their opinions	Socio-political context ⟶	
(3) continuous recruitment of community members			Socio-political context ⟶	During the eight months only 3 new members were added through personal contacts with resident members
(4) facilitation of self-sufficiency	Development of skills ⟶ Experience in planning, organizing and executing activities ⟶ Attendance of people allover the community to their activities ⟶	Links to other community groups through representatives Formal organization and role assignment	Membership characterized as being mainly female and elderly ⟶ Socio-political context ⟶	Six members left the group Lack of growth of group
(5) increasing consciousness-level	Increase in female participation Unwillingness to join civic group	Female coordinators elected for group	Socio-political context ⟶	

perspective may be seen. The quotations presented in Table 2, taken from the transcripts, include all direct remarks pertaining to the objectives being examined.

Tables 1 and 2 show residents' awareness of their resources. Activities were organized according to what residents could provide. For example, they refused our offer of a sports leader because they knew of such a person in the community. The number of activities the group organized is also an example of growth, since members had no previous experience organizing communal activities.

Table 2

Evaluation of Project's Intervention using Quotations

Objectives	Translated Quotations			
	For		Against	
	First 5 meetings (May - July)	Last 5 meetings (November - December)	First 5 meetings (May - July)	Last 5 meetings (November - December)
Facilitate the (a) identification and development of community resources so that we could work with community residents in (b) activities or tasks that would lead to the solution of their problems as perceived by both groups.	"I have two barrels" "I can bring flour and fish" "I know someone who has that machine" "I can draw propaganda leaflets" "I can get ribbons" "I can make contacts for a bus" "I can sell tickets" "I have two pails" "I can get juice"	"There's a sports leader in the community" "We can set up a theatre play for kids" "I could get the church for the activity" "The meeting can be at my house"		"We can't give the Xmas party 'cause we have no money" "Our funds? What funds?"
(1) development or strengthening of a sense of community among residents	"What you get for your community is for you and for others" "We have a commitment to the community and it means giving" "We should all share; the community should know us. We should work for the community without political or economic goals"		"We'll never have an united group. This community is asleep"	"Sometimes it's not good to invite all the community because they harm things" "The community doesn't cooperate" "If you organize a shoe factory the children are born feetless" "The community is emotionally and mentally disunited"
(2) facilitation of task group development	"Once we've decided we should follow through" "Lets seek a consensus" "Decision-making is easier when you write things down. It's like having a computer"	"We've got to decide. Either we do or we don't. We're so ambivalent today" "I told you it wouldn't work if we didn't plan ahead of time"	"I think December will come and we won't do anything" "Evaluating isn't necessary" "We turned back a previous decision. I hope this doesn't happen again"	"We've got to decide. Either we do or we don't. We're so ambivalent today"

Table 2

Evaluation of Project's Intervention using Quotations

Objectives	Translated Quotations			
	For		Against	
	First 5 meetings (May - July)	Last 5 meetings (November - December)	First 5 meetings (May - July)	Last 5 meetings (November - December)
	"We turned back a previous decision. I hope this doesn't happen again"	"We need all members here to decide about group structure"		
	"We talked about too many irrelevant things"	"We start at 6:00. If you are not here you find out what has happened"		
	"We're learning to organize picnics"	"I didn't like this meeting because we didn't do as planned"		
	"For the next time we all have more know-ledge so we can plan better"	"We were not enthusiastic"		
		"This group has been very use-ful. We will try to conti-nue what we have learned up to this date"		
		"I learned to make decisions outside of my home, with other people"		
		"I learned to share. To meet new people. To let all give their opinions and then decide. To deal with unpleasant moments and to deal with group forma-tion"		
(3) continuous recruitment of community members	"We need more people"	"If they don't come we'll go to them"	"We'll always be the same"	"If people haven't come, it's because they don't want to"
		"The fact that we are few should not stop us"	"If we don't get him, he won't come"	"We are very few people"
			"Few people are attending"	

Table 2

Evaluation of Project's Intervention using Quotations

Objectives	Translated Quotations			
	For		Against	
	First 5 meetings (May - July)	Last 5 meetings (November - December)	First 5 meetings (May - July)	Last 5 meetings (November - December)
(4) facilitation of self-sufficiency	"We should collect the funds" "The activities have been successful, good. We were all satisfied" "We met by ourselves and followed the agenda you left" "People in the community know us they know where to come" "We've been asked for another picnic"	"She (the facilitator) is one vote" "___ and I are going to lead this group and move it right along" "If you follow me meetings will continue. If not I'll withdraw and won't come back" "If we stay organized we shouldn't have problems"	"Someone from outside had to organize us" "You are our strength" "I wanted you as our leaders to come" "We need help from government groups" "Without you we can't do anything"	"The community doesn't cooperate with the group" "We do what people want us to. People expect us to fix the roads or collect the garbage" "Some people confuse us with the civic group" "There hasn't been enough time to develop the project. I would have liked to have more time"
	"All the group work is good" "I understand that a lot of people know about the group"	"We will continue to grow. You were the first push"		"We've been linked to the civic group because of our participation in the assembly" "Other people won't think we're important after you've left"
(5) increasing consciousness-level	"All opinions are good but together we'll achieve more" "You (the men) don't suffer, It's women who are in charge of the children" "Everything is conditioned by mr. money" "If this were 1984 (election year) things would be different" "One feels better when one does something positive like this"		"There are people that don't deserve us. I wouldn't go near them"	"Let's leave it like this. If God want us to suffer, then let's suffer"

A sense of community did not seem to develop. The data point to the creation of a strong sense of cohesion among group members and to explanations of community apathy for their lack of numerical growth. Although residents express the value of their work for the whole community, they are frustrated by the community's lack of support. The recruitment data are supportive of this analysis. The lack of new members could be explained by (a) deficiency of recruitment efforts, (b) lack of real interest of group members for the incorporation of other people, (c) community apathy, (d) opposition of other community groups, (e) characteristics of group members, and (f) the kind of activity the group was working with.

The lack of achievement of these two objectives, recruitment and a strong sense of community, could have strong negative implications for the group's survival. Among others effects, group members can feel overburdened and tired after time has elapsed, and the community may begin to perceive the group as a closed clique.

The skills development component seems to have been well satisfied. The group increasingly took over more complex group functions and also expressed awareness of their learning. They mentioned the usefulness of their newly acquired skills for future activities. The skill that seems to have improved the least was that of decision-making; those most strongly developed included planning and evaluation.

The self-sufficiency evidence tends to show that most of the reasons given for continuing self-sufficiency are relative to the group (internal) and those given for the lack of continuity are relative to the community (external). Events and quotations that favor self-sufficiency relate mainly to group skills, experiences, organizational structure, and leadership. There are also quotations that evidence their growing independence from the interveners. The factors against self-sufficiency are mainly a lack of community cooperation, being perceived as part of the civic group, community expectations of their work, and their own low status in the community. Whether or not their skills and experiences counteract these external forces is yet to be seen. A good sign is the residents' awareness of these factors. This increased awareness and the facilitation of the development of a "sense of self-sufficiency" seem to be positive results.

The last line in Tables 1 and 2 presents evidence of consciousness raising. Male-female relations was the most frequently mentioned or acted on area and some comments were made regarding community-wide versus individual connotations of events and understanding of Puerto Rico's socio-political situation. Overall, however, there are few comments to evidence change in this area. Their scarcity may be due to (a) our emphasis on skill building, (b) the subtlety with which ideological interventions were made, (c) residents' resistance to discussion of value-laden issues due to a cultural norm of non-confrontation, (d) the preliminary nature of this analysis, or (e) the ineffectiveness of our intervention.

To summarize, the best results of the project relate to skill development, identification of community resources, and facilitation of a sense of internal self-sufficiency. We were less effective in developing a strong sense of community, facilitating recruitment, or increasing consciousness levels. This leads me to fear the gradual dissolution of the group, or what could be worse, the continuation of a group that supports society's prevailing values.

MAJOR UNRESOLVED ISSUES

The major problems which our community efforts continue to encounter include: our stance relative to national politics, community leadership, skill versus consciousness raising emphasis, and duration of the project.

National Politics

In Puerto Rico there are three major positions regarding our political status. They include those favoring statehood, commonwealth, or independence. The island parties that represent the first two positions have been in power on various occasions. Pro-independence sectors have always been a minority.

The status issue is strongly present in Puerto Ricans' everyday lives. It is not only an ideological issue. It also reflects strongly on the day to day needs of people, government benefits, jobs, and resources they may or may not obtain. In very concrete terms, favoring or saying you favor the party in power is beneficial. On the other hand, favoring independence leads to stigmatization and discrimination.

Since this is such a pervasive issue on the island, it is of importance to the residents and affects our intervention. When we present ourselves as a university and CMHC group, residents question us indirectly about our political preferences. Our response up to this point has always been that this is not a partisan organization and that we are interested in the community as a whole. This is true in the sense that the members of our project come from different political parties. However, most of the members of our directing team are of a particular ideology and our values are clearly pro-independence. Thus, there is a contradiction between our available means for recruitment and our ideological stance. However, as "academics" we are not free to express these contradictions. This creates serious controversies in the community.

The vital questions it raises are: (1) If we maintain our partisan anonymity will the community feel betrayed? (2) If we choose to openly express our ideology will our community integration goals be impossible to achieve? (3) If a particular group of residents chooses to work with us, and their political partisanship is well known, should we refuse, or should we accept? Does our supposed neutrality hinder our consciousness-raising efforts by forcing us to remain outside of partisan political issues? The answers to these questions can only be found in community efforts with non-academic ties where partisan positions can be stated.

Community Leadership

In the development of this and other projects, we have thought much about the best strategies for working with already established community leaders. This is due to the fact that most of the literature on community development states that leaders serve as facilitators of change, provide information, and serve as linkages to other residents (Ander-Egg, 1980; Burghardt, 1982).

Our experience shows this to be only partially true, and even then not necessarily useful to our goals. The community leaders we have worked with are continuously struggling to maintain their leadership by providing insufficient or incorrect information, impeding leadership development of other residents, performing tasks for others, and controlling their resources.

Originally, in other projects, we initiated efforts with leadership groups and struggled to affect their decision-making processes so that greater community involvement would be feasible. We were not successful in increasing participation of other groups or individuals. Our second choice of strategy, the one presented here, was to work on problems that were different from the ones leaders were working on. For this purpose we organized residents who did not possess resources other than knowledge of the community. We were boycotted by the established leadership in this second effort, although not as adamantly.

Again questions are raised. If we work with already established groups, do we impede other residents' development? However, if we do not work with leaders do we foster community infighting which is contrary to our collective goals? Is it possible to work in both directions? A conclusive answer cannot yet be reached.

Skills versus Consciousness Raising Emphasis

This case study shows that although our interventions were meant to facilitate consciousness raising, in effect we did not succeed. Although this, in part, defeated our purposes, I now question the validity of our original decision. I wonder if it is appropriate to emphasize consciousness raising before residents have concrete skills and feelings of competence with which to face and act upon their newly discovered reality. If the answer is that both aspects have to be undertaken simultaneously, is it possible? Does our training equip us for this task? Before these interventions are carried out, do different subject areas of consciousness raising need to be specified and ordered according to their importance? Will some of these areas be compatible with skill building and others not? This challenge awaits future projects.

Duration of Project

The first projects I coordinated did not set time limits. We wanted residents to take this as a demonstration of our commitment, and we ourselves though that our departure could be monitored during the intervention. However, this resulted in false expectations on the residents' part and burnout on ours.

Thus, this project established a definite deadline. Although we saw the need for this, we really had no way of measuring the time that was to be allotted in order to reach our goals. We also had no way of controlling external events (i.e., the student strike) which interfered with our progress. The time limit had to be broad enough to allow for skill development and consciousness raising, but short enough to avoid the creation of dependency. This points to the need for the development of clear-cut criteria with which to establish a time frame for community development.

In summary, our major unsolved issues relate to (a) the generation of collective feelings and actions in a highly politicized community, (b) the development of new leaders without alienating other established groups, (c) the balance between skill development and consciousness raising, and (d) the establishment of criteria for time limits on community projects.

CONCLUSIONS: THE ILLUSION OF EMPOWERMENT

Did our intervention facilitate the empowerment of the residents of Esfuerzo? What are the limits of empowerment efforts within our colonial context? These are the two final issues that are raised and they are tightly intertwined.

The answer to the first one, if we view empowerment as a process where people gain greater control over their lives, must be positive. Residents that participated in Proyecto Esfuerzo gained new skills, feelings of competency, and insights that should enable them to achieve greater control over some aspects of their community life. Even though our goals were not achieved in other areas, these should be enough for them to have a different, more affirmative, perspective of their role in their community.

However, if our interest in ideological analysis is to foster the development of an alternate ideology, one characterized by the values previously presented, then this was not achieved. We may have even fostered the illusion that our society allows for this kind of empowerment.

I am convinced that our society does not allow this. Ours is a society which, along with the economic and political facts previously presented, is characterized by an ideology of conservatism and pro-American values (Macksoud & Serrano, 1982). These emphasize (a) an electoral definition of democracy, (b) the prevalence of a conservative vision of law and order, (c) uncritical acceptance of United States dominance over Puerto Rico, (d) rigid value stances that acknowledge only clear-cut definitions of right and wrong, (e) individualism, (f) veneration of the right to private property, (g) the belief in the governmental duty to protect this right, (h) protection of the free market, and (i) intolerance towards dissidence (Buitrago, 1972; Greenberg, 1977). The latter has been demonstrated through the constant and active persecution of pro-independence group members (Pabon, 1972).

Given these conditions, I am convinced that our project achieved the goals it did because its goals and strategies were and are unknown to people in power, because we are working with low-status people who are not recognized as a threat, and because we did not choose to deal with problems which directly confront governmental institutions.

The weakening of the ideology described above must continue to be our main goal. Although we attacked some of its components (rigid value stance, intolerance of dissidence, and individuality), there are other more partisan political issues which we did not pursue because of: (a) the political anonymity and nonpartisan position that our institutional affiliations demand, (b) our decision not to deal with the relocation issue which would have directly confronted government inefficiency and the inequality of service provision, (c) our lack of historical and political preparation, (d) the skill versus consciousness raising issue mentioned previously, and (e) the absence in the community and the nation of an organization which could responsibly continue our intervention at the societal level.

Of these facts the first and last are, in my opinion, most important. Our institutional links strongly determine the limits of our intervention. This was, after all, an effort sponsored by an academic and a governmental institution directed by professionals and students. I do not mean to say that these efforts should stop. It is apparent that they have some beneficial effects for those who participate in them. However, at this time ideological analysis of a more political nature has not been pursued mainly because we believed that residents would follow-up with a striving organization pursuing such goals. Thus, we have partially fostered an illusion of empowerment. Newly gained control by residents over their lives has been achieved within an oppressive colonial context. Residents can not yet confront that context. Yet it continues to determine their lives and, in many ways, their thoughts.

Our future efforts must be directed toward more effective development of the content and process of ideological analysis, collaboration with autonomous community projects which exist on the island, and the diffusion of our experience to these and other organizations that share our goals and values. Our hopes lie with the Puerto Rican people who in the long run, with, without, or despite our efforts, will fight to obtain a society where empowerment is no longer an illusion but a reality.

REFERENCE NOTES

1. Colón Parrilla, A. *Los desempleados: Estudio etnográfico sobre la problemática personal y su visión del desempleo en P.R.* Unpublished M.A. Thesis, University of Puerto Rico, 1982.
2. *Programa del Partido Independentista Puertorriqueño* (1980). Unpublished Manuscript. (Available at Roosevelt Ave., Río Piedras, P.R.).
3. Pargament, K., & Myers, J. *The individual system spiral: Towards an integrated foundation for community psychology.* Paper presented at the annual convention for the American Psychological Association, Washington, D.C., 1982.
4. Perfecto, G., & Santiago, L.C. *Encuentro del cristianismo y la psicología social-comunitaria en un esfuerzo investigativo con énfasis en la participación de la comunidad.* Unpublished M.A. Thesis, University of Puerto Rico, 1982.
5. Serrano, I., & Alvarez, S. *Proyecto Ingenio: Un nuevo enfoque en el desarrollo de comunidad.* Unpublished document, University of Puerto Rico, 1981.
6. Serrano-García, I., Lopez-Garriga, M., & Rivera, E. Toward a social-community psychology. *Journal of Community Psychology,* Under revision for publication.
7. Serrano, I., Suárez, A., Alvarez, S., & Rosario, W. *El Proyecto Buen Consejo: Un escenario de adiestramiento y cambio social.* Paper presented at the International Seminar of Community Psychology, La Habana, Cuba, 1980.
8. Serrano, I. *Community "interventions within research" as a partial response to poverty.* Paper presented at the annual convention of the American Psychological Association, Washington, D.C., 1982.
9. Martí, S., & Serrano-García, I. Needs assessment and community development: An ideological perspective. *Preventions,* Under revision for publication.
10. Alvarez-Hernández, S. *Definición de liderato de una comunidad puertorriqueña.* Unpublished M.A. Thesis, University of Puerto Rico, 1981.
11. Serrano-García, I., López, G., & Rosario, W. *Problematizacíon, Concientización y Liberación.* Unpublished document, 1980.

REFERENCES

Ander-Egg, E. *Metodología y práctica del desarrollo de comunidad.* Espana: UNIEUROP, 1980.
Berríos, R. Independence for P.R.: The only solution. *Foreign Affairs,* 1977, *55,* 555-561.
Buitrago, C. *Ideologia y conservadurismo.* Río Piedras: Ediciones Bayoán, 1972.
Burghardt, S. *The other side of organizing.* Cambridge, Mass: Schenkman, 1982.
Fanon, F. *The wretched of the earth.* N.Y.: Grove Press, 1968.
Freed, H. N. The community psychiatrist and political action. *Archives of General Psychiatry,* 1967, *17,* (2), 129-134.
Freire, P. *Pedagogía del oprimido.* Mexico City, Siglo 21, 1974.
Goldmann, L. Conscience reele et conscience possible conscience adequate et fausse conscience. In L. Goldman (Ed.), *Marxisme et science humanes.* Paris: Gallemaird, 1970.
Greenberg, E. *The American political system.* Cambridge, Mass: Winthrop, 1977.
Irizarry, A., & Serrano-García, I. Intervención en la investigación: Su aplicación en el Barrio Buen Consejo, Río Piedras, P.R. *Boletín de AVEPSO,* 1979, *2,* 6-21.
Keiffer, C. The development of empowerment: The development of participatory competence among individuals in citizen organizations. *Division 27 Newsletter,* 1982, *16* (1), 13-15.
Macksoud, S., & Serrano, I. El mito de la democracia: Apuntes sobre la cultura política puertorriqueña, *Revista del Colegio de Abogados,* 1982, *43* (3), 359-402.
Memmi, A. *The colonizer and the colonized.* Boston: Beacon Press, 1965.
Pabón, M. *La cultura política puertorriquena,* Río Piedras: Xaguey, 1972.

Rappaport, J. *Community psychology: Values, research and action*. N.Y.: Holt, Rinehart, & Winston, 1977.

Rappaport, J. In praise of paradox: A social policy of empowerment over prevention. *American Journal of Community Psychology*, 1981, 9 (1), 1-26.

Rogers, M. Instrumental and infra-resources: The bases of power. *American Journal of Sociology*, 1975, 79 (6), 1418-1433.

Rothman, J. *Planning and organizing for social change: Action principles from social science research*. N.Y.: Columbia University Press, 1974.

Ryan, W. *Blaming the victim*. N.Y.: Random House, 1971.

Sarason, S. *The psychological sense of community: Prospects for community psychology*. San Francisco: Jossey-Bass, 1974.

Seligman, M., Greer, J., & Maier, S. The alleviation of learned helplessness in the dog. *Journal of abnormal and Social Psychology*, 1968, 73, 256-262.

Empowerment and Synergy: Expanding the Community's Healing Resources

Richard Katz

ABSTRACT. This paper suggests an alternative to the commonly-held "scarcity paradigm" of thinking about valued human resources, which assumes individuals must compete because resources are scarce. The alternative—the "synergy paradigm"—is empitomized in "synergistic community," where valued human resources are renewable and expanding, and distributed equitably to members, so that what is good for one is good for all and the whole is greater than the sum of its parts. Three field studies present cross-cultural evidence for the functioning of empowerment within a synergistic paradigm. Empowerment is considered as access to and control of valued resources; the specific valued resource focused upon is community healing. The studies suggest that community healing resources can become renewable and expanding, as can the process of empowerment which accesses them. Community members share these resources, combining conflicting resources into unexpectedly effective treatment packages. Given present inequities in resource distribution, transformative education is offered as one means to support a shift in thinking toward synergy.

What might be called a "scarcity paradigm" dominates Western thinking about the existence and distribution of a wide variety of resources. This paradigm assumes that valued resources are scarce: their presumed scarcity in fact largely determines their value. It further assumes that individuals or communities must compete with each other to gain access to these resources, struggling to ac-

I appreciate the help of Oliva Espin, Maxwell Katz, Bill Lamb, Niti Seth Salloway, Bob Sedgwick, Laura Stephens-Swannie and Bobbi Sykes, who all gave generously of their clarifying comments. Portions of this paper are based on material appearing in Katz, 1981, 1982b; and Katz and Rolde, 1981. Reprints may be requested from Richard Katz, Program in Counseling and Consulting Psychology, Harvard Graduate School of Education, Nichols House, Appian Way, Cambridge, MA 02138.

201

cumulate their own supply, resisting pressures to share. But the relation of actual scarcity of particular resources to cooperation or competition remains an empirical question. The relationship may differ according to the resource in question as well as the social structure governing access to and control of that resource. Water is a scarce and valued resource for the !Kung people of the Kalahari Desert, while building materials for their shelters are a plentiful and valued resource. Yet both resources are used in a collaborative manner by the !Kung (Lee, 1979).

It is the thesis of this paper that resources created by *human activity and intentions,* such as helping and healing, are intrinsically expanding and renewable, and need not be assumed under a scarcity paradigm. Yet the scarcity paradigm has come to dominate the Western view of generating and distributing even these *human* resources. Helping is seen as existing in scarce supply. Value, expressed in varying fee schedules, becomes entrained to scarcity. People are forced to compete with each other for their share of helping, to trust "market place" mechanisms that it will be a "fair" share *despite* continuing evidence of inequities in distribution. It can be argued that the scarcity paradigm functions in this instance more as an ideology than an empirically derived framework.

Evidence exists that there is an alternative paradigm, based on synergy, which can free such human resources from the grip of scarcity and competition. The term synergy describes a pattern by which phenomena relate to each other, including how people relate to each other and other phenomena (Fuller, 1963; Benedict, 1970; Maslow, 1971; Katz, 1982b). A synergistic pattern brings phenomena together, interrelating them, creating an often unexpected, new and greater whole from the disparate, seemingly conflicting parts. In that pattern, phenomena exist in harmony with each other, maximizing each other's potential. Within the synergy paradigm, a resource such as helping expands and becomes renewable, yet it can remain valuable (Katz, 1981, Note 1). The resource is activated by individuals and communities who function as its guardian and not its possessor, and who, often guided by the motivation of service to others, allow the resource to be shared by all members of the community. Increasing amounts of the resource become increasingly available to all, so that collaboration rather than competition is encouraged. Paradoxically, the more the resource is utilized, the more there is to be utilized.

The process of empowerment, and its companion resource of

power, can and too often has been cast into the scarcity paradigm. Rappaport's (1981) helpful definition of empowerment as a process of *"enhancing the possibilities* for people to control their own lives" (emphasis added) offers a way out of this limiting construal. Empowerment becomes limited when questions about its functioning are framed within the scarcity paradigm. For example, there is the well-intentioned question: "How do we generate what must be a *limited* amount of empowerment and then distribute it wisely and justly?" Then there is unfortunately the perhaps more typical, though unexpressed, question: "How do we empower 'those' people and still reserve for ourselves all the resources we now have?"[1] Within the synergistic paradigm, empowerment assumes new potential. "Control over their own lives" becomes a renewable, expansively accessible resource, as does the process of empowerment itself.

This paper summarizes observations from field studies on the functioning of empowerment within a synergistic paradigm. It proposes that when empowerment is viewed as a self-generating and generative resource, it is intrinsically suited to that paradigm. The emphasis in the paper is on community healing systems, including community mental health in the West. The focus is on access to and control of healing resources, especially the power to heal. The term "healing" rather than "helping" is used to suggest a more generic and inclusive process (Katz, 1983). As these healing resources expand and access to them increases, empowerment expands.

The observations are drawn from three studies of community healing systems: a three month field study conducted in 1968 among the Kalahari !Kung, who live primarily as hunter-gatherers (e.g., Katz, 1982b); a twenty-two month field study conducted in 1977-1978 in the outer Fiji Islands, where subsistence is primarily by fishing and farming (Katz, 1981); and an interview study conducted in 1976 with clients and providers at an urban community mental health center in the United States where I worked for four years in consultation and education (Katz & Rolde, 1981). Standard ethnographic methods, including participant observation, spot observations, and interviewing, were used in the first two studies. In addition, psychological tests were given to matched samples of healers and non-healers to delineate specific healer characteristics and attitude scales were given to the community to delineate charac-

---

[1]My thanks to one of the anonymous reviewers of this paper for suggesting this question.

teristics of healing systems. This paper considers the implications of these field studies and their possible applications to increasing community healing resources.

This field data provide support for the concept of "synergistic community," which can be seen as an empowering environment, in which the potential for empowerment increases synergistically. Empowerment is not limited to or identifiable with individuals; it becomes a resource beyond the self. It occurs across individuals and within communities. It also suggests that we can turn to "education as transformation" (Katz, 1981) as a method, and "natural" support systems as vehicles for generating and distributing such a renewable and expanding resource.

THE CONCEPT OF EMPOWERMENT: TOWARD A SYNERGISTIC PARADIGM

Empowerment deals with the generation and distribution of power, in the form of access to and control of resources (Rappaport, 1977, 1981). The emphasis is on establishing equity in that distribution or what amounts to a redistribution, so that those who are presently disenfranchised and oppressed can have a fair share of the power. Berger and Neuhaus (1977, quoted in Rappaport, 1981) argue for empowering "poor people" to resist the "encroachment of megastructures," a power rich people already possess. They say this would involve spreading that power to resist "around a bit more" so that, for example, poor people can also resist their neighborhoods becoming the "playthings of utopian planners." Others speak more to the fundamental nature of change implied by empowerment. As Freire (1968, 1970) says, an essential aspect of the empowering process is that power must be taken from the oppressors by the oppressed. He posits that the oppressors will be forced to realize the immorality of their position and thence give up their power.

Though the concept of empowerment contains potential for an equitable distribution of community resources, the potential is severely restricted when it functions within the scarcity paradigm. Within that paradigm, when there is competition for scarce resources, the likely result is an oppressive situation of "haves" and "have-nots." Despite Rappaport's insistence on "collaboration" and Freire's on "dialogue" between helper and helped, those who have more power can easily become oppressors, or in gentler terms, "experts." Even the best intentioned experts can create expectations and structures whereby an *initial* reliance on their knowledge endures. Those who seek to empower continue to direct the process of empowerment, and those who seek to become empowered continue to look outside themselves for advice.

Rogers (1979), in his discussion of "personal power", moves the concept of empowerment squarely into the realm of human meaning-making, stressing the *perceived* sense of power. But empowerment is an actual as well as perceived sense of power, an observable effect on socio-political structures as well as a subjective experience (Keiffer, 1982). Rogers would establish the possibility of empowerment as a limitless resource if self-understanding were the only obstacle. But his relative emphasis on the perceived sense rather than the actual exercise of power, and on personal experience rather than social structures, does not attend sufficiently to sociopolitical obstacles to self-understanding and especially to expressing that understanding in action. Within the synergistic paradigm, the sense of empowerment is not divorced from social structure. In a synergistic community, individual and social change are intimately linked, enhancing each other's effect.

Fortunately, there are elements from which we can construct a bridge toward a more synergistic conception of empowerment. Fundamental evidence has been provided by cross-cultural studies (e.g., Bourguignon, 1977; LeVine, 1979), which demonstrate, for example, the existence of the self embedded in community in most non-Western cultures. Extensive sharing, so essential to synergy, but absent in the West, flows from this experience of self and community. The Western value of individualism, with its implication of an individualistic self, separate and separating from others and community, supports a competition for scarce resources. In contrast, in the Fiji Islands, for example, self is defined and experienced contextually, dependent on how one fulfills one's social obligations (Katz, 1981). Independence is valued as a community resource, not a vehicle for personal achievement. Creativity emerges in connection with others. The sacred dance-songs (*mekes*) exist as they are performed by the community; their beauty resides in the intricate and delicate interrelationships between performers, and performers and audience.

The Western assumption that the individual is inherently in conflict with her or his community also supports the scarcity paradigm, pitting the two against each other. Community psychology, for example, often sees one of its tasks as reducing the conflict between individual and community so that the needs of both can be satisfied (Rappaport, 1977). Turning again to Fiji, we find such an antagonistic relationship is not assumed. One's sense of self is defined by one's place in the network which constitutes one's community. When Fijians visit another village, they are received as a representative of their *village*. After expressing this representative function, they can emphasize their more idiosyncratic personal characteristics. Personal meaning-making is encouraged, but as a resource to be shared with the community, not as a means to accumulate personal prestige or rewards.

Certainly in Fiji there is a movement toward separation as well as connectedness, a tension between individual and community aims. This dialectic seems inherent in the human condition. But Fijian values and assumptions about self and community offer a synergistic alternative, wherein extensive connectedness supports a sharing which can allieviate the tension.

Cross-cultural research also establishes the reality within community life of transpersonal resources which are of (ultimate) value to the community. Spiritual power, for example, is a resource which comes from beyond the community and is often a basis for healing power (Fogelson & Adams, 1977). Though spiritual power can be accumulated, even hoarded by individuals in certain situations, it is intrinsically suited for communal utilization in other situations. Such communal concepts and contexts of power facilitate the functioning of an "empowering environment." Western concepts of healing power draw primarily upon an intra- or inter-personal base, even when functioning in technological systems. Community psychology has missed the opportunity of utilizing transpersonal resources by relegating them to the institutions of religion (Sarason, 1977).

Two other writers help make this transition from a concept of empowerment existing within the scarcity paradigm to one existing within the synergy paradigm. The work of Freire (1968, 1970) has been very influential in establishing the intrinsic and extensive connections between individual and community empowerment. He points out the impossibility of achieving one without the other. Freire demonstrates in a compelling and practical way how the resource of power expands when individuals work together to change the system. Most painfully, he also demonstrates how such power remains scarce, with the oppressed being denied access to that limited resource. This occurs when individuals are kept apart from each other and from a perceptive engagement with institutions by the deadening "culture of silence." As a calculated breakdown of that information exchange which leads to Freire's concept of "conscientization," the culture of silence is the very antithesis of synergy.

In a different vein, Rappaport (1981) has established the possibility for community psychology to take seriously a synergistic concept of empowerment. In his "praise of paradox" as an essential ingredient in community psychology, he discusses the importance of divergent, often conflicting solutions to problems. He brings this non-linear thinking into a central position in the *practical* work of the interventionist. The concept of synergy, with its apparently illogical combinations and consequences, where elements which may be in conflict are combined with an unexpectedly bountiful result, relies on just such non-linear thinking. His appreciation of the concept of empowerment as a source of images which can stimulate action, suggests the exponential effect of synergy, producing results far beyond the elements at hand. In this last point, Freire also makes an essential contribution as he discusses the evocative strength of the root words and symbols which are at the core of his literacy work. As Freire says, he is committed to "teaching worlds, not words" (Personal communication, June, 1982). This generativity is critical to synergy.

The writings of Fuller (1963) and Benedict (1970) are central to the concept of synergy being presented in this paper. They help suggest a framework for an efficient interpretation of field data (e.g., Katz, 1981, 1982b, 1982c) that leads one to deduce the model of "synergistic community" (Katz, Note 1). Synergistic community is a perspective for understanding the functioning of synergy within a community as well as a guideline for increasing that synergy. In the context of a "synergistic community," empowerment expands in an exponential fashion. Communities empower and become empowered.

A synergistic community can be defined as one in which:

1. A valued resource is renewable, expandable, and accessible.
2. Mechanisms and attitudes exist which guarantee that the resource is shared equitably among community members.
3. What is good for one is good for all.
4. The whole is greater than the sum of the parts.

The field data also suggests that synergistic community is established by "rituals of transformation" in which participants experience a transformation of consciousness. This is not necessarily a major, intense or radical alteration of consciousness. It is often a subtle shift in perspective. Nor is the ritual necessarily a dramatic or clearly demarcated event. It can be an event of ordinary dimensions. This transformation seems to bring on a (new) way of experiencing self as embedded in and expressive of community. By establishing a transpersonal bonding between people so that individuals realize and activate communal commitments, these rituals can activate expanding and renewable resources. New solutions to problems become possible; or old problems are seen in a new way and cease to be problems. When individuals sense their deep connectedness, and realize they do not have to compete for scarce resources, these new solutions are encouraged. It can be argued that such transpersonal connectedness, and the sharing of resources which accompanies it, are essential to the survival of the human species (Rappaport, 1978).

Synergy, it seems, is an inevitable aspect or phase of community. It exists in a necessary dialectical relationship with its opposite. Most communities function primarily on the scarcity paradigm, but they require at least brief moments of synergy in order to hold them together. When we speak of synergistic community, we are talking about both the phase of synergy that is intrinsic to community and those particular communities in which the balance is toward synergy, where, relatively speaking, there is more sharing and connectedness and the valued resources are renewable and equitably distributed. But also, it seems that a community cannot always function synergistically. In Turner's (1969) framework, anti-structure cannot exist without structure.

Synergistic community can exist even though its members are not altruistic in the usual sense of that word, namely intentionally wishing to share or help others. Sometimes the structure of synergistic communities is the dominant feature, overriding any individual motivations. Members can act out of what they perceive as their own best, even individual interests, but the structure makes what is good for one, good for all.

There are many examples of synergistic communities, where synergy and empowerment are merged. What may seem like an unrealizable ideal in the West is a lived actuality in other parts of the world and within various cultural minorities in the West. We can turn now to two such communities, the !Kung and the Fijians, and learn more about the actual operation of empowerment within a synergistic paradigm.

THE HUNTING-GATHERING !KUNG:
AN ANCIENT HUMAN COMMUNITY

In the late 1960s, when I did field work among the !Kung of the northwestern Kalahari Desert in Botswana, they were living primarily as hunter-gatherers. That mode of adaptation is rare today, though representative of what was the universal pattern of human existence for 99% of cultural history (Lee & DeVore, 1968). It is generally agreed that the basic dimensions of human nature were forged during that huge span of history when people lived as foragers (Lee & DeVore, 1968). A study of community healing among the !Kung therefore has the potential to generate crucial insights into the nature of community and its healing resources.

The !Kung community is characterized by sharing of resources and egalitarianism (Lee, 1979; Lee & DeVore, 1976; Marshall, 1976). Their primary ritual, the all night healing dance, epitomizes these characteristics (Katz, 1982b; Lee, 1968; Marshall, 1969). In the crucible of intense emotions and the search for protection which is the healing dance, sharing and egalitarianism are put to the test, relied upon as vehicles for survival. The healing power, or *n/um*, is the most valued resource at the dance (Katz, 1982b). It is a renewable resource which becomes expansively and equitably accessible to all as it is activated. It is released by the community, and through its healing effects, helps to recreate and renew that community. Though existing in its most intense form at the dance, n/um has a primary significance for the !Kung in all aspects of their life. Its synergistic functioning harmonizes with and helps maintain !Kung life. The !Kung community illustrates principles of a "syneristic community." The !Kung approach to healing is an exemplar of the potential released when empowerment functions within a synergistic paradigm.

!Kung healing involves health and growth on physical, psychological, social and spiritual levels; it affects the individual, the group, the surrouding environment and the cosmos. Healing is an integrating and enhancing force, far more fundamental than simple curing or the application of medicine.

The central event in the healing tradition is the all night dance (Katz, 1981, 1982a, 1982b). Sometimes as often as four times in a month, the women sit around the fire, singing and rhythmically clapping as night falls, signaling the start of a healing dance. The entire camp participates. The men, sometimes joined by the women, dance around the singers. As the dance intensifies, *n/um* ("energy") is activated in those who are healers, most of whom are among the dancing men. As n/um intensifies in the healers, they experience *!kia* ("a form of enhanced consciousness") during which they heal everyone at the dance. The dance usually ends before the sun rises the next morning. Those at the dance confront the uncertainties of their experience and reaffirm the spiritual dimension of their daily lives. "Being at a dance makes our hearts happy," the !Kung say.

A healer talks about the !kia experience:

> You dance, dance, dance, dance. Then n/um lifts you in your belly and lifts you in your back. . .N/um makes you tremble, it's hot. . .When you get into !kia, you're looking around because you see everything, because you see what's troubling everybody. (Katz, 1982b, p. 42)

As healers learn to control their boiling n/um, they can apply it to healing. They learn to heal, to "see the sickness and pull it out."

A powerful healer spoke of the feeling !kia gives, that of becoming more essential, more oneself: "I want to have a dance soon so that I can really become myself again." A transcendent state of consciousness, !kia alters a !Kung's sense of self, time and space. !Kia makes healers feel they are "opening up" or "bursting open, like a ripe pod."

Through !kia, the !Kung transcend ordinary life and can contact the realm of the gods and the spirits of dead ancestors. Sickness is a process in which the spirits try to carry a person off into their realm. In !kia, the healer expresses the wishes of the living to keep the sick person with them and goes directly into the struggle with the spirits. The healer is the community's emissary in this confrontation. When a person is seriously ill, the struggle intensifies. If a healer's n/um is strong, the spirits will retreat and the sick one will live. This struggle is at the heart of the healer's art, skill and power. In their search for contact with transcendent realms and in their struggle with illness, misfortune and death, the healing dance and n/um are the !Kung's most important allies.

Fiercely egalitarian, the !Kung do not allow n/um to be controlled by a few religious specialists but wish it to be spread widely among the group. All young boys and most young girls seek to become healers. By the time they reach adulthood, more than half the men and 10% of the women have become healers. Still there is no stigma attached to those who do not become healers. An unlimited energy, n/um expands as it boils. It cannot be hoarded by any one person. The !Kung do not seek !kia for its own sake, but for its healing protection. At the healing dance, n/um is shared by everyone; all are given healing. As one person experiences !kia at the dance, others likely will follow. Though !kia may be experienced most intensely in the healers, they are channels to aid in the distribution of that n/um to those at the dance.

The dance provides healing in the most generic sense: it may cure an ill body or mind, as the healer pulls out sickness with a laying on of hands; mend the social fabric, as the dance promotes social cohesion and a manageable release of hostility; protect the camp from misfortune, as the healer pleads with the gods for relief from the Kalahari's harshness; and provide opportunities for growth and fulfillment, as all can experience a sense of well-being and some a spiritual development.

These integrated functions of the dance reinforce each others, providing a continuous source of curing, counsel, protection and enhancement. The healing dance is woven into !Kung hunting-gathering life without undermining the execution of everyday responsibilities. Healers are first and foremost hunters and gatherers, their primary obligation being to help in subsistence activities. A public, routine cultural event to which all have access, the dance establishes community, and it is the community, in its activation of n/um, which heals and is healed.

Education for healing among the !Kung is a process of transformation. To heal depends upon developing a desire to "drink n/um," not on learning a set of specific techniques. Teaching consists of helping students overcome their fear, helping them to regulate the boiling n/um and resultant !kia so that healing can occur. The n/um must be hot enough to evoke !kia, but not so hot that it provokes debilitating fear. Accepting boiling energy for oneself is a difficult process because n/um, painful and mysterious, is greatly feared. The healer's education stresses not the structure of the dancing, but the importance of dancing so one's "heart is open to boiling n/um"; it emphasizes not the composition of the healing songs, but singing so that one's "voice reaches up to the heavens."

The experience of !kia brings profound pain and fear, along with feelings of release and liberation. N/um is felt as "hot and painful, like fire." A respected healer described another dimension of this fear: "As we !Kung enter !kia, we fear death. We fear we may die and not come back!" When potential healers can face the fact of death and willingly die, they can overcome fear of n/um, and there can be a breakthrough to !kia. An older healer talks about this death and rebirth:

> (In !kia) your heart stops. You're dead. Your thoughts are nothing. You breathe with difficulty. You see things, n/um things; you see spirits killing people. You smell burning, rotten flesh. Then you heal, you pull sickness out. You heal, heal, heal. Then you live. Your eyeballs clear and you see people clearly. (Katz, 1982b, p. 45).

This "education as transformation," which teaches the !Kung to become healers, also supports their continual efforts at healing. It is a process of education which is not restricted to the healers. The entire community journeys into and through the transformations.

The !Kung establish some basic principles in our consideration of empowerment within a synergistic paradigm. First, the healing power (n/um)—the most valued resource at the dance and one of the most valued resources in all community life—is an expanding and renewable resource. It is released by the community, and expands as it is activated, becoming accessible throughout the community. The activation of n/um creates a synergistic system in which an act of healing means that not less but still more healing is available. Because of !Kung's egalitarian social structure, this resource is distributed fairly throughout the community.

Second, their approach to healing creates an "empowering environment," which intensifies access to and the effects of the healing power. Empowerment increases manyfold because it is the community, as well as its members, which is empowered. The healer's journey is an intensified version of the community's. It is the community which heals and is healed; all have access to healing. The healing dance is an intensified expression of community life. Healing is integrated into daily life, making extensive use of community support networks. It is directed toward prevention as well as treatment and assumes both as processes in the re-establishment of community balance.

Third, a model of "education as transformation" is suggested which can move empowerment toward a synergistic paradigm. This education stresses a transformation of consciousness which connects the healing power with the healer and the community. This combination increases empowerment, as the three parts working together produce a whole greater than the sum of the parts.

FIJIAN HEALING: THE CHALLENGE OF SPECIALIZATION OF FUNCTION

The three generic principles of empowerment and synergy established by the !Kung also appear among rural, indigenous people of the Fiji Islands. This fact is particularly interesting because the Fijians, who practice fishing and farming, have a very different mode of adaptation from the hunting-gathering !Kung. They are more hierarchically organized and have more specialization of function, including the existence of a variety of specialized healers (M. Katz, 1981; Nyacakalou, 1975, 1978; Sahlins, 1962). The Fijian approach to community healing suggests further principles which have a particular relevance to contemporary industrialized societies of the West, where specialization of function is extreme (Katz, 1981).

Ceremonial life is essential in Fiji, promoting economic and social exchange and celebrating the religious dimension (Spencer, 1941; Thompson, 1940; Ravuvu, Note 2). The present field research (Katz, 1981) shows that three main elements characterize Fijian ceremonies generally and the healing ceremony in particular: the *Vu* ("ancestors"), the *mana* ("spiritual power"), and the *yagona* ("a plant with sacred use") that brings this power to humans. Mana, the ultimate power, is an invisible, irreducible force that "makes things happen." As Fijians say, "Mana is mana," and its effects are often described as miraculous.

Fijians conceive of sicknesses in two major categories with different etiologies. The "true" or "real" sicknesses are caused by natural events. For example, one may have painful joints from being in the cold ocean too long while fishing. The second type, "spiritual" sicknesses, are caused either by witchcraft or by some violation of cultural norms, punished directly by the ancestors. While Fijians may seek Western medicine for treating "true sicknesses," both true and spiritual sicknesses are brought to the traditional Fijian healers. The same symptom pattern often can express either etiology.

In times of doubt, crisis or illness, the spiritual healer is the primary community resource. No problem is excluded from his or her domain, but the majority of cases are illnesses with accompanying physical symptoms. Requests for help range from a boy with a swollen neck, to a childless women who wishes to become pregnant, to a family seeking protection against other's evil intentions, to an entire village wanting to make amends for violating a sacred custom. As one villager remarked about the spiritual healer in her village: "He can't get sick, because without him, we would all be lost." Compared to non-healers, healers are rated as more highly "respected" and "hard working," and closer to the "ideal Fijian"; they remain fully contributing community members.

The healing ceremony, centering around the ritual exchange of yagona, typically begins when the client comes to the healer with a request for help whether it be for protection or a cure. The client incorporates the request within a ritual presentation of yagona to the healer. The healer accepts the yagona on behalf of the ancestors from whom he or she draws healing power. Yagona may be prepared with water and drunk by the healer, but that is not necessary. In that very act of acceptance, the critical initial exchange between healer and client is completed, and the healing is accomplished. In that moment, the mana is said to become available, making possible accurate diagnosis and selection of an effective treatment. The client returns after four days for the conclusion of the treatment or, if needed, further treatment in the same or some new direction. Herbs and massage are used in about 20 percent of the instances to carry out the healing.

Mana, like n/um, is the most valued resource in the healing ceremony. It is omnipresent. Though meant for the protection and healing of humans, mana can be turned to opposite purposes. Only by following the *gaunisala dodonu,* the "straight path," can persons direct mana toward healing and thereby release it within a synergistic paradigm. A highly respected Fijian healer spoke about the education of the healer:

> The mana, the spiritual power, is close at hand here in Fiji. Some of us are called to bring that power to the people for healing. That can be frightening, but the hard part is just beginning. To become a healer we must follow the straight path . . .and also find it. That is a long and difficult process. (Katz, 1981, p. 58).

The path itself is not straight, but the way one travels it should be. The path is discovered by traveling it.

Traveling the straight path means living out certain attributes that characterize the ideal Fijian. The straight path provides a concept of ideal development for all Fijians, an aim pursued with special intensity by healers. The education of healers is therefore an education for living in an ideal manner. The healer's education becomes a paradigm for education in and of the community.

The healer's character creates the possibility of healing work, and the development of character marks the continuation and deepening of that work. Information about healing techniques is available only to those with character. There is respect for the technical aspects of healing, but character precedes and provides the context for healing technology.

The following attributes are often mentioned when prescribing the way a healer must live in order to follow the straight path: telling and living the truth; love for all, so that all who come receive help; proper or traditional behavior; humility; respect for others and tradition; single-mindedness; and service, so that the power is used only to heal and not for personal gain. Though these attributes are often phrased in terms of the healing work per se, they generally prescribe the way a healer, and by extension all Fijians, must live.

The healer is constantly tested to betray the attributes that define the path. Increased healing power is determined by how one meets increasingly severe tests. For example, the healer's increasing empowerment must be reflected in the mutual empowerment of the community.

A first vision lays the foundation of the healing work—the connection with the ancestor who will be the source of power, and the commitment to use that power for healing. It inspires the appearance of the path and sets in motion a life long process one can call "envisioning." Envisioning is more than carrying out the intent of the first healing vision; it requires a continuous recreating and reshaping of that initial vision into an unfolding life pattern. Envisioning involves advice and instruction from a teacher, if there is one; subsequent visions; lessons learned from one's patients; and most of all, the actual practice of healing and learning to live with that practice in one's community.

Healer-client case records were gathered over a one year period to document patterns of utilizing healing resources within one Fijian village. These data demonstrate the use of a variety of healing resources in the search for protection and help (Katz & Lamb, Note 3). Clients become empowered in their efforts to procure healing because of both their own extensive knowledge of the available healing resources and the healers' collaborative relationship with each other and clients which helps translate that knowledge into action and actual accessibility. In the final analysis, it is the community which is empowered, because healers as well as clients, all of whom are community members, gain increased control over their health and their lives through this free flow of information. Finally, clients *with the help* of healers put together what we might call "treatment packages"—combinations of different healing resources to treat one illness—synergistically maximizing the quality of their healing.

In the village of approximately 100 persons, the healing specialists included a Western-trained Fijian female nurse, who ran a small dispensary and four traditional healers—one male spiritual healer, two female massage specialists and one female herbalist-massage healer. There were numerous other informal healers, mainly women who knew of herbs or other treatments for particular ailments. The dominant resources both in terms of patient usage and perceptions in the village were the spiritual healer and the nurse. All the healers knew each other well, and they turned to each other for treatment of their various illnesses.

Each of the traditional healers was asked to keep a systematic case book, recording all their contacts with clients, including information about complaint and treatment. The nurse was already doing this, and the spiritual healer had kept an informal, but incomplete, record. Working with the traditional healers in this manner was especially rewarding as they were able to see the full history of their service to the people of the village and recognize more clearly areas of special strength.

During that year, 500 persons visited the various healers, 26% from the home village, another 18% from the neighboring village, and the rest from the surrounding area. There were 1,125 client-healer interactions in which a client sought help for a particular complaint. In 5% of these interactions, more than one type of healer was consulted. Overall, nearly 79% of the client-healer contacts were with the nurse, 13% with the spiritual healer; but the latter tended to see each of his clients more times, so that the actual time spent in their respective healing efforts was more equal.

The most frequent complaint brought to all the healers was aches and pains, which accounted for 35% of all the complaints during the year. There were also distinctions in illnesses treated. The nurse saw nearly all the cuts and wounds, while the spiritual healer saw all the requests for preventive help against misfortune. Yet areas of overlap in regard to symptoms as well as areas of specialization prevailed. Clients visited different healers for the same complaint, depending on their own and the healer's diagnosis about etiology. Healers and clients maintained distinctions between the way different healers worked, citing the dominance of spiritual factors and the mana for the traditional healers and the dominance of Western medicines and medical training for the nurse. Similarities were also recognized, such as the requirement that all healers serve the people.

Of particular interest were those instances where a client saw both the nurse and a traditional healer for the same illness. We could call this the usage of "mixed-healing paradigms," as the treatment package contains different healing resources which are theoretically in conflict. There were more visits per healer during these instances of mixed-healing paradigms than when only one type of healer was seen. But though they received more service when utilizing these combinations of different healers, such clients had fewer sicknesses and expressed less general anxiety than clients who did not use these combinations. Usage of mixed paradigms seems to have been a pragmatic strategy, maximizing sources of healing and/or receiving a different kind of help when another type had failed, rather than an activity of persons who are sicker or more anxious than others.

While reaffirming the three generic principles about empowerment and synergy expressed by the !Kung, the Fijian approach suggests two additional principles. First, extensive information about the variety of healing resources available in one's community is essential to empowering people to become active, effective users; maintaining that variety during actual usage brings a synergy to the empowerment. Fijian healers and clients maintained rather than glossed over certain crucial distinctions between types of healing resources, including fundamental differences in the respective conceptions of and responses to health and illness. Community members were empowered to select their own treatment, including the construction of individualized "treatment packages" which combined the efforts of these different healers, enhancing preventive and treatment opportunities. Second, extensive collaboration between clients and healers and between healers is necessary to support such flexible and varied usage. Healers supported these usage patterns by recognizing the different assumptions of each healing system; by respecting the distinctive work of the other; by understanding the strengths and limitations of each system, *especially* their own; and by being knowledgeable about and willing to make referrals between systems (Katz, 1982d).

THE UNITED STATES: HOW CAN SYNERGY SURVIVE?

Health care in the United States provides a most serious challenge in the increased functioning of empowerment within a synergistic paradigm. The society at large is precariously tilted toward the scarcity paradigm, and the search for and delivery of health services must operate within that paradigm. Empowerment as a process becomes a scarce resource.

But if synergy is an intrinsic phase in or aspect of all communities, there must be forces in the industrialized and urbanized West tending toward synergy. In the community mental health system, one example is consumers' increasing use of combinations of different healing resources, or what can be called "mixed healing paradigms" (Katz & Rolde, 1981). Expressing their own empowerment, consumers begin to forge "treatment packages" combining healing resources which are theoretically in conflict, what we are calling "mixed healing paradigms." These apparently "illogical" combinations, in synergistic fashion, produce a more effective total healing resource than either one resource can when functioning separately. Unfortunately, this force toward synergy in empowerment is not supported by the providers of these services. The providers, through their failure to collaborate with each other and with the consumers, cut off the free flow of information about their health services and the actual exchange of these services. The specialization of function in the West results in a restriction of access to and control over resources. Providers in the United States have yet to learn the principles of collaborative service so clearly illustrated in Fiji.

Data on this use of mixed healing paradigms comes from interviews with two kinds of persons associated with an urban community mental health center: clients who were engaged in both traditional therapy and some alternative change system, though the two approaches to change were theoretically in conflict; and providers in the respective systems (Katz & Rolde, 1981). By traditional therapy we meant dynamically-oriented psychotherapy (see Freedman et al., 1975); and by an alternative change system we included both alternative therapies such as Alcoholics Anonymous (A.A.) (see Alcoholics Anonymous, 1955, 1957) and alternatives to therapy such as spiritually-oriented approaches based on eastern meditation and spiritual disciplines (see Trungpa, 1970).

There is a literature suggesting productive relationships between these conflicting approaches to change. Jung combined a therapeutic and spiritual emphasis in his work, especially in the later years. Katz (1973) proposes the concept of "preludes" and "paths" to distinguish different emphases and phases in the growth process. One could, for example, consider psychotherapy as a prelude, and a spiritual system as a path, and have a harmonious, synergistic combination. But for the persons we interviewed such combinations, which represent already integrated systems, were not available. Instead, these clients were forging their own "treatment packages," trying to make a synergistic combination. These treatment packages contained theoretical elements which were in conflict, especially from the perspective of providers. The consumers may or may not have known about such conflicts, and if they did, they emphasized whatever theoretical compatibility there may have been as they sought to reduce conflict in usage and maintain access to the total treatment package.

Many of these theoretical conflicts express a basic difference in conceptions of reality and epistemology. For example, spiritual approaches see themselves as meta-therapies, suggesting that work on spiritual issues will solve "therapy-type" problems. One dynamically-oriented therapist, whose patient had become a devotee of an eastern guru, remained convinced that her client's meditative experiences fit the definition of psychotic thought processes. As she put it: "The client's old thought patterns which we before called psychotic now find a new structure in his devotional religion. It may be effective coping, but I think much of it is the same old crazies." The devotee, operating within the framework of his spiritual discipline, believed that the view of reality held by his therapist was not only false but destructive. This case illustrates that though there are differences in points of *fact* between psychotic episodes and religious revelations, most often these differences are obscured by avidly held differences in point of *view* (see e.g., Scheff, 1971). The lack of collaboration between therapist and client prevents a careful consideration of the nature and extent of both kinds of differences, which could lead to more effective healing.

Theoretical differences also occur over what is to be treated, about what is defined as a "disease." Whereas traditional therapy seeks the removal of symptoms and their underlying causes as a key to making a person "better," A.A. stresses that removing the symptoms, the drinking behavior syndrome, does not cure the disease of alcoholism. A.A. emphasizes that though one has stopped drinking, one remains "sick" or vulnerable; one is a sober or recovering alcoholic. It is just this rememberance of their disease that helps keep the alcoholic sober.

Theoretically, traditional therapy and these alternative approaches to change are difficult to combine. Stated in the extreme, a client cannot be fully and simultaneously involved in two systems of change that consider each other's view of reality as distorted, each other's definition of health as misguided, and each other's methods as ineffective, irrelevant or harmful. *Practically,* a different picture emerges. In the effort to maximize the delivery of help, consumers will make pragmatic decisions to combine these theoretically conflicting systems. They shape theoretical incompatibilities to accomodate pragmatics.

The actual trend toward combinations, which we found to be on the increase, can build on certain practical characteristics which could bring these different change systems together. There is for example a possible complementarity in time-scale. Dynamic therapy is relatively short-term—usually functioning as a time-bounded intervention in the life-course; spiritual disciplines, relatively long-term—usually functioning as a structure for ongoing participation throughout the life-course. The most powerful force toward combination, however, is the series of pragmatic decisions consumers make to maximize the delivery of help. For example, dynamic therapy, with its interpersonal goals is used in combination with a spiritual approach with its metaphysical goals and their functioning with a spiritual approach with its metaphysical goals and their functioning on two different *levels* is stressed.

What might we learn about encouraging empowerment and synergy from this interview study on community mental health services? We see again that the free flow of information about the variety of healing resources available, and the ability to construct combinations from that variety, increases empowerment. The combinations come from a pragmatic need for help, with no loftier motivations necessary. Again, we can appreciate the synergistic effects on empowerment as it is maximized in unpredictable ways from seemingly "illogical" combinations, or what we are calling "mixed-healing paradigms." But we also see that these synergistic effects are curtailed, even short-circuited because all the relevant elements are not participating. Emphasizing their theoretical differences, practitioners do not provide information which would facilitate combinations, and generally do not support the combinations once made. If synergy is to have its full impact, all relevant elements must be operating within the synergistic paradigm. Empowering consumers can only go so far; it can go so much further if providers contribute their share, becoming part of the empowering process. Most important, we learn that there are *points of view* and *points of fact*. Combinations of healing resources can be prevented because of either or both kinds of differences. Expanding these resources depends on a collaborative consideration by provider and consumer of these differences so that they do not arbitrarily obstruct combinations.

ENCOURAGING EMPOWERMENT AND SYNERGY

We have posited that synergy is inherent in all communities; that synergistic community is a phase in or aspect of the life of every community. How might that synergy be encouraged in the industrialized West, and in particular in a way that enables empowerment to increase manyfold? Given the characteristics of the dominant culture in the West, where for example the three principles activating empowerment and synergy among the !Kung are relatively absent, this aim can seem idealistic. The fact that synergy is more of an actuality in minority cultures within the United States provides mixed support for that aim. Oppression too often results in these minority communities. While the resource such as healing is shared *within* the minority community, the community itself exists in a larger society where healing and other political and economic power resources are neither expanding nor shared. Yet the aim, linked as it is to key survival issues, seems worth the struggle.

The lessons from the !Kung and the Fijians about empowerment and synergy are provocative, even inspiring, but we cannot apply them without careful thought about questions of econiche. To what extent are the central features of those lessons culture-dependent and embedded in specific demographic, economic, technological and other sociocultural conditions? !Kung and Fijian societies both differ from the industrialized West on all those dimensions, as well as differing from each other. The necessity of describing the !Kung and Fijian material in English can create an illusion of familiarity with these two cultures in the Western reader. This presumption of familiarity is sometimes compounded by the erroneous and demeaning assumption that traditional healers represent "prescientific" or "primitive" doctors. The degree to which particular aspects of the lessons are embedded in the patterns of economic and social adaptation characteristic of those two societies remains an empirical question. While particular aspects may be culture-specific, there are aspects that seem applicable across cultures. Focusing on those potentially transcultural aspects, as well as the lessons drawn from our community mental health center study, suggests ways of encouraging empowerment within a synergistic paradigm in our own culture.

To establish the empowering environment which is found in a synergistic community requires a radical paradigm shift—a major shift in the way persons experience meaning and process and interpret data (Kuhn, 1970). Experiencing the self embedded in community as a desirable state, along with the sense of the separate and separating self, is but one example. In a synergistic community, self and community work toward the common good while seeking to fulfill their own perceived needs. As healing is given, more rather than less becomes available. These apparently "illogical" events can be accepted or even encouraged when the synergy paradigm prevails. If the paradigm shift is truly radical, it must involve new socio-political structures which initiate and express these new ways of making sense of experience.

Perhaps the most important element within this synergy paradigm is the fact of expanding, renewable resources. If empowerment is to increase exponentially, it must establish access to and control of expanding, renewable resources. N/um in the !Kung healing approach, mana used according to the straight path in the Fijian approach, and the emerging consumer knowledge in the United States community mental health approach are expanding resources which set the stage for such empowerment.

The free flow and exchange of information about healing resources seems to be a critical factor. Such an exchange creates pathways between resources and people, consumers and providers. It stimulates combinations of healing resources which can in a synergistic manner produce effects far beyond what is possible from the separate parts. This is especially so in combinations which could be labelled "illogical" from the perspective of linear thinking. These combinations can produce surprising and unexpected increases in empowerment.

The free flow of information will reveal limits to the knowledge-base of various providers. Providers, especially, must give up their needs for a sense of omnipotence and omniscience, and their insistence on defending professional territories and prerogatives (Light, 1980), if this exchange of information is to occur. In accepting their own vulnerability, providers can forge a collaboration with consumers, whose very status accentuates their vulnerability. Vulnerability can be a source of strength as it places knowledge and skill in the realistic context of human communication and competence. In the Freirian sense, an exchange of knowledge about healing resources can be liberating. For it is not merely healing systems we are talking about but world views and perceptions of reality.

Rituals of transformation are the essential link in introducing synergistic community (Katz, 1981, 1982a, 1982b). In the area of healing, these rituals connect the healing power, the healing and the community. By providing experiences of transpersonal bonding, the rituals enable individuals to sense their deep interconnectedness and realize their communal responsibilities for their own and other's health. By providing new social structures and allocations of political and economic resources, they enable people to express their interconnectedness in actual behaviors.

"Education as transformation" is one method for encouraging these rituals of transformation (Katz, 1981, 1982c). Though this model of education can focus on healers, it also speaks to the education of clients and consumers, and of the community which supports them both. Education as transformation is one way to insure that the valued resource of healing is not trapped within personal constraints or hoarded to fulfill the needs of only certain individuals. It can introduce humility before and respect of the healing process.

Central to this model of education is a transformation of consciousness, a new experience of reality in which boundaries of the self become more permeable to an intensified contact with a transpersonal realm or a realm beyond the self. A sense of connectedness results that joins the healing power, the healer and the community. During the transformation, the emphasis is on the psychological process of transition rather than on the nature of the barriers crossed or stages reached. Through envisioning, this transformation of consciousness keeps recurring, as the person continually recreates the experience of transition.

A second principle in the model is that the experience of transformation, which makes healing possible, does not remove the healers from the context of daily living nor diminish their everyday responsibility. The service orientation is a third principle. The healer's commitment is to serve as a vehicle that channels healing to the community rather than to accumulate power for personal use.

The emphasis on character as a critical context for healing and healing technology is a fourth principle. It is qualities of heart—courage, commitment, belief and intuitive understanding—that open the healers to the healing potential and keep them in the healing work. Healing technologies become available to those with the necessary character. Technologies serve the healing aim, but they do not justify or measure the healing work.

A fifth principle is that transformation sets in motion an inner development in the healer that is not manifested or rewarded by enduring changes in external status. A final principle is that healing stresses the proper performance of the healing ritual rather than a discrete outcome. The cure of a patient assumes importance in the larger context of the community's healing ritual, which seeks a general sense of balance throughout the community. Since the balance is dynamic, it needs continual attention; it is not always achieved. Proper performance demands that the healer serve as a focal point of intensity, embodying an unswerving dedication to healing and reaffirming the community's self-healing capacity.

If education as transformation is one possible intervention, then the existence of natural support systems (Caplan & Killilea, 1976; Katz & Bender, 1976; *Journal of Applied Behavioral Science*, Special Issue, 1976) is another. These support systems are usually functioning as synergistic communities. They pose a radical challenge to all aspiring professionals, no matter how well-intentioned their wish to empower others. Helping these support groups may not require any professional help, but the offering of oneself and one's own knowledge under the same conditions as other members, especially being vulnerable to the same risks they face. One then enters the group as a participant rather than a helper, let alone an expert.

The healing contact is made when both healer and healee can experience their own vulnerability in such a way that they go beyond themselves and their own personal needs. In that way they connect with each other and a realm beyond themselves, where communal efforts are logical and natural. A healing community can result, creating an empowering environment where empowerment and synergy become merged.

REFERENCE NOTES

1. Katz, R. *Synergistic community: Expanding educational resources.* Program in Counseling and Consulting Psychology, Harvard University, Cambridge, MA, 1983.
2. Ravuvu, A. *Fijian religion.* Unpublished article. University of the South Pacific, Institute of Pacific Studies, Suva, Fiji, 1976.
3. Katz, R., & Lamb, W. *Utilization patterns of "traditional" and "western" health services: Research findings.* Paper presented at the annual meeting of the National Council on International Health, Washington, DC, 1983.

REFERENCES

Alcoholics Anonymous. *Alcoholics anonymous* (2nd ed.). New York: Alcoholics Anonymous World Services, 1955.

Alcoholics Anonymous. *Alcoholics anonymous comes of age: A brief history of A.A.* New York: Alcoholics Anonymous World Services, 1957.

Alcoholics Anonymous. *Twelve steps and twelve traditions.* New York: Alcoholics Anonymous World Services, 1953.

Benedict, R. Synergy: Patterns of the good culture. *American Anthropologist,* 1970, *72,* 320-333.

Berger, P.L., & Neuhaus, R.J. *To empower the people: The role of mediating structures in public policy.* Washington, DC: American Enterprise Institute for Public Policy Research, 1977.

Bourguignon, E. *Psychological anthropology.* New York: Holt, Rinehart and Winston, 1979.

Caplan, G., & Killilea, M. (Eds.). *Support systems and mutual help.* New York: Grune & Stratton, 1976.

Capr, J. Youth's need for social competence and power: The community building model. *Adolescence,* 1981, *64,* 935-951.

Fogelson, R., & Adams, R. (Eds.). *The anthropology of power: Ethnographic studies from Asia, Oceania and the New World.* New York: Academic Press, 1977.

Freedman, A., Kaplan, H., & Sadock, B. *Comprehensive textbook of psychiatry-II* (2nd ed.). Baltimore: Williams & Wilkins, 1975.

Freire, P. *Pedagogy of the oppressed.* New York, NY: Seabury Press, 1968.

Freire, P. Cultural action for freedom. *Harvard Educational Review,* 1970, Monograph Series No. 1.

Fuller, B. *Ideas and integrities.* New York: Macmillan, Collier Books, 1963.

Journal of Applied Behavioral Science, Special issue: Self-help groups. 1976, *12* (6).

Katz, A., & Bender, E. (Eds.). *The strength in us: Self-help groups in modern world.* New York: Franklin Watts, 1976.

Katz, M.M.W. *Gaining sense at age two in the outer Fiji Islands: A cross-cultural study of cognitive development.* Doctoral Dissertation, Harvard University, 1981.

Katz, R. *Preludes to growth: An experiential approach.* New York: Free Press, 1973.

Katz, R. Education as transformation: Becoming a healer among the !Kung and Fijians. *Harvard Educational Review,* 1981, *51*(1), 57-78.

Katz, R. Accepting "boiling energy": Transformation and healing. *Ethos,* 1982, *10*(4), 344-368. (a)

Katz, R. *Boiling energy: Community healing among the Kalahari !Kung.* Cambridge, MA: Harvard University Press, 1982. (b)

Katz, R. Commentary on "Education as Transformation." *Harvard Educational Review,* 1982, *52*(1), 63-66. (c)

Katz, R. The utilization of traditional healing systems. *American Psychologist,* 1982, *37*(6), 715-716. (d)

Katz, R. Toward a paradigm of healing. *The Personnel and Guidance Journal,* 1983, *61*(8), 494-497.

Katz, R., & Rolde, E. Community alternatives to psychotherapy. *Psychotherapy: Theory, Research and Practice,* 1981, *18*(3), 365-374.

Kieffer, C. The emergence of empowerment: The development of participatory competence among individuals in citizen organizations (dissertation summary). *Division of Community Psychology Newsletter,* 1982, *16,* 13-15.

Kuhn, T.S. *The structure of scientific revolutions.* (2nd ed., enlarged). Chicago: The University of Chicago Press, 1970.

Lee, R.B. The sociology of !Kung Bushman trance performances. In R. Prince (Ed.), *Trance and possession states.* Montreal, Canada: Bucke Memorial Society, 1968.

Lee, R.B. *The !Kung San: Men, women and work in a foraging society.* Cambridge, England: Cambridge University Press, 1979.

Lee, R.B., & DeVore, I. (Eds.). *Man the hunter.* Chicago: Aldine, 1968.

Lee, R.B., & DeVore, I. *Kalahari hunter-gatherers: Studies of the !Kung San and their neighbors.* Cambridge, MA: Harvard University Press, 1976.

LeVine, R. *Culture, behavior and personality* (2nd ed.). Chicago: Aldine, 1979.

Light, D. *Becoming psychiatrists: The professional transformation of the self.* New York: W. W. Norton, 1980.

Marshall, L. The medicine dance of the !Kung Bushmen. *Africa,* 1969, *39,* 347-381.

Marshall, L. *The !Kung of Nyae Nyae.* Cambridge, MA: Harvard University Press, 1976.

Maslow, A. *The farther reaches of human nature.* New York: Viking Press, 1971.

McClelland, D. *Power: The inner experience.* New York: Irvington, 1975.

Nayacakalou, R. *Leadership in Fiji.* Oxford, England: Oxford University Press, 1975.

Nayacakalou, R. *Tradition and change in the Fijian village.* Suva, Fiji: University of the South Pacific, 1978.

Rappaport, J. *Community psychology: Values, research, and action.* New York: Holt, Rinehart & Winston, 1977.

Rappaport, J. In praise of paradox: A social policy of empowerment over prevention. *American Journal of Community Psychology,* 1981, 9(1), 1-25.

Rappaport, R. Adaptation and the structure of ritual. In N. Blurton-Jones & V. Reynolds (Eds.), *Human behavior and adaption, 18.* New York: Halsted Press, 1978.

Rogers, C. *Carl Rogers on personal power.* New York: Delacorte, 1979.

Sahlins, M. *Moala: Culture and nature on a Fijian Island.* Ann Arbor, MI: University of Michigan Press, 1962.

Sarason, S. *The psychological sense of community: Prospects for a community psychology.* San Francisco: Jossey-Bass, 1977.

Scheff, T.J. *Being mentally ill: A sociological theory.* Chicago: Aldine, 1971.

Spencer, D. *Disease, religion and society in the Fiji Islands.* New York: Augustin, 1941.

Thompson, L. *Southern Lau, Fiji: An ethnography.* Honolulu: Bishop Museum, 1940.

Trungpa, C. *Meditation in action.* Boulder, CO: Shambala, 1970.

Turner, V. *The ritual process.* Chicago: Aldine, 1969.

Thoughts on Empowerment

Robert Hess

We hold these truths to be self evident: That all men are created equal; that they are endowed by their creator with certain inalienable rights; that among these are life, liberty, and the pursuit of happiness; that, to secure these rights, governments are instituted among men, deriving their just powers from the consent of the governed; that whenever any form of government becomes destructive of these ends it is the right of the people to alter or to abolish it and to institute a new government, laying its foundation on such principles, and organizing its powers in such form as to them shall seem most likely to effect their safety and happiness.

Over two centuries ago, Thomas Jefferson, in this one sentence of uncommon eloquence, clarity, and power, laid the cornerstone of American political philosophy—the empowerment of a people. But still, after all these years, we continue to struggle with the application of this philosophy to our nation's internal political affairs. Today there remains discord over the efforts of our various minority groups to achieve legal and social empowerment. And in a more circumscribed area, prevention, we hear empowerment, being put forth, again with uncommon eloquence, by Julian Rappaport (1981) as an ideology which should replace the present ideology of prevention in mental health. Finally, we find ourselves as editors devoting an entire volume to increasing the understanding of empowerment, an understanding which only now appears to be emerging.

The difficulty in understanding and applying Jefferson's philosophy and related ideals lies in the dynamics which result from the interplay of concepts and principles espoused. Take, for example, the interplay of the two concepts of freedom and equality. According to Rappaport (1981, p.3), "if we maximize one we find that the other is necessarily minimized." The interplay of the two concepts is complex. Minimal freedom can exist contextually with minimal equality. Rappaport's statement suggests that the interplay of Jefferson's concepts is a dynamic with fluidity, tension, and movement. As a result, attempting to apply such a philosophy is akin to balancing a scale, a multidimensional one at that, which is slowly pivoting to and fro as weights in the form of societal variables beyond our control are not too gently loaded on one side or the other. But, despite the difficulty, because we sense that Jefferson's philosophy is fair, noble, and wise, we continue to struggle in application and understanding rather than giving up.

The articles in this volume assist us in our struggle for understanding by giving examples of the means, ends, the process of empowerment. They are rich in content but they are even richer in the concerns and questions that they raise. It is entirely in line with our present level of understanding of empowerment that this volume ends not with premature answers but with personal questions, concerns, and points for consideration.

My first point for consideration relates to the perception of how power is obtained. Some might perceive it as something that is taken; others might perceive it as something that is given. Because this volume focuses on the powerless, it might be construed as supportive of the former perception. Empowerment, however, is a dynamic; it is both taken and given. The powerful do not, except in extreme and often violent cases, have their power taken away. Instead, the powerless usually exert pressure which eventuates in the powerful giving away some of their power.

If we view power as both taken and given, we must take more of a systems approach to the study of empowerment. We must study not only how the powerless attempt to take power but also how the powerful give power. It is the dynamic that is of crucial importance in understanding empowerment.

A systems approach which focuses on dynamics causes us to also examine the interplay of the interventionist with the powerless and powerful. Questions are raised regarding how the interventionist enters the system. Should they come in only on invitation; or should they, as in Biegel's article, enter without invitation? How an interventionist enters a system obviously leads to changes in process but does it also lead to differences in outcome?

Of special interest in regard to outcome is how the interventionist "fits" into the system, especially in regard to his or her values. Do people become "empowered" when the values they adopt and the actions that these values guide coincide with those of the interventionist? When values and actions do not coincide, have people not been "empowered"? Who should be the judge—the interventionist or the people?

Serrano-Garcia's article provides contrasts that raise questions, the answers to which might lead to a better understanding of how values and philosophy guide the actions of interventionists. In one instance, the people they were working with wanted to hold a "private" Christmas party for them but they refused to participate saying it should be a community party. Neither side budged and the party was not held. In another instance, the Propaganda Group overruled them in regard to how information should be disseminated.

Why did Serrano-Garcia and her colleagues refuse to be overruled in one instance but not in the other? It is not difficult to see that the differing actions were in accord with their values but if their goal was to empower the people they were working with, should they have set aside their values in both cases and gone with the will of the people? Or should they have considered themselves as being an integral part of the system and allowed their values to intrude? The degree to which an interventionist should impose their values on a system is a matter of continuing concern, debate, and study.

Another concern raised by these articles, especially by the article by Fawcett and his colleagues, has to do with the negative effects of empowerment. As empowerment is a dynamic, it must have negative as well as positive features. Fawcett and his colleagues discuss some of the negative effects of their technology. What were some of the negative effects of the other interventions? Such effects are usually not reported but need to be looked for and shared to improve our understanding of empowerment.

In closing, some final thoughts need to be shared with readers. First is the belief that the philosophy of empowerment, if used as a guide to our actions, will lead to profound changes in what we do. For example, rather than imposing our expertise on people in the form of parenting groups, stress management courses, etc., if we are guided by empowerment, we will retain this expertise but will use it as a tool for empowerment within the context of an equal partnership with people in our community.

My second thought stems from the article by Katz. He describes an intangible energy, an expanding and healing power, that is generated by groups such as the !Kung in their healing rituals. It is a power which exists not only in such healing rituals but also at times when people gather together to share in a common purpose or experience. It may be found in groups as varied as fundamentalist religious groups, sports teams, work groups, and self-help groups. It is that moment when the power of individuals in the group becomes totally synchronous, yielding a renewable and expanding power greater than the group itself. The group becomes, according to Katz, a synergistic community.

Synergistic communities need to be a special focus of study because they appear to be major structural elements in the building of large scale empowerment and healing. However, this study must be guided by the philosophy of empowerment, leading us to study in partnership with these communities and within the context of their meaning and values. Measures and techniques that are not true to the phenomenon will not yield the proper understanding, a point which may be derived from the article by Maton and Rappaport.

My third and final comment returns us to Jefferson's concepts. As noted earlier, the interplay of these concepts is a dynamic, the fluidity of which necessarily places limitations on large scale empowerment within the context of our society. The empowerment of the powerless only takes place, in general, to the extent allowed by those with power. Power is not easily given up; compromises are not easily made; inequities continue to exist. However, this does not mean that empowerment is an illusion; it just means that we have an extremely long way to go before we understand it to the point where it truly becomes the larger reality.

REFERENCE

Rappaport, J. In praise of paradox: A social policy of empowerment over prevention. *American Journal of Community Psychology*, 1981, *9*, 1-25.